RUSSIAN
MINSTRELS

*University
of
Pennsylvania
Press
1978*

Russell
Zguta

RUSSIAN
MINSTRELS

A History
of the
Skomorokhi

For
my mother
and father

Молилася, турбувалась,
День і ніч не спала,
Малих діток доглядала,
Звичаю навчала.

"Розрита могила"

Т. Шевченко

Designed by Tracy Baldwin
Composition by Deputy Crown, Inc., Camden, N.J.

Library of Congress Cataloging in Publication Data

Zguta, Russèll.
  Russian minstrels.

  Includes index.
  1. Clowns—Russia. I. Title.
PN1955.Z47   791.1'2   78-53331
ISBN 0-8122-7753-8

Contents

v

Illustrations

Acknowledgments

Russian Minstrels had its genesis in the spring of 1970 in Finland, where I was spending the academic year as a Fulbright Research Fellow working at the University of Helsinki Library. In addition to providing a most pleasant environment in which to work, the Helsinki Library staff contributed in no small measure to my research effort, both in 1969–70 and again in the summer of 1972. I am especially grateful to Miss Elizabeth Tokoi, the Slavic Librarian, and Miss Tytti Talja for their patience and diligence in ferreting out obscure materials. I wish also to thank the staffs of the Finnish National Museum and the Folklore Institute for their generous assistance.

Some of the research was done at the New York Public Library (Slavonic Division), to whose expert staff I am indebted. The book could not have been completed without the aid of the efficient Inter-Library Loan service of the University of Missouri-Columbia. I am particularly grateful to Anne Edwards, whose tireless efforts on my behalf facilitated research even at some distance from the major depositories of sources. Through every stage of the project the Research Council of the University of Missouri-Columbia provided generous financial aid. Margaret Hein-Steck and Phyllis Boechler both did a superb job of typing the final draft.

Portions of Chapters 4 and 5 appeared previously as articles. I wish to thank Richard M. Dorson, editor of the *Journal of the Folklore Institute,* and James R. Millar, editor of the *Slavic Review,* for permission to incorporate material from the articles in the book.

Finally, my most sincere thanks go to Professor Felix J. Oinas of Indiana University, whose perceptive criticism, kind encouragement, and willing assistance helped bring the project to a successful conclusion, and to my wife, Nancy, who had the unenviable task of reading, correcting, and typing the first draft of the manuscript.

 *Introduction*

The *skomorokhi* can truly be described as the forgotten class of Russian medieval society. For nearly seven hundred years, from the eleventh through the seventeenth century, they provided both peasant and burgher, both low and high born, with entertainment ranging from dancing bears and puppet shows to the recitation of serious heroic verse. Yet they have been the subject of only two brief monographs and a handful of specialized essays. These have by no means done justice to the professional entertainers who are credited not only with the preservation of aspects of native culture but also with the birth of Russian ballet, theater, and secular music.

The reason frequently cited for the scholarly neglect of the Russian minstrels is scarcity of sources, particularly for the early period of their professional existence. A few bitter denunciations in the chronicles and other ecclesiastically inspired literature, and some widely scattered references in official medieval documents—these at first glance appear to be the only traces left by the *skomorokhi* on the pages of Russian history. How could it be otherwise, some may argue: they were, after all, the cultural spokesmen of a basically oral, peasant society. Many of them were itinerant. All were subject to relentless persecution by the church. Even though with time some of them gained respectability and became members in good standing of a particular community, as a group they had no formal organization or anything resembling a traditional guild structure. Under the circumstances, it is remarkable that the *skomorokhi* left as much of an imprint on Russian history as they have.

As far as the written record is concerned, the historian does face some insurmountable problems. Even such relatively hard statistical data as those found in the cadastres, census books, and customs duty records from the late fifteenth, sixteenth, and seventeenth centuries are woefully incomplete and must be used judiciously. This makes it necessary to rely heavily on other disciplines, such as ethnography and archeology, to fill in the many lacunae. The problem thus becomes not so much one of sources as of methodology.

The literature on the *skomorokhi* can best be described as limited in quantity and uneven in quality.[1] The earlier of the two monographs on the subject, A. S. Famintsyn's *Skomorokhi na Rusi* (Saint Petersburg, 1889), is both hopelessly out of date and somewhat superficial and narrow in scope. It draws too heavily on literary and linguistic evidence of dubious historical value. The more recent study, A. A. Belkin's *Russkie skomorokhi* (Moscow, 1975), has a useful review of the secondary literature and the major theories on the origins of the *skomorokhi* and a valuable analysis of the relationship between the legitimate folk theater and the dramatic activities of the Russian minstrels.[2] There are, however, two serious flaws in Belkin's book. By basing his treatment of the place of the *skomorokhi* in Russian society on documents associated with the popular uprisings of 1068, 1547, and 1648, he imposes an artificial sociopolitical framework on his subject.[3] In the process he neglects a large body of documentary, ethnographic, and artistic evidence essential to a fuller understanding and appreciation of the *skomorokhi*. Second, Belkin's discussion of the cultural contribution of the *skomorokhi* is limited to drama, leaving one with the impression that he intended to write a history of the Russian theater to 1650, not a history of the *skomorokhi*.

Without a doubt, N. Findeizen has made one of the most significant contributions to the study of the *skomorokhi* in his superb history of Russian music, which devotes a lengthy section to them.[4] The merit of Findeizen's work lies chiefly in his making the long overdue break with the two prevailing methodological approaches to the study of the *skomorokhi*—the literary and the linguistic. Exponents of these schools have, since the late nineteenth century, been immersed in controversy either over the interpretation of certain *byliny* passages or over etymological minutiae concerning the name *skomorokh*, making little progress toward a better understanding of the institution itself.[5] Findeizen avoids these fruitless debates and concentrates on writing good history. He exploits such previously untapped sources as the Novgorod and Muscovite cadastres, on the basis of which he draws a map illustrating the geographic distribution of the *skomorokhi* throughout medieval Russia.

Except to a handful of specialists interested in the early history of the performing arts in Russia, the *skomorokhi* are virtually unknown in the West: my own essay in the *Slavic Review* and several pages in the Chadwicks' study of Russian oral literature are all that one will find on the subject in English.[6] This neglect is the more unfortunate since, in terms of broad cultural influence, the *skomorokhi* are perhaps of greater significance to Russia than the *Spielmänner* are to Germany or the *jongleurs* to France.

In the following pages I intend, first, to subject the existing sources to rigorous scrutiny and, second, to introduce new evidence from other disciplines in the hope of creating something like a mosaic, as E. K. Chambers did in *The Mediaeval Stage*, one of the classic studies of the West European minstrel. The main objective of this study is to trace the history of the *skomorokhi* from their origins in pre-Christian times to their dispersal in the seventeenth century, when they ceased to function as a professional class. From the time that they first became the subject of serious scholarly research in the mid-nineteenth century, the origins of the *skomorokhi* have been the concern primarily of etymologists and folklorists. Historians, while generally aware of their role in the cultural life of Muscovite Russia, have shown little interest in the earliest period of their history. It is not unusual, for example, for historians to describe the beginnings of *skomoroshestvo* as "obscure" or "shrouded in mystery," and then somewhat apologetically hasten onto the terra firma of the Novgorod and Muscovite periods (fifteenth through seventeenth centuries), where the evidence for the activities of the Russian minstrels, while not overwhelming, is at least less ambiguous and incontrovertible.

The question of origins is of particular interest here because on it hinges an underlying premise of this study—that were it not for the *skomorokhi*, whom I believe were originally priests of the pagan religion of the Eastern Slavs, much of what is regarded as native in Russian culture might not have survived. In other words, it was not as professional minstrels, as is normally assumed, that the *skomorokhi* made their most significant contribution to Russian music, dance, theater, and oral tradition, but rather as former cult leaders. It was in this capacity that they became, after 988, the heirs of a discredited native, pagan culture, which they kept alive for hundreds of years in the face of intense persecution and pervasive foreign (Byzantine and Western) influence.

My second objective is to dispel the widely held notion,

common among scholars in the West in particular, that the *skomo-rokhi* were little more than traveling buffoons, an unruly lot of vagrants who appealed only to the lowest ranks of society. Illustrative of this unfortunate typing is the following passage from C. R. Smith's translation of Iu. M. Sokolov's classic study of Russian folklore, *Russkii fol'klor*: "The *byliny*, these songs which are so diverse in their historical content, penetrated into the North through the medieval popular poets and musicians, the so-called 'buffoons' and clowns, analogous to the French *jongleurs*, [and] the German *Spielmänner*. . . ."[7] One may legitimately ask why the French *jongleurs* and German *Spielmänner* have retained their professional identity in this passage, while the Russian *skomorokhi* have been transformed into clowns and buffoons.

Other, less glaring, examples can be cited to illustrate the low regard in which the *skomorokhi* have, with little justification, traditionally been held. "Minstrelsy in Russia," writes R. N. Leonard, "never reached the stage of a fine art as it did in the West. . . . The Russian minstrels enjoyed neither privilege nor dignity."[8] And in a recently published essay on early Russian keyboard music, J. Spiegelman describes the *skomorokhi* simply as "roving bands" of "musical vagabonds" and concludes his description by saying that "these minstrels were not the respected artists that their western counterparts were, and their art probably never reached a high degree of refinement. . . ."[9]

There is some truth to these harsh judgments if one has in mind some of the itinerant *skomorokhi* of the sixteenth and seventeenth centuries. The *Stoglav*, as well as other sources, reminds us that some of the itinerant minstrels had indeed degenerated into lawless brigands by the mid-sixteenth century. These, however, by no means constituted a majority. As we know from numerous cadastral and census entries, many of the *skomorokhi* had, by the late fifteenth century and perhaps even earlier, taken up permanent residence in towns and villages throughout Muscovy. Some had become small landowners; others, shopkeepers; one, a restaurateur. In a word, the noninitinerant *skomorokhi* evolved very early into a distinct socioeconomic class, although they maintained their professional identity and continued to practice their ancient craft. As for the alleged lack of privilege and dignity accorded the Russian minstrels, one can point to Ivan IV's special importation of the most talented *skomorokhi* from Novgorod and vicinity to his court in Moscow, several of whom he rewarded handsomely by integrating them into his elite corps of *oprichniki*, and to the fact that in the reign of Michael Romanov, some of the *skomorokhi* were in a position to make petitions of grievances directly to the tsar.

Finally, this study focuses on the important question of the legacy of the *skomorokhi* to the performing arts and oral literature, and illustrates, with specific examples where possible, the nature of that legacy. Even where there is an awareness that the *skomorokhi* have made a contribution to some area of Russian culture, there is too often an accompanying vagueness as to the precise nature of that contribution or how it was made. It is not enough to say, as one authority on the Russian ballet recently did, that "the *skomorokhi* did much to spread the art of dancing in ancient Russia,"[10] and to stop there.

In conclusion, I hope that this study will be more than just a history of the Russian minstrels, for I intend it also as a modest overview of certain aspects of Russian popular, or low, culture that have hitherto received little attention. Through it I hope to demonstrate how that purportedly pagan, native culture was preserved and disseminated by a few talented men and became ultimately a source of inspiration to men of genius in a more recent age.

1
Origins
and Early
History

In the introduction to his *Skomorokhi na Rusi*, A. S. Famintsyn notes that whether one traces the origins of the *skomorokhi* to Byzantium or to Western Europe, there is little doubt that, by the eleventh century, they had become an integral part of the cultural life of the Eastern Slavs. Furthermore, according to Famintsyn, the period from the eleventh through the seventeenth century can justifiably be labeled "the epoch of the *skomorokhi*," particularly as regards the early history of secular music in Russia.[1] Underlying Famintsyn's remarks are two basic assumptions: first, that the origins of the *skomorokhi* are foreign, either Byzantine or Western European, and second, that these origins can be traced back to the eleventh century only. The same historical framework has for many years served as a model for most, though not all, scholars interested in the *skomorokhi*. A thorough re-evaluation of both a priori assumptions is not only long overdue but absolutely essential if the *skomorokhi* are to be accorded their rightful place in the cultural history of the Eastern Slavs.

The question of the origins of the *skomorokhi* is somewhat reminiscent of the continuing debate over the origin of the Rus', both the people and the name. (As Professor Valentin Kiparsky, the distinguished linguist of the University of Helsinki, recently pointed out in conversation, the word *skomorokh*, like *Rus'*, is a veritable gold mine for etymologists, affording limitless possibilities for comparative linguistic analysis.) As has been the case with the Rus', the etymological roots of the *skomorokhi* have been sought in a variety of languages and cultures, among them Greek, Arabic, French, Scandinavian, Italian, and Old Slavonic.[2] However, the ety-

1

mological explanations for the origins of the *skomorokhi* have proven less than convincing to historians, no doubt because of the apparent inability of linguists to approach the subject dispassionately, without a compulsion to prove that the *skomorokhi* were of foreign origin in both name and profession. Only Šafařik and Il'inskii, the two spokesmen for the Old Slavonic school, have sought native etymological roots for the *skomorokhi*,[3] and even they have failed to explore the possibility that the *skomorokhi* may have deep cultural and historical roots in native soil.

The unquestioning acceptance by Famintsyn and others of foreign origins for the *skomorokhi* is the more puzzling since, as early as the mid-nineteenth century, two widely respected scholars, I. Beliaev and A. Afanas'ev, had provided evidence of the minstrels' strong links with Russia's native pagan past. In the first scholarly piece devoted exclusively to the *skomorokhi*, published in 1854, Beliaev writes that there was a long-standing tradition of participation by *skomorokh*-like musicians in wedding ceremonies and memorial rites among the early Eastern and Western Slavs.[4] Although he does not call these early pagan musicians *skomorokhi*, Beliaev implies that they were related to the latter, if not in name, at least in function.

In his important two-volume study of Slavic mythology, *Poeticheskiia vozzreniia slavian na prirodu* (1865), Afanas'ev elaborates on Beliaev's remarks on the origins of the *skomorokhi*. He points out that the early pagan musicians, or proto-*skomorokhi*, of whom Beliaev speaks were involved not only in wedding and memorial rites, but also in the numerous seasonal festivals that punctuated the calendar year. According to Afanas'ev, the pagan Slavs were animists and tried to invoke and appease nature by performing certain ritual ceremonies, which invariably included music, song, and dance. During these cyclic religious observances, the proto-*skomorokhi* donned masks, danced, played musical instruments, and generally performed the function of priests or cult leaders. As evidence of the importance of the *skomorokhi*-priests to the pagan cult of the early Slavs, Afanas'ev cites the virulent and persistent attacks upon their successors, the professional minstrel-entertainers, by both ecclesiastical and secular authorities.[5]

Two other nineteenth-century scholars, A. I. Ponomarev and A. Sobolevskii, took issue with the various etymological theories that claimed foreign origins for the *skomorokhi*. In a critical review of A. I. Kirpichnikov's important article on the *skomorokhi*, which had appeared in 1891, Sobolevskii suggested that rather than continue to engage in futile etymological speculation, his colleagues should turn their attention to traditional survivals of old Russian culture, such as the *Maslenitsa* (pre-Lenten spring festival), in which originally the *skomorokhi* and later their spiritual successors played an important role as late as the nineteenth century.[6]

Several years after the appearance of Sobolevskii's review, an attempt was made to explain the origins of the *skomorokhi* along the lines he had suggested. In the absence of a well-defined priestly class among the early Slavs, wrote A. I. Ponomarev, it was necessary to entrust the rites and rituals connected with the pagan cult to an amorphous group of cult leaders that included the proto-*skomorokhi*. As paganism progressively lost more ground to Christianity, the rites and rituals associated with it either became extinct or were transformed into ordinary folk games and festivals. As for the cult leaders, many of them ceased to function professionally, while others, to wit, the *skomorokhi*, adapted easily to the changed circumstances and became professional entertainers, or *veselye liudi*.[7]

Origins

When the *skomorokhi* first appear on the pages of eleventh-century historical sources, they have already emerged as an established Kievan sociocultural institution. An entry in the Primary Chronicle for 1068 describes them in the following words: "With these [that is, pagan practices and superstitions] and other devices the devil deceives us, with all manner of enticements he draws us away from God, with horns and *skomorokhi*, with *gusli* and *rusalii*."[8] At first glance one might be inclined to dismiss the "enticements" enumerated here as rhetoric used freely by the chronicler-monk to condemn all popular worldly amusements; indeed, scholars have frequently given the passage that interpretation. But is that in fact what the chronicler meant?

The 1068 entry begins with the factual statement that the Polovtsy have for the second time—the first attack occurred in 1061—invaded the land of Rus'. Three of the Rus' princes, Iziaslav of Kiev, Sviatoslav of Chernigov, and Vsevolod of Pereiaslavl, marched against them, and a battle ensued on the river Al'ta (L'to) below Kiev from which the Polovtsy emerged victorious. It was this national calamity that prompted the chronicler to launch into a lengthy tirade on the wickedness of his countrymen, whom God was obviously punishing for their sins. "When any nation has sinned," he writes, "God punishes it by death or famine or barbarian incursion. . . ." After drawing heavily on the Old Testament prophets to develop and illustrate the theme of divine retribution, the chronicler comes to the heart of his argument. "Do we not live like pagans as long as we attach superstitious significance to meetings? For he turns back who meets a monk or a swine. Is that not pagan? It is part and parcel of the devil's teaching to adhere to such divinations."[9] It is in this paragraph, devoted to pagan survivals among the people, that the reference to the *skomorokhi* occurs. What the chronicler is concerned with here is not the worldliness of his countrymen, but rather their residual paganism.

Having placed it in its proper context, we must examine this passage in greater detail. The four devilish enticements singled out by the chronicler are *trubi* ("horns"), *skomorokhi*, *gusli*, and *rusalii*. The first term mentioned, *trubi*, is the most obvious and least difficult to render into English. The other three have no English equivalents and are basically untranslatable. *Skomorokhi* may be described as versatile entertainers; *gusli* as a stringed musical instrument; *Rusaliia* (plural *Rusalii*) as a folk festival corresponding roughly to Midsummer. There is an obvious generic relationship between the *trubi* and *gusli*—both are musical instruments. Less obvious is the relationship between the *skomorokhi* and the *Rusalii*. In the eyes of the chronicler, however, there is clearly a symbiotic relationship among the four.

It is evident from the chronicles and other sources that with the advent of Christianity all musical instruments were looked upon as pagan and held in contempt by the church. Nestor condemned both horns and *gusli*. When the eleventh-century Kievan monk Isaac was confronted in his cell by demons trying to tempt and torment him, they were playing loudly on flutes, *gusli*, and tambourines.[10] There was, we know, a long tradition of instrumental music, both sacred and profane, among the Eastern Slavs prior to their conversion.[11] However, by accepting Byzantine Christianity, the Kievan Slavs also inherited the Byzantine tradition of vocal liturgical music. Like many other aspects of Kievan culture, native music was labeled pagan and *officially* proscribed.

There is a closer relationship than may at first appear between the *skomorokhi* and the two musical instruments singled out by the chronicler. From earliest times music was an integral element in the pagan cult of the Slavs, used in magic rites, conjurations, and charm incantations. In fact, both the *gusli* and the horn were quite early identified among the Slavs, as among many other primitive peoples, with magic and the occult.[12] Thus Buslaev, in describing the pan-Slavic origin of the word *gusli*, notes that in Sorbian *gusslowasch* once meant "to practice witchcraft" and that a *gusslowař* was a male witch. In Polish *gusli* formerly meant "witchcraft," while among the Kievan Slavs, Buslaev maintains, the word once carried a connotation of pagan worship or sacrifice, and the Sorbians, or Wends, after their conversion attached to it the meaning "pagan altar."[13] According to K. W. Wojcicki, the nineteenth-century Polish literary historian, the *gęslarzy*, or pagan priests, in 1034 spearheaded a violent anti-Christian reaction in Poland, which resulted in the destruction of churches and the murder of many priests and monks, particularly in Cracow and Gniezno.[14] Wojcicki traces the history of these Polish *gusli* players to prehistoric times and identifies them with the pagan cult of the Western Slavs.[15]

While it was the *gusli* that eventually became the musical instrument most closely identified with the *skomorokhi*, the horn, in its various forms, also played an important part in their professional activities, both religious and, later, secular. In the earlier, pre-Christian period, we know that horns were used extensively by the pagan priests of the Baltic Slavs.[16] Much later, in a *Paterik* dating from the fifteenth century and in the prologue to one from the sixteenth, we find the word *skomorokh* used to render the Greek expression for "fife player."[17] In many of the surviving sixteenth-century cadastres, *skomorokh* is used interchangeably not only with *gusel'nik* ("*gusli* player"), but also with *dudnik* and *rozhechnik* ("fife player").[18]

The fourth and last of the pagan practices singled out for censure by the chronicler is *Rusalii*, described earlier as the folk festival corresponding roughly to Midsummer. The name *Rusalii* is probably of classical origin and has been traced to the *rosalia* (*rosaria, dies rosae*) of the ancient Romans, among whom it signified the days on which ancestors were commemorated with garlands of roses placed upon their graves. The placing of the roses was frequently accompanied by special rites and songs at the gravesite. The Slavs are believed to have borrowed this commemorative feast from the Romans via Thrace and Macedonia. It eventually spread throughout the Slavonic world, developing its own national and regional peculiarities wherever it appeared.[19] The Kievan Slavs celebrated the festival of *Rusaliia* as early as the fourth century A.D. According to B. A. Rybakov, it was a week-long celebration that began on 19 June and ended on 24 June, culminating on that date with *Kupalo*, more commonly known in the West as Midsummer, or the Feast of Saint John the Baptist.[20] With the advent of Christianity, *Rusaliia* was incorporated into the Kievan liturgical cycle and became identified with the week preceding Trinity Sunday, or Pentecost. It continued to be regarded as a festival of the dead or a festival of ancestors; however, in keeping with the spirit of the new religion, the emphasis shifted from ancestor worship to the

shadowy world of those who had the misfortune of dying an un-
natural death, particularly women who drowned and infants who
died unbaptized. The theme of the festival, as reflected in the
numerous songs and rites associated with it, now revolved around
the warding off of malevolent *rusalki* from one's person, home,
fields, and village community.[21]

Like horns and *gusli*, the *Rusalii* were closely identified by
the chronicler with the *skomorokhi*. That *Rusalii* and *skomorokhi*
were frequently spoken of in the same breath and, with time, became interchangeable can be demonstrated.[22] In the *Zlatustroi*, a
collection of Byzantine didactic and homiletic literature dating from
the late twelfth century, one finds the Greek expression for "pagan
games" rendered into Slavonic as *skomrakhi* (a South Slavic equivalent of *skomorokhi*) and *rusalii*.[23] In a thirteenth-century commentary on the writings of Saint Paul, incorporated into the so-called
Isbornik, or *Sbornik*, the good Christian is admonished to avoid
all contact with the *skomorokhi* and their games, or *rusalii*.[24] Another thirteenth-century source, the "Slovo sv. Nifonta o rusa-
liiakh," makes no distinction between the two and condemns the
skomorokhi as the personification of *rusalii*.[25] Finally, the *Azbukov-
nik*, a kind of encyclopedic lexicon published anonymously in numerous editions during the seventeenth century, contains this entry
for *Rusaliia: "igry skomorosheskiia"* ("games of the *skomorokhi*").[26] The fusion of *Rusalii* with *skomorokhi* has become
complete.

Clearly, the author of the Primary Chronicle intended to
identify the *skomorokhi*, in no uncertain terms, with paganism. The
task before us now is to define the role of the *skomorokhi* in the
pagan cult of the Eastern Slavs, both before and after their conversion to Christianity. First, however, we must trace the main
features of the pre-Christian religion of the Kievan Slavs.

Until the tenth century, Kievan paganism was an amorphous
phenomenon. Each of the Slavic tribes that made up the Kievan
state had its own preferred gods. It was not until Vladimir the
Great had consolidated his authority in Kiev (978–80) that an
attempt was made to standardize the religion of the state and thus
raise its prestige in the eyes of the world. The standardization took
the outward form of an open-air sanctuary in Kiev that brought
together into one pantheon the gods of the various Slavic tribes,
providing also a powerful symbol of the political unity of the newly
expanded Kievan realm.[27] While there was no well-defined priestly
class to oversee this newly reorganized pagan cult, there were the
traditional *volkhvy*, wisemen or Magi, who exercised considerable

influence, especially among the urban class.[28] They were the overseers of public worship and sacrifice, practiced medicine and surgery, and were invested with judicial authority.[29] Their fame as soothsayers, particularly among the well to do, was widespread. Even the highly subjective, ecclesiastically inspired Primary Chronicle, when relating the circumstances surrounding Prince Oleg's death in 912, notes with obvious respect and awe the soothsayer-*volkhv*'s prediction of the precise manner of Oleg's death.[30]

It must be emphasized that the *volkhvy* were a distinctly urban and upper-class phenomenon. The evidence we have for this is twofold. First, they possessed a more than rudimentary philosophical system that would have had little appeal for, and would have been largely incomprehensible to, the illiterate masses. Second, they drew their support from the larger towns and cities, and, for the most part, restricted their activities to them. This was particularly true during the eleventh century, when they tried to instigate a pagan reaction against Christianity in ·Kiev, Novgorod, Rostov, Suzdal, Iaroslavl, and Beloozero.[31] Concerning their philosophical system, an entry in the Primary Chronicle for 1071 describes two *volkhvy* defending their beliefs before one of Prince Sviatoslav's boyars; what they have to say about God, creation, and the role of Satan or evil in the universe bears a striking resemblance to Manichaeism, or dualism.[32] It is not at all unlikely that the concept of dualism was introduced into Kievan Rus' by the *volkhvy*. It was probably borrowed from Bulgaria, where it enjoyed considerable popularity during the tenth and eleventh centuries under the name of Bogomilism.[33] The *volkhvy* may have circulated their philosophical ideas among the educated through the medium of the *Glubinnye knigi* (literally "Books of Depth, or Deep Wisdom"), about which, unfortunately, we know very little.[34]

Official paganism did not endure long in Kievan Rus', giving way in 988 to Byzantine Christianity. As for the *volkhvy*, some fled and sought refuge among the Baltic and Balkan Slavs. Others became nominal Christians and awaited the opportunity to reverse the tide of Christianity, as indeed they attempted to do in 1071.[35] The old priestly class, meanwhile, was replaced by a new one, which continued to minister primarily to the faithful in the cities, among whom Christianity found its firmest roots. The majority of the people in the countryside remained largely unaffected by the new religion and persisted in the practice of the tribal cult of their ancestors.[36] The Metropolitan of Kiev, Ioann II (1080–89), aptly characterized this peculiar dichotomy between the urban and rural classes in matters of religious practice: "You say the marriages of the simple folk are not blessed or wed [by a priest], but only boyars and princes are wed, and the simple people take their wives like concubines with dances, music, and noise."[37]

To return to the question posed prior to our digression into Kievan paganism: what precisely was the role of the *skomorokhi* in the pagan cult of the Eastern Slavs? We can begin by focusing once more on the Primary Chronicle's enumeration of pagan practices common among the Kievan Slavs. Assuming that the chronicler did not draw up his list haphazardly (a valid assumption, I believe, in view of the evidence cited above), we can derive from it some important clues about the early activities of the *skomorokhi*. We know that in Kievan times both horns and *gusli* were essential to the performance of various pagan rites, including magic, conjuration, divination, healing, and the casting of charms or spells. The chronicler's identification of the *skomorokhi* with these instruments seems to imply that they were closely associated with the pagan rites in which the horn and *gusli* were widely used. Some scholars have even suggested that, in view of the magical powers attributed to music by the early Slavs and the intimate relationship of the *skomorokhi* to music and musical instruments, the *skomorokhi* may have been members of a powerful, secret, religious fraternity with extensive, and no doubt exclusive, rights over the occult arts in Kievan Rus'.[38]

Evidence of the widespread reputation for magic and sorcery that the *skomorokhi* enjoyed can be found in the Chronicle of Pereiaslavl-Suzdal. An entry for the year 1070 contains the following curious passage: "There was at that time a famine in the district of Rostov when two crafty men arrived from Iaroslavl saying: 'We know who holds the answer [to the food shortage].' And they went along the Volga and asked that a number of the most distinguished women be brought to them, saying that some of these affected the grain supply, some the fish, some the furs. Then the inhabitants [from the surrounding areas] brought them their mothers, and sisters, and wives, while they, by means of magic in the fashion of the *skomorokhi*, stabbed each of the women in the back and then before all the people took wheat from some, and from others honey, furs, and fish. They thus killed many women and took what they had for themselves."[39] The implication of the reference to "magic in the fashion of the *skomorokhi*" seems to be that by the end of the eleventh century, magic and *skomorokhi* had become synonymous.

In the *Kormchaia kniga* of 1282, in the section entitled "On Sorcery," there is an intriguing reference to "those who drag around bears or other animals with them for the purpose of omen reading."[40] Since there is in this same section a separate reference to the *volkhvy*, it is presumably the rustic *skomorokhi* who are here implicated in divination through the use of animals, particularly bears. The bear, like the *gusli*, eventually became a trademark of the *skomorokhi*-entertainers.

As late as the seventeenth century, on the eve of their formal proscription by Aleksei, the *skomorokhi* were still feared and respected for their ability to cast spells. A story attributed to Simon Azarin, an elder of the Trinity–Saint Sergius Monastery, is illustrative. In a village not far from the monastery, a band of *skomorokhi*-entertainers gave a performance and solicited voluntary contributions at its conclusion. A certain woman in the audience refused to make a donation, whereupon, says the author, the *skomorokhi* cast a spell upon her, making her deathly ill, and warned of even worse evils that would befall her in the future.[41]

An echo of their former reputation as warlocks has been preserved until recent times in some of the customs and traditions surrounding a peasant wedding in Russia. In the province of Viatka, for example, it is customary for the best man, always an avowed sorcerer, to lead the wedding party to the church, chanting a prescribed series of incantations to ward off evil from the bride and groom.[42] From the *Stoglav* of 1551 we learn that for a long time the *skomorokhi* had the distinction of escorting the wedding party to the church, preceding even the cross-bearing priest.[43] It was in their role as warlocks that the *skomorokhi* left a lasting imprint on the peasant wedding.

Finally, in a strange, though by no means unique, fusion of the pagan and the Christian, one finds the *skomorokhi* identified in folk literature with the two patron saints of physicians, Cosmas and Damian. In the *bylina* "Puteshestvie Vavily so skomorokhami" (frequently also "Vavilo i skomorokhi"),[44] repeated reference is made to these two third-century Eastern saints, who, according to popular Christian legend, were philanthropic physicians who offered their services gratis to the people. During the reign of Diocletian they were accused of witchcraft by their anti-Christian persecutors and put to death as martyrs.[45] It is probably no mere coincidence that these two popular Russian saints, healers by profession and warlocks by allegation, were chosen as patrons by the *skomorokhi*.

We have examined one facet of the many and varied activities of the *skomorokhi* in their professional relationship to the people in the countryside. We can learn more about this relationship by taking a closer look at the *Rusalii*, noted by the chronicler as one of the more persistent pagan festivals. Whereas the association of the *skomorokhi* with horns and *gusli* provides some insight into the personal side of their priestly functions, their identification with the *Rusaliia* will reveal the communal, or social, aspect of their activities.

The week-long observance of the *Rusaliia* traditionally marked the high point of both the agricultural year and the summer festival season. Its strong agrarian overtones are manifested in the belief that the *navki* or *mavki*, who have spent the winter in their traditional dwelling place, nearby waters, have now to be escorted into the fields and ultimately into the grain itself to secure a good harvest. Housewives make a path by sprinkling milk on the ground, leading away from the water to the edge of the fields, where the head of the household places a piece of bread for the female water spirits. Once the spirits have passd from the water to the grain, it is safe to bathe in the water without fear of being drowned by the *mavki*.[46]

As was noted earlier in this chapter, the *Rusaliia* festival has over the years undergone a basic change in emphasis. In its original form, and probably down to the mid-seventeenth century, it was primarily a memorial observance or festival of the dead, marked by the remembrance of one's ancestors. It was with this earlier phase of the *Rusaliia* that the *skomorokhi* were identified and in which they played such a singular role (recall the *Azbukov-nik's* definition of *Rusaliia* in the seventeenth century as "games of the *skomorokhi*"). In light of the close relationship between the *skomorokhi* and the *Rusaliia*, it seems likely that it was Aleksei's harsh condemnation and official proscription of the *skomorokhi* and their "devilish games" in 1648 that marked the beginning of the gradual shift in emphasis in the festival from memorial observance to agricultural feast.

With the aid of two pre-seventeenth-century sources it is possible to reconstruct, if only partially, the earlier version of the *Rusaliia* festival. The *Stoglav* of 1551 contains the more complete description of the festival. On the Saturday before Trinity Sunday (the eighth Sunday after Easter), men and women gather in village graveyards for a memorial observance. There is first a period of loud and mournful lamentation on the graves of individual ancestors. Then the *skomorokhi* begin playing their musical instruments while the mourners cease crying and commence dancing, clapping their hands, and singing "Satanic songs."[47] In the "Life of Saint Nifont," which dates back at least to the twelfth century, there are several additional details about the *Rusaliia*. Most significant is the revelation that animal masks were widely used during the festival; while some of those overseeing the ceremonies (that is, presumably, the *skomorokhi*) beat on tambourines or played bagpipes and fifes, others donned animal masks and "made sport of man."[48] There is a strong suggestion here of sacred drama, which may have been an integral part of the celebration.[49] What is particularly important for us, however, is the presiding role of the *skomorokhi* in these early *Rusaliia* festivals.

At the opposite end of the calendar year, in late December and early January, corresponding more or less to the winter solstice, there was another important and quite ancient festival period known as *Koliada*.[50] Among the Eastern Slavs, the *Koliada* festival originally focused on the theme of rebirth, of renewed hope in the revival of nature, signified by the beginning of the sun's gradual return. Our primary source of information about the early *Koliada* is the extensive cycle of ritual songs associated with it. These have been preserved, with some textual changes, to be sure, for hundreds of years in oral and, more recently, written form.[51] The *Koliada* songs are not as emphatic as the *Rusaliia* songs in identifying the *skomorokhi* with this winter festival, but they nonetheless leave little doubt that there once was a close relationship between the two. Generally speaking, the *skomorokhi* have left their imprint on the *Koliada* songs in two ways. There are, first of all, songs in which they are mentioned by name and described as itinerant minstrels coming with their *gudki* (musical instruments resembling the modern cello) to entertain the master of the house and his guests.[52] Then there are the numerous shorter songs that have a light, humorous, and even insouciant or bawdy air about them, which are the unmistakable creation of the *skomorokhi* themselves.[53] In both instances the surviving *koliadki* reflect a later stage in the development of the *Koliada* cycle of songs when the *skomorokhi* had already become established professional entertainers. They tell us little about the earlier *Koliada* festival.

For this we must turn to the so-called mythological songs, considered by many to be the oldest of the *koliadki*. These are generally distinguished by their dialogue form (an echo of their former representational and dramatic character) and their pervasive themes of creation and rebirth.[54] One Ukrainian song in this group, from the district of Chernigov, is of particular interest. It has as its central figure the goat, the ancient symbol of fertility of the soil among the Eastern Slavs and many other peoples, and as its central theme the securing of the harvest by the death and resurrection of the goat-grain. The song opens with an exhortation to the goat-grain to procure a plentiful harvest for its master. In spite of warnings, the goat wanders off to the neighboring village, where he is mortally wounded and dies. A *mikhonosha* (literally "sack carrier") is summoned to revive the dead goat. He does so by blowing with his fife, or *dudochka,* into the goat's vein (that is, his reproductive organ). The goat-grain revives and goes out into the fields, where it will now secure a bountiful harvest of oats, barley, and wheat.[55]

Among the noteworthy features of this Ukrainian *koliadka,* which is known to have been acted out as late as 1915, are its dramatic character and the pivotal role of the *mikhonosha* in the story. This is undoubtedly one of the oldest East Slavic fertility rites to survive intact to our own day.[56] The use of masks, an integral part of the performance, can be traced back at least to the eleventh century. According to most scholars, it was probably the ritual plays connected with the *Koliada* festival that the eleventh-century Bishop of Novgorod, Luka Zhidiata, had in mind when he warned his flock to shun *moskoludstvo.*[57] Also noteworthy, as Evreinov and others have pointed out, is the striking similarity between the Slavic rituals involving the goat-grain and the rustic Dionysia of ancient Greece.[58]

The role of the *mikhonosha* (Russian *mekhonosha*) in this *koliadka* requires additional comment and explanation. In recent times the term has been applied to the person responsible for looking after (or, literally, carrying) the sack containing the donations made to the performers in *Koliada* skits and plays.[59] Earlier, the name seems to have been applied to the *skomorokhi* in a similar context. In the folksong about Gost' Terentii, for example, the *skomorokh* who carries the sack with the unfortunate husband in it is referred to as a *mekhonosha.*[60] It is quite likely that formerly *skomorokh* and *mekhonosha* were used interchangeably and that the *mekhonosha* called upon in the *koliadka* to revive the slain goat is, in fact, a *skomorokh* performing one of his medico-magical priestly functions. Here, as in the *Rusaliia* festival, the dominant role of the *skomorokhi* in the religious life of the community is vividly reflected.

Finally, the *skomorokhi*-priests played the same role in a somewhat different kind of festive celebration, one that was no less communal in scope than the *Rusaliia* and *Koliada.* Of all the events that touched the life of the early Slav, none was of greater significance to the individual, his clan, and his community than marriage.[61] A wedding was truly an act of the clan and of the community; in time the ceremonies grew into a lengthy and elaborate ritual involving, actively or passively, every member of the community, beginning with the matchmaking and ending with a great feast on the day following the nuptials.[62] The whole was given a distinctly dramatic character with stereotyped roles for all the principals. In fact, the usual way of referring to the customs

and rituals associated with a wedding was by the phrase *igrat'
svad'bu* ("to play a wedding").[63]

In describing the marriage customs of the early East Slavic
peoples, the Primary Chronicle notes that only the Poliane had a
fixed custom whereby the groom did not himself have to go and
fetch a wife; rather, she was brought to him in the evening, while
her dowry was brought after her on the following day. As for the
other tribes in the Kievan region—the Drevliane, Radimichi,
Viatichi, and Severiani—they took their wives forcibly, by capture,
arranging festivals between their villages precisely for that purpose. In the words of the chronicler: "They would come together
for games, for dancing, and for all manner of devilish amusements
and would then seize wives for themselves, and each took any
woman with whom he had reached some understanding."[64] The
notion that a wedding was a type of community festival persisted
among the majority of the people long after the introduction of
Christianity. The words of Metropolitan Ioann II of Kiev cited
earlier attest to that.

To better appreciate the role of the *skomorokhi* in this important community function, it is necessary to keep several things
in mind. First, among the Eastern Slavs, as among many other
peoples, magic, both prophylactic and productive, was considered
indispensable for a successful and happy marriage. Second, it was
not the bridal couple or their parents, but rather the matchmakers
and the attendants of the bride and groom, particularly the *druzhko*
(Russian *druzhka*), or best man, who directed from start to finish
the long and drawn-out wedding drama. It was the *druzhko's* responsibility to keep all manner of evil away from the bridal couple
through the use of prophylactic magic and, equally, if not more,
importantly, to ensure their future fertility, wealth, and good
health through the use of productive magic.[65] Under the circumstances, who was better suited than a *skomorokh* to serve as aide
to the groom and preside as master of ceremonies over the wedding
fete?[66]

Evidence that the *skomorokhi* once served in both capacities
can be found in a variety of different sources. In the *Stoglav* of
1551, for example, there is a stern condemnation of the widespread
custom of allowing a *skomorokh* to escort the wedding party to the
church ahead of the cross-bearing priest, apparently a reference
to a long-standing tradition, predating the involvement of the
priest in the marriage ceremonies, of dominance by the *skomorokhi*
over the entire ritual.[67] Even as late as the mid-nineteenth century, one could still find in some areas of Russia a sorcerer serving
as *druzhka*, or best man. His place was at the head of the wedding

procession reciting a prescribed set of incantations to ward off the evil eye, the loose woman, the heretic, the slanderer, and so forth from the bridal couple.[68]

Echoes of the participation of the *skomorokhi* in the wedding celebration can be heard in surviving wedding songs that mentioned them by name and allude to their function as masters of ceremonies.[69] Moreover, a peculiar custom known as "gypsying," recorded by Chubinskii in several areas of the Ukraine, also reflects the community spirit and festival atmosphere that once permeated the Slavic wedding. After all the food and drink provided by the wedding hosts has been exhausted, the guests who remain (and are sober) don masks and costumes (men exchange clothes with women). Then, to the accompaniment of music, they sally forth into the village among relatives, friends, and neighbors of the bride and groom and help themselves to whatever they chance upon in the way of food. The money they are able to cajole or steal is used to buy more vodka. And so the wedding festivities continue.[70] According to Niederle, the use of masks and costumes, particularly men dressing up as women and vice versa, was once an integral part of the ancient Slavic wedding rite.[71] One might note that the *Kormchaia kniga* of 1282 singles out for special censure the practice of men exchanging clothes with women.[72] It is entirely possible that the Ukrainian custom of gypsying is a corrupt version of an earlier wedding ritual in which the *skomorokhi* took a leading part.

I began this chapter by questioning the a priori assumption, enunciated by Famintsyn and others, that the *skomorokhi* were basically of foreign origin (either Byzantine or Western) and that their history can be traced only as far back as the eleventh century. Taking a cue from Afanas'ev, who identified the *skomorokhi*, albeit vaguely, with the pagan cult of the early Slavs, I have broached the question of origins from the perspective of what we know of the early functions of the *skomorokhi* in their sociocultural and religious milieu. Unlike Famintsyn and others, who have relied heavily on oral tradition, particularly the *byliny*, I turned instead to existing historical and literary sources convinced that, meager though they were, they would still prove intrinsically more reliable and revealing. A close reading of the Primary Chronicle and other early references to the *skomorokhi*, supplemented by ethnographic evidence, allows us to draw two tentative conclusions: first, that in their origins the *skomorokhi* appear to be a distinctly native phenomenon, intimately related to the pagan religion of the Eastern Slavs; and second, and more to the point, that the earliest *skomorokhi* were probably pagan priests, the rustic counterparts of the urban *volkhvy*, who ministered to the people of the countryside in a variety of ways, ranging from fortune telling and healing to presiding over their sundry community festivals and celebrations.

Early History

While it may be impossible to say with any degree of certainty how far back the origins of the *skomorokhi* extend, one can reasonably begin their history as professional minstrels with the date 988. In fact 988, which marks the official conversion of Kievan Rus' to Christianity, was only the first of three turning points in the long history of the *skomorokhi*. A second such turning point came in 1571, during the reign of Ivan IV, when the geographic center of their activity shifted from Novgorod to Moscow, marking the beginning of a period of rapid decline. This decline culminated in a third and final turning point, their formal proscription by Aleksei in 1648.

In spite of Vladimir's effort to swiftly and thoroughly transform his people from a nation of heathens to one of enlightened Christians, he fell far short of his ideal. To be sure, many of the pagan idols in Kiev and the other cities were torn down and publicly dishonored. It was urban paganism, however, that was officially disavowed and forsaken.[73] The majority of the people in the countryside were largely unaffected by the conversion and would not be affected for a long time to come; they continued to practice the ancient cult of their ancestors and to call upon the *skomorokhi* for spiritual guidance. As for the *skomorokhi* themselves, life was never the same again. In the eyes of both ecclesiastical and secular authorities they were virtually the embodiment of paganism, and, with their close ties to the people, a very real threat to the new religion. Consequently they were anathematized and became the object of continuous abuse and persecution: all references to them from the eleventh century on vividly attest to that.[74]

How did the *skomorokhi* adjust to these new circumstances? Some probably went into exile like their urban counterparts, the *volkhvy*. Others may have forsaken their pagan ways and become Christians. The majority undoubtedly took a different course, one that enabled them to achieve a modicum of accomodation with the authorities and at the same time to continue their multifarious activities among the people. They transformed themselves into professional minstrel-entertainers after the fashion of the Byzantine mimes and German *Spielmänner*, or *Spielleute*, who had by the eleventh century evidently become a familiar sight in the larger cities of Kievan Rus'.

Paradoxically, these foreign entertainers seem to have been far less objectionable to the Kievan ecclesiastical authorities than the native *skomorokhi*; I say "paradoxically" because along with Byzantine Christianity, Kiev also inherited Byzantine church law with its ascetic idealism and inherent mistrust of all things worldly. In the period following the iconoclast controversy, however, Byzantine rigorism had lapsed and with it the enforcement of the canons prohibiting secular entertainment.[75] In Kiev, as in Byzantium, the prohibitions against secular entertainment were largely unenforced and unenforceable. The young and fledgling church in Kievan Rus' was far more concerned with eradicating paganism than with mere worldliness or secularism.

It can be readily demonstrated that both the mimes and the *Spielmänner* had at one time or another visited Kievan Rus', bringing with them the brand of entertainment for which they were famous. The *Kormchaia kniga Riazanskaia* from 1284, for example, cautions the faithful against imitating or following in the footsteps of the *shpil'many*, a term obviously derived from the Middle High German *spilman*, meaning "mime," "actor," "dancer."[76] Some scholars (Vostokov, for example) maintain that the *Spielmänner* made their original appearance among the Eastern Slavs as early as the tenth or eleventh century, leaving behind not only their name, but something of their craft as well.[77] In its variety the repertoire of the *Spielmänner* resembles that of the later *skomorokhi*: they played sundry musical instruments; sang; danced; recited epics, fables, proverbs, and riddles; presented theatrical skits and puppet shows; walked on tightropes; leapt through hoops; and juggled knives and other objects.[78]

We have a reasonably accurate idea of how the German *Spielmänner* made their way into Kievan Rus' as early as they did. It was, of course, in the very nature of their profession to be peripatetic, but equally important is the fact that many were engaged in trade, a convenient avocation for those who had to travel extensively anyway. As merchants they dealt primarily in cloth and trinket jewelry.[79] This leads us to the larger question of early German–East Slavic relations.

There were not only commercial contacts, but also cultural and diplomatic ones, between the Eastern Slavs and the West, dating, in some instances, to the beginning of the tenth century.[80] With respect to Germany (or, more accurately for the later Kievan period, the Holy Roman Empire), the Raffelstätter customs statute of 906 is the logical starting point for considering the course of commercial relations between the two peoples. Among the foreign merchants coming to Germany mentioned in article six of this document are the Boemani and the Rugi;[81] while *Boemani* is an obvious reference to the Czechs, *Rugi* can only be interpreted as Rus'.[82] Also mentioned are the chief items of trade between the Rus' and the Germans: wax, slaves, and horses. The road from Kiev to Germany originally passed through Cracow and Prague, terminating in Regensburg, or Ratisbon, which by the eleventh century had evolved into the most important center of Kievan commercial activity in Germany.[83]

Kiev itself, by virtue of its strategic location on the major overland and water routes between the Far East and the West and between Byzantium and Scandinavia, had by the tenth century already begun to attract merchants from the far corners of the earth, including, of course, Germany. The Kievan merchants were frequently called upon to act as middlemen on behalf of their Western counterparts for goods imported from the Orient and Byzantium. By the twelfth century, according to Ediger, Kiev stood alongside Breslau, Prague, Vienna, Augsburg, and Regensburg as an important eastern European commercial center.[84] During the course of the twelfth century, several other Rus' cities, notably Novgorod, Pskov, and Smolensk, became actively involved in the German trade.[85]

Reinforcing the commercial ties between Kievan Rus' and Germany were diplomatic and cultural contacts. These can be traced back to the mid-tenth century, when the Kievan ruler, Princess Olga, began negotiations with Otto I of Germany to secure a Latin hierarchy for the fledgling Christian community in Kiev. Olga herself had become a Byzantine Christian in 955. Two years later she made a state visit to Constantinople in the hope of acquiring a ranking ecclesiastic, perhaps one independent of both patriarch and emperor, to head the Kievan church.[86] Failing this, she turned to the West. In 959 she dispatched legates to Otto I at Ingelheim, who shortly thereafter, in 960, designated a newly consecrated bishop, Libutius of Saint Alban's Monastery in Mainz, to proceed to Kiev. Libutius's departure was delayed, however, and soon after his appointment he died. The mission was next entrusted to Adalbert from the monastery of Saint Maximinus in Trier. Adalbert did go to Kiev, but for some unknown reason his mission apparently failed, for he returned to Germany in 962.[87]

In 973 there was further evidence of continuing diplomatic ties between the Rus' and the Germans. On the occasion of the Reichstag held that year in Quedlingburg, the last imperial Diet to be presided over by Otto I (who died that same year), there was in attendance an embassy from the Rus', sent by Vladimir's predecessor, Iaropolk.[88] In the course of the eleventh century, Germans from different walks of life traveled to Kiev, and some left vivid accounts of their visits. About 1008 Saint Bruno of Querfurt, on his way to convert the Pechenegs, stopped in Kiev, where, as he writes in a letter to the emperor, he was most graciously received by Vladimir himself. The latter personally escorted the missionary monk to the border of his frontier.[89] The chronicler Thietmar of Meresburg (975–1018) was greatly impressed by the wealth of Kiev, while Adam of Bremen (d. 1074) considered the capital of Rus' a worthy rival of Constantinople.[90]

As Father Dvornik has ably demonstrated, there were close cultural ties between Kievan Rus' and the Holy Roman Empire during the eleventh and twelfth centuries as well. Dvornik bases his conclusion in part on a series of Latin prayers dating back to Kievan times, which have survived to this day in Russia in Slavonic translation. Not even the Schism of 1054, Dvornik contends, could sever the strong cultural ties between Kiev and the West.[91]

Against this background of East Slavic–German relations during the Kievan period, the assumption of Spielmänner influence on the skomorokhi is plausible. A clearer understanding of the nature of this influence can be gleaned from a reference in the introduction to the Chronicle of Pereiaslavl-Suzdal. Here the dress of the skomorokhi is likened to the krotopolie (knee-length girded tunic) worn by the Latins, that is, by Western Europeans.[92] By the end of the eleventh century, the skomorokhi could be distinguished by their dress, which they had in all probability borrowed from the visiting Spielmänner. This change of costume was no doubt intended primarily to convince the Kievan authorities that the native minstrels had indeed become like their Western counterparts.

Because Byzantine commercial, diplomatic, and cultural ties with Kievan Rus', particularly after 988, are well known and documented, they require no elaboration here. It is only reasonable to assume that the Byzantine mimes exerted an influence on the skomorokhi equal to, if not more pervasive and enduring than, that of Spielmänner. As the immediate successors of the classical Greek and Roman mimic tradition, they commanded a far wider audience than their medieval German counterparts. This assured their popularity, not only in the Hippodrome, but in the precincts of the imperial palace as well.[93] It was undoubtedly such mimes who entertained Princess Olga on her state visit to Constantinople in 957 at a banquet given in her honor in the palace of Justinian.

The entertainment included theatrical performances, singing, dancing, and "other games."[94]

There is reason to believe that Iaroslav the Wise had not only witnessed mimic performances but was even quite fond of them.[95] At least one other Kievan prince seems to have enjoyed and actively supported this type of entertainment as well. Nestor, the biographer of Feodosii Pecherskii, describes the saintly monk's visit in 1073 to Prince Sviatoslav II of Kiev. "One day our blessed and God-bearing Father, Feodosii, went to see the Prince. And coming into the chamber where he was [banqueting] he sat down and saw before him many entertainers. Some were playing stringed instruments, others were singing, still others played the *organon*. All were playing and making merry as is the custom before the Prince [that is, at court]." Feodosii, according to Nestor, mildly rebuked Sviatoslav for his indulgence in such frivolous, worldly pastimes, and the latter saw to it that in the future whenever the venerable monk had scheduled a visit the entertainers were kept discreetly out of sight.[96]

How can one be certain that the entertainers whom Feodosii saw performing before Sviatoslav were in fact Byzantine mimes and not native *skomorokhi* as some have alleged?[97] First, as living symbols of Kiev's pagan past the *skomorokhi* would scarcely have been welcome at court, where the clergy had frequent and easy access. Both Nestor, in the 1068 entry in the Primary Chronicle, and Feodosii Pecherskii himself, in one of his Instructions dating from the same period, had in no uncertain terms condemned the *skomorokhi* as nefarious pagan holdovers.[98] If these were *skomorokhi* who were entertaining Sviatoslav, then surely they would have been recognized as such by Feodosii and Nestor, and Sviatoslav would have received more than just a mild rebuke for worldliness from the saintly monk. More significant for establishing the identity of the entertainers is Nestor's reference to the *organon* as one of their musical instruments (the other being the *gusli*). Until recently this reference has puzzled scholars. The word is obviously of Greek derivation, where it can mean "tool" or "implement" as well as "musical instrument."[99] Its meaning here will become clearer after we examine some recent archeological findings that have cast new light on the famous staircase frescoes of the Kievan Saint Sophia.

No discussion of the early history of the *skomorokhi* would be complete without some consideration of these controversial staircase, or "*skomorokhi*," frescoes. The consensus among art historians is that the cathedral of Saint Sophia in Kiev was largely the creation of Byzantine masters, both in its architectural design and its interior decoration.[100] It was begun by Iaroslav the Wise in 1037 and was probably consecrated around 1046, with a second consecration taking place sometime in the 1060s, when the interior was completed.[101] The frescoes in question adorn the staircase leading up to the gallery where the Prince's private pew was once located, which is now a choir loft. The secular nature of the frescoes can be explained by the fact that they originally adorned the passage between the church and the palace, of which this staircase was a part.[102]

Depicted in the frescoes, on the extreme right, are two acrobats and, in the central portion, six musicians, two of whom are playing stringed instruments (one a trapezoid harp, the other a tanbur).[103] Also in the center are two squatting figures, who could be either actors engaged in a pantomime or perhaps singers accompanying the orchestra. One section of the frescoes, however, is quite enigmatic. Pictured on the extreme left are two men standing behind what appears to be a miniature or puppet stage. A third person is shown standing in front of the stage, apparently pointing to it. Veselovskii thinks it entirely possible that this part of the fresco depicts a troupe of Byzantine puppeteers preparing to give a performance.[104] According to Nicoll, who groups the two squatting figures in the center with the three on the extreme left, all five of the non-musicians pictured can be described as actors taking part in a play.[105]

In the summer of 1964 the Kievan staircase frescoes underwent their third restoration (the first had been made in 1843, and the second in the 1920s) and some intense scrutiny by scholars. The happy results of this latest restoration provided the basis for an important essay that demonstrated beyond all doubt that what some had thought to be either an early example of the Byzantine puppet theater or a mimic theatrical performance was in fact a Byzantine pneumatic organ.[106] It is now possible to resolve several of the long-standing questions regarding the influence of Byzantine mimes on Kievan culture and their relationship to (or, more accurately, confusion with) the *skomorokhi*.

First, with respect to the use of the word *organon*, there is every likelihood that Nestor was referring to a Byzantine organ played by Byzantine musicians or mimes, and not native *skomorokhi*. Second, the fully restored fresco should lay to rest once and for all the popular but erroneous notion that the entertainers pictured here are native *skomorokhi*—a Byzantine pneumatic organ in the hands of the simple, rustic minstrels seems highly improbable. Clearly, the extreme left section of the fresco belongs with the central portion, and together they form a musical ensemble of Byzantine mimes. Judging from Nestor's description of Feodosii's visit with Sviatoslav in 1073, this was quite a popular form of entertainment at the Kievan court, at least in the eleventh century. Finally, it is evident both from this fresco and from Nestor's reference to the *organon* that one must now add the Byzantine pneumatic organ to the list of musical instruments known to the Kievan Slavs by the early eleventh century.[107]

While the Western *Spielmänner* provided the *skomorokhi* with a distinctive new costume, the Eastern mimes introduced them to an assortment of new acts, largely of an acrobatic or gymnastic variety. This was their forte, as one can readily judge from the right side of the staircase fresco, as well as from other sources. Liutprand of Cremona, visiting Constantinople in 949, describes a mimic entertainment that he witnessed at the Byzantine court. A man came in carrying on his head, without using his hands, a wooden pole with a crosspiece; and two boys appeared and performed various tricks on the crosspiece. What particularly impressed Liutprand was the ability of the man carrying the pole to keep it properly balanced, even when there was only one boy performing on the crosspiece.[108]

In addition to the foreign influences that enabled the *skomorokhi* to transform themselves, at least outwardly, from pagan priests to legitimate entertainers, there was an important native influence that cannot be overlooked. The source of this influence was the *gusliari*, or Kievan court poets, about whom more will be said later. They were responsible for creating a brilliant heroic tradition in Kievan Rus'. Contrary to what the Chadwicks and other scholars have maintained, the *gusliari* were as distinct from the *skomorokhi* in their origin and professional character as they were in their dress. The *skomorokhi*, as we have seen, very early adopted a rather flamboyant costume consisting of a brightly colored, knee-length, girded tunic, which made them stand out from the rest of the population as Western or foreign.[109] The *gusliari*, on the other hand, dressed in the more conservative costume of the day, a plain, loose-fitting, ankle-length tunic.[110] The two did, however, share a common, and one might add fortuitous, love for the *gusli*, which eventually facilitated a merger between them. As the Kievan heroic age waned and with it the economic support and patronage of the prince, and as oral tradition began to give way to written literature, the Kievan court singers found it not only necessary, but quite natural, to cast their lot with the *skomorokhi*. In the process of this amalgamation, the *skomorokhi* became heirs to a rich body of oral heroic poetry, or *byliny*, which added an important dimension to their professional repertoire.

The metamorphosis was now complete. With the help of the *Spielmänner*, the mimes, and the *gusliari*, the *skomorokhi* had by the twelfth century evolved into a new class of professional minstrels with a versatility and appeal that made them welcome, not only in the village street, but in the town square as well. To be sure, they continued to maintain a strong spiritual link to the pagan tradition that gave them birth: this is apparent from the continuing abuse and persecution of the ecclesiastical authorities, who were evidently not in the least convinced that the new *skomorokhi* were different from the old. Partly as a result of this persistent persecution in the Kievan lands, but mostly out of political and economic necessity, the *skomorokhi*, like many other people at this time, began to drift northward and northeastward to Lord Novgorod the Great and the newly emerging Muscovite lands. While they would not totally escape persecution in the north— after all, the process of Christianization was proceeding apace even in the most remote areas of Russia—they would nonetheless find here a freer life that would enable them to preserve and disseminate much of the native pagan culture to which they had fallen heir. This was particularly true of Novgorod and its lands, where the *skomorokhi* not only found a new home but something approaching a golden age as well.

2
A New Life in the North

The exodus of the *skomorokhi* from Kievan Rus' and their migration northward probably began shortly after their transformation into professional minstrel-entertainers. The migration coincided, by and large, with the rapid disintegration of the Kievan state in the twelfth and early thirteenth centuries. Kiev's political decline had commenced in the mid-eleventh century. A long period of interprincely rivalry and strife that followed the death of Iaroslav the Wise in 1054 was accentuated by the constant threat of foreign incursions from the Cumans in the south and economic catastrophe. The loss of Tmutorokan in the late eleventh century was a severe blow to Kiev's Oriental trade. Furthermore, the Cumans threatened to sever the main artery of Russo-Byzantine trade, the Dnieper waterway, while Byzantium itself, following the signing of a treaty in 1082 with Venice, became less and less interested in trade with Kiev. The final blow to Kiev's vital economic ties with Constantinople came after the Fourth Crusade and the founding of the Latin Empire (1204–61), when all normal commercial relations between the two ceased.

During this transitional period in their history, the Russian minstrels continued to become progressively more professionalized and secularized. From the late eleventh century until 1571, there is no mention of the *skomorokhi* in the chronicles. There are, however, references to them in other contemporary sources. In the so-called "Pravilo," a collection of fifty-three church canons attributed to Maksim, Bishop of Belgorod (1187–90), the penitent sinner is warned to shun "the dancing games of the unclean and abhorrent before God *skomorokhi*."[1] The *Pchela*, a twelfth-century Slavonic translation of aphorisms from the Hellenistic philosophers, mentions the *skomorokhi* in the same context as prostitutes and describes them as having a reputation for singing villainous songs.[2] The monk Georgii of Zarub, in a sermon dating from the mid-thirteenth century, describes the *skomorokhi*, along with such other evils as slander, envy, and covetousness, as thoroughly heathen and consequently to be shunned by the good Christian. In the same sermon Georgii upbraids the *skomorokhi* for their worldly philosophy of life, which, he says, is the direct antithesis of the Christian ethic.[3]

Given the exclusively ecclesiastical provenance of these sources, their negative and uncomplimentary portrayal of the *skomorokhi* comes as no surprise. What is surprising, however, is the change in emphasis. There is no longer a preoccupation with the paganism of the *skomorokhi*; rather, they are now branded as sinful, worldly, and villainous. In fact, only the monk Georgii attempts to identify them with paganism, and only in the sense that they are not truly Christian, just as slander, envy, and covetousness are un-Christian. Thus, in the waning days of their association with Kievan Rus', the *skomorokhi* appear to be gaining wider acceptance as secular, professional minstrels.

Upon leaving the strife-torn Kievan lands in the twelfth and early thirteenth centuries, the *skomorokhi* proceeded in two directions: directly north toward Novgorod and northeast toward Vladimir-Suzdal.[4] In both areas they left indelible traces of their early settlement and widespread activity by giving their name to numerous villages and hamlets—a total of twenty-nine in the five lands (*piatini*) of Novgorod.[5] Their primary objective, however, was Novgorod and Pskov (a *prigorod*, or dependency, of Novgorod).[6] As a flourishing political, economic, and cultural center, this "Venice of the North," as Novgorod was frequently called, prided itself on its virtual independence of Kiev, its democratic spirit, and its comparative liberalism. At no time, for example, were secular music and entertainment proscribed in Novgorod until Aleksei's universal ban on the *skomorokhi* in 1648. Pskov, even before it became politically independent of Novgorod in the early fourteenth century, was in its own right an important commercial center, and, by virtue of its close association with Novgorod, it shared in the splendid cultural achievements of the mother city.

The migration and resettlement of the Russian minstrels in the north were completed by the late thirteenth and early fourteenth centuries. Evidence for this can be found in the series of initials, or miniature letter-figures, from Pskov, Novgorod, and Riazan, which art historians have identified as depicting *skomo-*

rokhi. The earliest of these initials dates from the late thirteenth or early fourteenth century and is found in a Pskovian Psalter.[7] According to some critics, this richly ornamented Psalter is among the earliest known manuscripts to include the full human figure in its teratological ornamentations.[8] The initial in question is an Old Slavonic **T** depicting a standing *skomorokh* dressed in a knee-length tunic and playing a five-string triangular *gusli.* His appearance here seems quite inappropriate, since Psalm 39, which the initial introduces, has nothing to do with music or musicians.

The earliest of the Novgorod initials date from 1323 and are found in the *Evangelie nedel'noe,* or collection of Sunday Gospels. Stasov reproduces six of the letter-figures from this early fourteenth-century manuscript. Two are in the form of the Old Slavonic letter **Р** and four in the form of **В**. Of these six, two are animal tamers in the act of giving a performance; the animals they are handling are stylized dogs. The other four can be described as actors; one is sitting, another standing, and two are crouched on one knee, holding an axe and a cane respectively.[9] All are wearing costumes similar to the *krotopolie,* described as the standard attire of the *skomorokhi* in the Chronicle of Pereiaslavl-Suzdal.[10] In addition, several of the figures are wearing elaborate headdress.

In another group of Novgorod letter-figure initials, taken from a 1355 edition of the *Evangelie nedel'noe,* two actors and a juggler are represented, both in the form of the letter **В**.[11] A third version of the *Evangelie nedel'noe,* dating from 1358, contains an initial **Р** depicting a musician playing an oval, nine-string *gusli* (using a feather as a plectrum) and simultaneously dancing. Above and to the left of the letter-figure are inscribed the words *gudi gorazdo* ("play skillfully"), probably added by someone other than the copyist-artist by way of marginalia.[12]

Perhaps the most interesting of the Novgorod initials are two from the mid-fourteenth century, one of which appears in a Psalter, the other in a Sluzhebnik, or Liturgicon.[13] Both are in the form of the letter **Д** and depict flamboyantly dressed musicians. The Psalter *skomorokh* plays the oval *gusli* and is pictured in a squatting position, as if engaged in a dance of a variety best described as *vprisiadku.*[14] Without a doubt, these two miniatures provide us with the most accurate visual description of early Russian minstrels to be found anywhere.

Among the miniatures from Riazan are four that depict performing *skomorokhi.* The earliest of the four, from the second half of the fourteenth century, is an initial from a liturgical *Sbornik* in the form of a **В**, depicting a dancing, *gusli*-playing *skomorokh.*[15] The other three are somewhat later, from the 1544 edition of the

Evangelie nedel'noe, and represent the letters **Ж**, **Ч**, and **Н**.[16] The two *skomorokhi* forming the **Ж** appear to be actors, as do the two forming the **Н**; **Ч** is represented by a *skomorokh*-juggler.

According to the art historians Nekrasov and Rozov, the Novgorod book illuminators made a significant contribution to the evolution of Russian teratological ornamentation and introduced the full human figure into this style of ornamentation. One can, in fact, speak of an important school of book illumination in Novgorod that flourished in the late thirteenth and early fourteenth centuries, whose influence was strongly felt throughout the northern and northeastern parts of medieval Russia.[17] Pskov and Riazan obviously came under the influence of this early Novgorodian school of illumination, which supplied the artistic inspiration for the initials I have been discussing.[18] The thematic inspiration was provided by the *skomorokhi* themselves, who, as these miniatures clearly show, were not only widely dispersed throughout the north and northeast by this time, but were evidently also so well known that the illuminators could use them as easily identifiable models. With their flamboyant, colorful costumes and versatility of repertoire (the initials show them as musicians, dancers, actors, jugglers, and animal tamers), they offered the artist a wide range of possibilities, enabling him to execute any letter in the Old Slavonic alphabet in singularly eloquent fashion.

Finally, the thoroughly nonsecular nature of the manuscripts in which these miniatures appear (that is, Psalters and Liturgicons), might lead one to conclude that the Russian minstrels found conditions in the north far more favorable to their professional development than those in the south, where no such miniatures of *skomorokhi* have been found. Although it is by no means unusual to see the intrusion of secular motifs into ecclesiastical ornament, particularly in the West, it is nonetheless ironic that the "pagan" *skomorokhi* should find their way into the church's official service manuals.

With the sole exception of the *Zlatoust*,[19] a late fourteenth-century translation of sermons and other didactic literature from the Greek Fathers, there are no further written references to the *skomorokhi* until the second half of the fifteenth century. In the *Zlatoust* the *skomorokhi* are condemned, along with a host of other worldly amusements, for preparing the road to perdition for themselves and their listeners.[20] It appears that, though the minstrels had found greater tolerance in the north, the church's official attitude toward them, particularly in the Muscovite lands, had changed little.

Their reputation and popularity continued to grow, nonetheless. Ironically, the church may have inadvertently contributed to their popularity by admitting their images into its official service books. An enigmatic fifteenth-century fresco from Meletovo, a village on the outskirts of Pskov, is a striking example of the church's uncertain response to the menace of the *skomorokhi* during this period of relative freedom in the north. According to the First Pskovian Chronicle, the stone church of Meletovo, dedicated to the Assumption of the Virgin Mary, was built in 1461, and its interior decoration was completed four years later.[21] In 1925 K. K. Romanov uncovered fragments of a fresco on the west wall and over the main entrance of the church. It was not until 1951, however, that Iu. N. Dmitriev for the first time attempted to analyze and interpret this anonymous fresco.[22]

At the very top of the fresco, dominating the whole, is the figure of the Virgin Mary, standing with head inclined toward another figure lying on a cot and covered from the neck down. In the center, below the couch and the Virgin, sits a clean-shaven musician on a high, spacious, and richly ornamented throne, holding a *gudok* in one hand and a bow in the other. To his left is a dancing woman with raised hands; on his right stands a group of men and women. Most intriguing is the barely visible inscription found to the left and right of the musician's head— ЯНТЪ СКОМОРОХ. Dmitriev and subsequently Likhachev have found the first word problematic.[23] There is no doubt, however, regarding the second word: it is the Old Slavonic for *skomorokh*.

The subject of this fresco puzzled scholars for quite some time; Dmitriev frankly admitted that he could not explain it.[24] Then in 1964 D. S. Likhachev found a short narrative tale entitled "O nekoem skomrase, khulivshem prechistuiu bogoroditsu" ("About a Certain *Skomorokh* Who Mocked the Virgin Mother of God") in a rare Old Russian literary anthology known as *Limonis*. Here, he was convinced, was the key to the Meletovo fresco. The tale relates the story of a certain *skomorokh* named Янн who, whenever he performed, invariably mocked and cursed the Virgin Mary. She appeared to him twice to admonish him to mend his ways, but this only made him intensify his blasphemy. Finally, she came to him a third time, and while he slept, touched his arms and legs with her finger. When he awoke he found himself dismembered, and from the shock fell dead on the spot.[25]

The points of comparison between the tale and the fresco are obvious. On the lower, or earthly, level, one finds the *skomorokh* entertaining with music and, presumably, irreverent songs about the Virgin Mary, who is shown standing with one arm outstretched toward the figure on the couch. Although the reclining

figure does not bear an exact resemblance to the seated figure—
Dmitriev calls it a female, Likhachev a male—both are clean
shaven. What is more significant, however, is the absence of arms
and legs on the reclining figure.

Two points need further elucidation. One involves the word
ӐНТЪ; the other, the composition or style of the fresco, particularly the rendering of the figure of the *skomorokh*. Both Likhachev
and Rozov have unsuccessfully tried to identify the name of the
skomorokh in the tale with the word **ӐНТЪ** in the fresco, with
Likhachev ultimately pointing out that the difference between the
two words does not affect the basic similarity between the tale
and the fresco. As he notes, at least one other version of the tale,
included by Metropolitan Makarii in his encyclopedic *Chet'i Minei*
("Monthly Readings") under the date 30 July, gives the name of
the *skomorokh* as Goino, which bears no resemblance at all to
Ӑнн.[26]

Somewhat more involved is the problem of style, particularly as it is reflected in the artist's conception of the *skomorokh-*
musician. Judging from the thirteenth- and fourteenth-century
miniatures we have examined, there seems to be little similarity
between the earlier *skomorokhi* and the one depicted in the fresco.
In the first place, the fresco *skomorokh* is dressed rather conserva-
tively, which contrasts sharply with the flamboyant attire of the
earlier *skomorokhi*.[27] One could, of course, argue that over a
period of one hundred years the *skomorokhi* had gradually shed
their Western-inspired dress in favor of more pedestrian native
attire. This was certainly the case by the early seventeenth century, as can be seen in the two illustrations of performing *skomo-*
rokhi in Olearius. The costume of the Meletovo *skomorokh* is less
puzzling, however, than his musical instrument (the *gudok*) and
the regal throne upon which he is seated. The musical instrument
most closely identified with the early Russian minstrels is the
multi-stringed *gusli*; they are pictured with this instrument in all
of the surviving miniatures. In fact, there is no reference to the
gudok in connection with the *skomorokhi* in any of the sources
until the first half of the seventeenth century. The spacious and
imposing Byzantine throne on which the musician is seated is of
the type frequently depicted in icons of the Saviour and of the
Mother of God dating from this period.[28] It is totally inappropriate
both to the story and to the *veselye molodtsy* ("merry lads"), as
the happy-go-lucky *skomorokhi* were commonly known.

According to Rozov, the artist who executed the fresco of
the *skomorokh* in the Meletovo church used a combination of
Byzantine stylistic devices to render the person of the musician.

As his model he chose not the native *skomorokhi*, but rather the serene and stately figure of King David the Psalmist, who is pictured in both the Kievan Sophia, the Novgorod Sophia, and other Novgorod churches, and in several Novgorodian and Pskovian miniatures from the thirteenth century. One miniature shows him holding a stringed instrument in one hand and a bow in the other. To his right stands a group of male musicians, while on his left a female dancing figure is depicted.[29] All of these details are reminiscent of the Meletovo fresco.

There was one obvious drawback to this unique portrayal of a native minstrel in classic Byzantine fashion—he bore little or no resemblance to real life. So, to remind worshipers and other viewers, who were used to seeing their *skomorokhi* in brightly-colored costumes with *gusli* in hand, that this was indeed a *skomorokh*, the artist added a brief explanatory inscription, **ЯНТЪ СКОМОРОХ**. He thus integrated the native literary theme of the fresco with its Byzantine style. One can only speculate about why the artist chose to render the Meletovo *skomorokh* in this unusual fashion. Perhaps the solemn setting of the fresco, in a prominent, public place inside a church, called for greater restraint and dignity than the Psalter initials. One cannot help but wonder also why such a painting was commissioned in the first place; was it, as Likhachev and Rozov have intimated, to combat some popular contemporary heresy involving the Virgin Mary?[30] We know that the *Limonis*, from which the legend depicted in the fresco was apparently taken, originally appeared in Bulgaria during the reign of Samuel (969–1018) as a tract against the Bogomil heresy.[31] We also know that during the second half of the fourteenth century the heretical movement known as the *Strigol'niki* gained wide currency both in Novgorod and Pskov, and that in the late fifteenth century the Judaizers came into prominence in the north. Both the *Strigol'niki* and the Judaizers tended to de-emphasize and even reject the divinity of Christ, by implication casting a shadow over Mary as well.[32] Were the *skomorokhi* connected somehow to either of these or to some other heresy, or were they simply being singled out once again as a threat to the church because of their persistent identification with the pagan elements of Old Russian culture?

I believe the latter to be the case. There is little doubt that paganism continued to permeate the social and cultural life of Pskov long after the introduction of Christianity and that the church authorities viewed this as a serious problem as late as the sixteenth century. This can be seen, for example, from the curious epistle of the monk Filofei dating from the 1510s. The epistle is addressed to the people of Pskov and describes in considerable detail the thoroughly pagan elements of the Feast of Saint John the Baptist (Midsummer or *Kupalo*), which it condemns in no uncertain terms. Filofei notes with horror that the entire city of Pskov runs wild on the eve of the festival and that the people engage freely in all manner of indecent Satanic games, music, dancing, and so forth.[33]

It is in light of the apparent pertinacity of pagan beliefs in Pskov that the inscription of the Meletovo fresco can perhaps be properly understood. While Dmitriev, Likhachev, and Rozov have all been concerned with reading the enigmatic word **ДНТЬ** as a proper name, I agree with N. Andreyev, who has observed that it is in fact the Old Slavonic abbreviation for Antichrist. Only when it is read thus can one appreciate the full significance of this singular fresco, which represents, in Andreyev's words, "a unique apotheosis of the Church's condemnation of that 'devil's brood,' the *skomorokhi*."[34]

We turn next to the northeast of Russia, where we have already encountered the late fourteenth-century Riazan miniature-initial depicting a performing *skomorokh*, the earliest evidence we have for the activities of the *skomorokhi* in this part of Russia. Because the Muscovite lands were more immediately affected by the Mongol conquest, it is likely that the *skomorokhi* were less numerous here than in the northwest, where political and economic conditions were more stable and consequently more favorable to their professional development. Even so, by the second half of the fifteenth century the Russian minstrels were becoming quite active here as well.

Revealing in this regard is a clause in a charter, or letters patent (*zhalovannaia gramota*), granted by Prince Iurii Vasil'evich of Dmitrov in 1470 to the Trinity–Saint Sergius Monastery (located some forty-eight miles north of Moscow). Here the *skomorokhi* are specifically forbidden to entertain in the villages and hamlets belonging to the monastery.[35] Allowing for the ecclesiastical status of the petitioner, it is nonetheless significant that the first reference to *skomorokhi* in Muscovite sources is a negative one. Similar charters granted to both ecclesiastical and non-ecclesiastical petitioners in the early sixteenth century also evince varying degrees of antipathy toward the *skomorokhi*: in some they are forbidden to set foot in specified towns, villages, and hamlets;[36] in others they are allowed to enter provided they refrain from loud or boisterous entertainment.[37] Thus, while the civil authorities may not have shared the Muscovite clergy's traditional contempt for the *skomorokhi*, they were willing to grant certain communities the right not to be entertained against their will. The tolerant atmosphere that enabled the Russian minstrels to flourish in the northwest evidently did not prevail in the northeast.

It is clear from references to the *skomorokhi* in Muscovite charters from the late fifteenth and early sixteenth centuries that the minstrel-entertainers in the northeast were considerably more mobile than their counterparts in the northwest, apparently because of the constant threat of sanctions and persecution by the church. One can better appreciate the nature and extent of this persecution by reading the anonymous "Instruction" on church discipline addressed to all clergy and faithful of the late fifteenth century, where the *skomorokhi* and those who associate with or listen to them are explicitly barred from Holy Communion for a year and are declared anathema (in effect, are excommunicated). Should any Orthodox Christian persist in his association with them, he is to be kept physically out of the church, his stipend for its upkeep is to be spurned, and no priest is ever to set foot in his house.[38]

Sixteenth-century sources confirm the Muscovite church's virulent opposition to the *skomorokhi*. Maksim Grek, the controversial Greek scholar-translator living and writing in Moscow in the 1520s, addressed himself at length to the subject in one of his "Instructions," "Slovo protiv skomorokhov." He begins by stating that the *skomorokhi* have learned their trade from Satan himself and by virtue of this are already cursed and damned; damned also are all those who allow themselves to be amused by the *skomorokhi*, as well as those in positions of authority who do not speak out openly and forcefully to condemn them. He is particularly disturbed by the relative ease with which the *skomorokhi* are able to travel from town to town and village to village, exposing numerous innocent souls to their scandalous entertainment. He lashes out at their sinful abuse of animals such as bears, whom they train to dance and engage in other Satanic games to the accompaniment of various musical instruments, and finally, he links them to witchcraft, which compounds their pernicious influence among the people.[39] Maksim's contemporary, Metropolitan Daniil of Moscow, is no less contemptuous of the *skomorokhi* and those who indulge in their evil amusements: a man who exposes his wife and children or other members of his household to their sundry diversions not only loses his own immortal soul but calls down the same fate upon his loved ones.[40]

So the Muscovite *skomorokhi*, faced with relentless hostility from the ecclesiastical authorities, found it not only necessary for professional reasons (in order to reach a wider audience), but also expedient for personal reasons (to elude the authorities), to take to the road. Their lot was not an enviable one. Sigismund von Herberstein, the German ambassador to Moscow in 1517 and again in 1526, writing about the severity of the weather in the winter of 1526, observed: "Of course, many itinerant people (*multi circulatores*) who are in the habit of wandering about these regions with dancing bears (*cum ursis ad choreas edoctis*) were found dead along the roads."[41] This brings to mind E. K. Chambers' poignant description of the medieval minstrel in the West: "To travel long miles in wind and rain, to stand wet to the skin and hungry and footsore, making the slow bourgeois laugh while the heart was bitter within; such must have been the daily fate of many amongst the humbler minstrels at least. And at the end to die like a dog in a ditch, under the ban of the Church and with the prospect of eternal damnation before the soul."[42]

It is possible to draw some conclusions from these sources about the Muscovite *skomorokhi*. First of all, in addition to becoming progressively more itinerant, they became more secular and professional; without abandoning their traditional stock in trade of music, song, and dance, they did expand their repertoire to include the trained bear act and the puppet theater, or *pozorishche*.[43] In spite of their secularization, however, they had by no means severed their ties with their pagan past, as Maksim Grek reminds us when he mentions the Satanic games (a reference to the seasonal festivals, such as *Rusaliia*) in which the *skomorokhi* continued to be actively involved, and when he identifies them with witchcraft.

More significant than the professional changes the *skomorokhi* had undergone by the sixteenth century was their evolution during this same period into a distinct socioeconomic class. This evolution can be clearly seen in the cadastres (*pistsovye knigi*), census books (*perepisnye knigi*), and customs duty records (*tamozhennye knigi*) which have come down to us from the late fifteenth through the eighteenth century. An invaluable source for the social and economic history of late medieval and early modern Russia, these statistical records also add a new dimension to our knowledge of the *skomorokhi*.

Only two scholars have to date made any serious effort to utilize the information on the *skomorokhi* contained in these records. On the basis of data from the cadastres and some other supplementary material, Findeizen constructed a map that graphically illustrates the dispersal of the *skomorokhi* throughout northern and northeastern Russia in the sixteenth and seventeenth centuries.[44] More recently V. I. Petukhov published an article in which he draws some general conclusions about their socioeconomic status during this period, basing his conclusions on statistical and related information culled from all three sources—cadastres, census books, and customs duty records.[45] While performing yeoman service in alerting scholars to a potentially invaluable source of new information on the *skomorokhi*, Petukhov missed the opportunity to fully exploit his findings by failing to thoroughly digest and to evaluate the raw material he had so painstakingly assembled.

It was the Mongols who introduced census taking in Russia in the mid-thirteenth century. According to the early chronicles, there was an enumeration of the population of Kiev and some other cities in 1246, while a general census was undertaken around 1257 and another in 1275.[46] These early censuses were used by the Mongols to facilitate the systematic collection of taxes and as a basis for military conscription. When the collection of the Khan's taxes was finally entrusted to the Muscovite princes in the early fourteenth century, the general census was discontinued, though individual princes continued to enumerate the peasants on their own land. There is no direct evidence that any general censuses were undertaken in Russia during the fourteenth and fifteenth centuries, though according to some scholars there is circumstantial evidence that one or more may have taken place, at least in the fourteenth century.[47] Unfortunately nothing remains of these early Mongol and Muscovite censuses. The earliest such records surviving are the Novgorod cadastres from the late fifteenth century. Essentially registers of real estate, they also contain some information from previous surveys. We know that there were several population and land censuses made in the first half of the sixteenth century, of which only a few have been preserved. Most, like the cadastral books from 1538–47, fell victim to the fires that periodically devastated Moscow.[48] More numerous, though by no means complete, are the records for the period beginning with the 1550s. During the seventeenth century a number of general censuses of Muscovite population and land tenure were undertaken, and many of these books have been preserved; among them are the general surveys of households made in the 1620s, 1646, and 1678, as well as an unfinished survey from the 1680s.[49] The last fiscal surveys of the old cadastral variety were attempted in the reign of Peter I, one in 1710 and the other in 1717, both of which proved unsuccessful.

Far less numerous than cadastres and censuses are the records of customs duties (*tamozhennye knigi*) from the towns of Muscovite Russia. These were compiled in the period from the sixteenth through the eighteenth century and provide statistical information on the annual duty paid by merchants when they brought their wares into a particular town or market. Unfortunately, only the books covering the period 1633–80 have been preserved and published; most of the earlier ones were destroyed in the Moscow fire of 1626.[50]

Taken collectively, the cadastres, censuses, and customs duty records provide the historian with an important source of information about the economic, social, and, to some degree, the political history of Muscovite Russia. Cadastres and censuses, for example, shed considerable light on the size and movement of both urban and rural populations; their social, professional, and economic composition; the size and quality of taxable land; and the relative importance of commerce and small industry. The customs duty ledgers, or at least those that have survived, are particularly useful as an indicator of the overall state of commerce and trade in Muscovite Russia during the seventeenth century. They also provide some inkling of the place of the small merchant in the economic life of the country, and such specific information as the type, price, and place of origin of the products sold in the marketplace.

The references to the *skomorokhi* in all three sources are both numerous and revealing. The cadastres and censuses provide information about the settled, or nonitinerant, *skomorokhi*, while the customs duty records furnish some rare insights into the lives of the more elusive traveling, or itinerant, minstrels. Although these statistical records are by no means complete or comprehensive, dictating caution in using them, they represent one of the few sources of concrete, relatively accurate information about the *skomorokhi* during the period when their fame and popularity were most widespread.

Looking at Findeizen's map, one cannot but be struck by the wide distribution of the *skomorokhi* throughout the Russian lands, from Pskov in the west to Kazan in the east and Belgorod in the south. One finds them in all of the major cities and towns, including Novgorod, Moscow, Riazan, Tver, Viatka, Tula, Mozhaisk, Toropets, Kolomna, Nizhnii Novgorod, and others. Some lived in the towns; others preferred rural hamlets and villages. When a number of them settled in a rural community, they frequently gave their name to it; thus, there were at least eighteen villages with the name Skomorokhovo in three of the five provinces (*piatini*) of Novgorod, dating back to the late fifteenth century.[51] In the Muscovite lands proper one finds, by the sixteenth and early seventeenth centuries, at least eight settlements bearing the name Skomorokhovo, and one each called Gusel'nikovo and Domerni-kov.[52]

On the basis of their geographical distribution one might say that the *skomorokhi* tended to follow the flag: wherever Muscovite political influence was carried, they soon followed. Kazan, which finally succumbed to the Russians in 1552, provides one illustration of this "cultural imperialism." By 1565, a mere thirteen years after its conquest, there were already eight *skomorokhi*, one of them a woman, in this distant outpost of Muscovite rule.[53] Other similar instances of rapid *skomorokh* penetration into newly acquired or newly colonized regions of the country can be documented.[54]

Petukhov calculates that during the second half of the sixteenth century forty-nine *skomorokhi* were registered in the Muscovite (including Novgorod) cadastres.[55] For the period from 1600 to 1648 Petukhov counts a total of seventy-nine *skomorokhi* entered in both the cadastres and census books.[56] According to my own calculations, based on information drawn from six separate cadastres and one census, there were no fewer than sixty-two professional minstrel-entertainers in greater Novgorod alone between 1495 and 1539.[57] What is the significance of these figures? For one thing, they show that prior to 1550 there was a far greater concentration of *skomorokhi* in the Novgorod lands than anywhere else. They also illustrate that with the final political humiliation of Novgorod at the hands of Ivan IV in 1570 there was a fundamental shift in the geographic center of their activity from the northwest to the northeast, a shift that becomes quite pronounced by the early seventeenth century. Finally, and perhaps somewhat surprisingly, these cumulative figures indicate an increase in the population of the minstrel-entertainers on the very eve of their formal proscription by Aleksei in 1648.

More indicative of the importance of the *skomorokhi* in the sixteenth and seventeenth centuries are certain comparative statistics that can be extracted from the cadastres and census books. For example, in the town of Iama, located north-northwest of Novgorod in the Vodskaia *piatina*, there were seven professional minstrels registered in a cadastre from 1500,[58] compared with a single butcher, baker, and tanner; two fishmongers and shoe-makers; three blacksmiths, carpenters, and potters; four tailors and professional herdsmen or shepherds.[59] Although we do not know the exact total population of Iama in 1500, we do know that there were 239 registered households, six of which belonged to *skomo-*

rokhi: one minstrel for every forty households.[60] A similarly high ratio of *skomorokhi* to registered households can be found in other Novgorod and Muscovite towns.

The ancient commercial center of Toropets, situated directly south of Novgorod and northwest of Moscow, numbered some 2,400 inhabitants in 1540–41, among whom there were seven *skomorokhi*. By comparison, there were eight bakers and shoemakers, seven blacksmiths, four butchers, and one tanner in the town.[61] In Kolomna, not far from Moscow to the southeast, there were eleven *skomorokhi* in 1578 out of some 3,000 inhabitants.[62] Mozhaisk, with an approximate population of 2,000 in the 1570s, had four professional minstrels.[63] Further to the south of Moscow, in Tula, there were five *skomorokhi*, out of a total male population of 840, registered in a cadastre from 1588–89.[64] Finally, far to the east, in recently conquered Kazan, there were eight minstrels active in the city by 1568.[65] The total Russian population of Kazan at this time has been estimated at about 7,000.[66]

Some tentative conclusions may be drawn on the basis of these comparative statistics. It is evident, first of all, that by the sixteenth century, and probably much earlier, the *skomorokhi* had gained wide acceptance as a distinct professional class; consequently, we find both their names and their profession duly recorded in the cadastres and census books, where they are accorded equal status with other craftsmen, such as bakers, shoemakers, tanners, silversmiths, and armorers. In the eyes of the secular, if not the ecclesiastical, authorities, they had come to be regarded as tax-paying members in good standing of the community. It should be noted, however, that this social acceptance was extended to the nonitinerant *skomorokhi* only—the wandering minstrel continued to be looked upon as a public nuisance by both secular and ecclesiastical authorities, as the local charters of immunity that enabled Muscovite towns and villages to refuse entry to itinerant *skomorokhi* attest.

In addition to becoming socially acceptable as a class, the *skomorokhi* had, by the sixteenth century, begun to play an increasingly important part in the cultural and social life of both urban and rural communities. This is reflected in some of the comparative statistics from the cadastres and census records cited above. Not only do these statistics show a relatively high ratio of minstrel-entertainers to total population, but, even more importantly, they show a proportionately high ratio of *skomorokhi* to other craftsmen in both essential and nonessential services; in fact, in many instances we find the *skomorokhi* outnumbering the butchers, bakers, shoemakers, carpenters, and other artisans in towns and villages alike. One can thus reasonably conclude that prior to 1648, when the *skomorokhi* were outlawed by Aleksei, the minstrel-entertainer was very much a part of the social and cultural life of the community. His talents were many, and he could be called upon to provide a variety of services, from overseeing a wedding to presiding over a myriad of cyclic festivals and celebrations.

While the cadastres and census books are useful as a source of demographic information, their real value to the historian lies in the economic data they contain about a wide spectrum of Muscovite population, including the *skomorokhi*. Many of the complete cadastral books provide detailed information about the type of landholdings; amount of arable land; quality of soil; expected harvest; amount of forest, meadow, or wasteland; land cultivated outside regularly tilled fields; abandoned fields (in addition to the regularly rotated fallow); number of occupied and empty peasant households; names and occupations of landholders; number of nontaxpayers (including soldiers, slaves, widows, male children, indigents, priests); and local nonagricultural industries, such as fishing, hunting, salt extraction, and tanning. Upon examining the cadastres, census books, and customs duty records, it becomes clear that many of the *skomorokhi* were well integrated into the economic structure of sixteenth- and seventeenth-century Russia. They could be found in the city and in the country, as taxpayers and with tax-exempt status. Some of them were relatively well to do, others eked out an existence as members of the lower taxpaying class (*molodshie liudi*), while still others were poor, landless peasants (*bobyli*), or even serfs, not infrequently living off the church as paupers. Some were engaged in business and commerce, and a few were involved in small industry. There were also *skomorokhi* who doubled as professional soldiers (*strel'tsy*). Women were not excluded from their professional ranks, and there is at least one recorded instance of a *skomorokh*'s son who became a priest.[67]

In the late fifteenth and early sixteenth centuries the *skomorokhi*, particularly those in the northwest, were more or less evenly distributed between town and country. During the course of the sixteenth century, however, they began to gravitate not only toward the northeast, but also away from the countryside and into the towns of the expanding Muscovite state. There were, of course, many factors responsible for this basic demographic change. Ivan IV's *oprichnina* and his forcible resettlement of many Novgorod *skomorokhi* in Muscovy in the early 1570s stand out as perhaps the most significant of these. Other factors, such as the greater economic and cultural opportunities afforded by the town, no doubt contributed to the urbanization of the *skomorokhi* in the northeast.

Economically and socially, both urban and rural minstrels, like most of the Muscovite population in the sixteenth and seventeenth centuries, fell into the broad category of *tiaglye liudi*, those liable to heavy taxes and, in some instances, compulsory labor (*tiaglo* literally means "burden"). Included among the *tiaglye liudi* were the free peasants living on state lands, serfs, and townspeople. Collectively these all came under the general heading of commoners, who were further subdivided into an upper (*luchshie*), middle (*srednye*), and lower (*molodshie*) class; this division into three classes was particularly common among the *posadskie liudi*, or city taxpayers.

While most of the *skomorokhi* can be described as commoners, or *tiaglye liudi*, some had achieved a degree of status and privilege as members of the lower service class, or *sluzhilye liudi*. These were apparently minstrels who had cast their lot with the military and who are designated in the cadastres as *strel'tsy*, the first regular troops in Muscovite Russia. They were organized into regiments (*prikazy*) in the mid-sixteenth century by Ivan IV. Originally their service was by contract, the length of service depending on the health and the ability of the individual; eventually service became lifelong as well as hereditary. The *strel'tsy* lived with their families in special suburban settlements and received, in addition to their homes, small plots of land and a salary from the government. They were also permitted to engage, taxfree, in trade and commerce on a limited scale and to make alcoholic beverages for their own use.[68]

Several *skomorokhi-strel'tsy* are recorded in the cadastres. One, by the name of Elka, is registered in the 1565–68 cadastre from Kazan; he is described as paying no taxes and living in a house on Zdvizhenskaia Street.[69] Another, Ontoshko Petrov by name, is entered in a 1585 cadastre from Pskov. He had a *dvor*, or homestead, in Sebezh, a suburb of Pskov, and also owned a plot of land (*ogorodok*) outside the town that measured eleven by seven *sazhen'*, or approximately 3,234 square feet.[70] He paid no taxes on either of these.[71] The 1621 cadastre from Nizhnii Novgorod contains the name of a *skomorokh-strelets*, Zakhar, living on the banks of the Volga River. His *izba*, or house, is designated as *ne tiagloe* (that is, "unburdened by taxes").[72] From these and other examples it appears that there existed during the sixteenth and seventeenth centuries a possibility of upward social mobility through military service for a few of the Muscovite *skomorokhi*.[73]

Some *skomorokhi* were prosperous enough to be included in

the middle group of the *tiaglye liudi*. In the town of Sviiazhsk, for example, there lived in the 1560s a *skomorokh* who owned two homes.[74] In Pskov in 1585, the *skomorokh* Ortemka owned a brick *bania* (public bath house or sauna) on which he paid a tax of one *grivna*.[75] A minstrel from Nizhnii Novgorod owned a small, but evidently profitable, eating establishment, a *povarnia* (literally, "kitchen"), which measured twenty-eight square feet and on which he paid a tax of one ruble in 1621.[76] Finally, the Moscow census of 1638 records a *skomorokh* by the name of Lubimko Ivanov who was apparently prosperous enough to have his own manservant.[77]

Even more numerous were the *skomorokhi* from the *srednye* class engaged in commercial activity as small shopkeepers and, to a lesser extent, traveling merchants. With respect to the latter, we learn that on 3 March 1636 five *skomorokhi* were assessed four *dengi* each by the customs duty officials in Ustiug Velikii when they brought some unspecified goods into the city.[78] A legal document from 1563 has survived which describes a *skomorokh*, along with several other merchants, as petitioning the tsar concerning his rights to engage in commercial activity in the village of Vesegonska, in the district of Uglich.[79] From this last example one can conclude that the *skomorokhi* had equal status and rights under the law with other commoners.

As for the *skomorokhi*-shopkeepers, some of these dealt, appropriately, in musical instruments and supplies, while others handled more conventional merchandise. In Kolomna in 1578, a *skomorokh* was operating a shop that sold strings for musical instruments.[80] In Mozhaisk in 1595, there were two such shops operated by *skomorokhi*, one located by the Nikolskii Bridge, the other on Bolshaia Street.[81] Several entries in the Muscovite customs duty records show that on more than one occasion large numbers of both musical instruments and musical supplies (such as strings) were brought into various towns for resale in local shops, some of which, presumably, were operated by *skomorokhi*. On 3 September 1633, for example, some 3,000 *domra* strings were brought to Ustiug Velikii by a wholesaler named Semen Fedorov Olgodaev.[82] On another occasion, fifty clay fifes were sold to local merchants in the same town by one Ivan Seliverstov.[83]

Among the *skomorokhi* who dealt in more essential, less specialized merchandise, there was one in Pskov in 1585 who owned a boot shop;[84] another in Viaz'ma in 1627 who ran a granary and presumably sold grain;[85] still another in Viatka in 1628 who was part owner of a shop selling fish.[86] Other *skomorokhi*-merchants, dealing in unspecified goods, could be found in Serpukhov, Riazan, and Viatka.[87] In Novgorod alone there were five commercial establishments or shops owned by *skomorokhi* in 1583.[88]

One conclusion that might be drawn from the foregoing discussion of the *srednye*, or moderately well-to-do, *skomorokhi* is that in order to achieve a modicum of economic security and prosperity the Russian minstrel found it necessary to supplement his professional earnings by engaging in some form of entrepreneural activity. There is in fact only one recorded instance in which an urban *skomorokh* appears to be prospering without some outside source of income: a certain Rodivonko, listed in the cadastre from Iama for 1500 and described as a *srednyi* taxpayer. His dwelling, along with those of six other *skomorokhi* described as *molodshie*, or of the lower class, was located on the Luga River.[89] Rodivonko's relative prosperity, one suspects, could be attributed to his being the most accomplished and popular of the seven minstrels living in Iama at this time.

The number of *skomorokhi* who ultimately reached the middle rung of the socioeconomic ladder was not great. Even in the period of their greatest popularity, the sixteenth and early seventeenth centuries, a majority of those living in the towns and nearly all of those in the countryside were firmly tied to the *molodshie* class, which was itself characterized by considerable economic stratification. There were, first of all, those among the *molodshie skomorokhi* who, though by no means prosperous, were able to maintain a certain degree of economic self-sufficiency. If they lived in the town they normally owned their own homesteads and supported themselves solely by their craft. Those in the countryside frequently owned land, which they worked as a means of supplementing their somewhat smaller professional earnings. Like other craftsmen living in the towns, the urban *skomorokhi* usually settled in specially designated quarters or streets, somewhat after the fashion of the medieval guilds. We have already mentioned, for example, the seven *skomorokhi* living along the Luga River in Iama. In Nizhnii Novgorod in 1621, there were three *skomorokhi* living on Il'inskaia Street.[90] Ustiug Velikii had four minstrels on Gulynia Street in 1630, while in Riazan they seemed to gravitate to an area of the city known as the Rezanski Gate.[91] Many of the Novgorod *skomorokhi* favored Dobrynia Street in the Goncharskii quarter on the Saint Sophia, or noncommercial, side of the city; there were at least four of them living here in 1581–84.[92] It is entirely possible that this street owed its popularity among the Novgorod minstrels to its namesake, Dobrynia, the legendary *bogatyr* of the Kievan cycle *byliny* and perhaps the most illustrious of all *skomorokhi*.[93]

Below the economically self-sufficient *skomorokhi* of the

lower class was a sizable group of minstrel-entertainers who found it difficult to survive on their own resources. A measure of the precarious economic condition of these *molodshie skomorokhi* is provided by the cadastres, where they are frequently described as sharing their dwellings (if in the town) or their farmland with others and paying taxes on them collectively. In Viatka in 1628, the two *skomorokhi* Vas'ka and Agafonko shared one dwelling, which was taxed as a single homestead.[94] In Riazan in 1626, the *skomorokh* Mikhailov owned a home in common with two other people, neither of whom was a minstrel, on which they paid a joint *obrok* of six *altyn* and four *dengi*.[95] In Mozhaisk, according to the census of 1544, the *skomorokh* Ivashko shared a taxable homestead with two non-*skomorokhi*.[96]

The practice of shared ownership of homestead and tax burden was even more common in the countryside than in the city. Though it was not unusual for two or three peasants to farm a single plot collectively, there are also instances of as many as thirteen and fourteen pooling their resources and engaging in what could almost be labeled communal agriculture. The 1495 cadastre from the Derevskaia *piatina* of Novgorod, for example, lists a homestead owned by the *skomorokh* Gridka and shared with thirteen other peasants in the village of Domashovo.[97] Judging from the properties' reported annual yield, the margin of profit for each of the shareholders was probably close to subsistence level.

There were also those among the *molodshie skomorokhi* who came under the general heading of *bobyli*, a class resembling the cotters (cottagers) in the West. Some of the minstrels in this poorest of classes were totally destitute, owning no property and living as wards of the church in hovels provided for that purpose. Four such *skomorokhi* are recorded in the Moscow census of 1638; two could be found in Tula in 1589; two others in Nizhnii Novgorod in 1621.[98] *Bobyli* dwelling in cities usually supported themselves as hired workers, *zakhrebetniki* or *dvorniki*. There were three *skomorokhi-zakhrebetniki* in Tula in 1589 and one in 1629, and six *skomorokhi-dvorniki* in Kolomna in 1578.[99] Some of the peasant *bobyli* owned small homesteads, with or without arable plots, on which they paid a minimal tax. There was at least one such landed homestead belonging to a *skomorokh* in the Shelonskaia *piatina* of Novgorod in 1539, and two other *skomorokhi* owned landless homesteads in the same general area.[100] A few of the poorest *skomorokhi* eventually sank even lower than the *bobyl'* class into a state of permanent servitude. The cadastre from Kazan for 1565–68, for example, numbers one *skomorokh* among the 137 serfs living in the city.[101]

One group of Muscovite *skomorokhi* were evidently in a class by themselves—the minstrels retained either by the tsar at court or by wealthy noblemen on their estates. Ivan IV was the first tsar to use *skomorokhi* as court entertainers. In 1572 he ordered that all of the *veselye liudi* from Novgorod and the surrounding area be rounded up and, together with their trained bears, transported to Moscow.[102] The Moscow census of 1638 records two homesteads on Bol'shaia Street, belonging to Feodor Tiutchev and Ondrei Shalkov, both of whom are described as entertainers of the sovereign.[103] Among the prominent Russian noblemen who were known to retain their own *skomorokhi* were Prince Ivan Shuiskii and Prince Dmitrii Pozharskii. In May 1633 four of Shuiskii's *skomorokhi* and two attached to Pozharskii's estate complained collectively to the tsar of having been unlawfully seized and detained by the nobleman Kriukov, who also relieved them of their cumulative earnings of thirty-seven rubles.[104] Even from the incomplete information that we have, it can reasonably be assumed that these court minstrels constituted a rather privileged class among the *skomorokhi*. They were well provided for by their patrons, and their absence from the cadastral tax rolls only confirms their unique socioeconomic status.

In addition to providing a glimpse of the social and economic status of the Russian minstrels, the cadastres, and to a lesser extent the census books and customs duty records, furnish us with evidence of their continuing artistic evolution and professionalization, particularly during the sixteenth and early seventeenth centuries. This is apparent from the large number of synonymous names—other than the usual generic *skomorokh*—used to describe the professional minstrel-entertainers in these sources. At least twelve distinct names can be singled out. In most cases they pertain to a performer's special skill or talent, and implicit in the variety of names is the wide-ranging versatility of the *skomorokhi*. Quite common by the mid-sixteenth century was the name *medvednik* ("bear tamer"),[105] evidence, no doubt, of the association between the bear and the *skomorokh* that reaches far back into Russian antiquity. By the end of the same century, the names *smychnik* ("fiddler"), *domrachei* (also *domernik* or *domershchik*, "*domra* player"), *rozhechnik* ("horn player"), *nakrachei* ("drum player"), *gudochnik* ("minstrel"), *strunnik* ("string player", and *dudnik* ("flute player") had also gained wide currency as synonyms for *skomorokh*.[106] Four others were added in the early seventeenth century: *veselyi* ("merry one"), *tsymbal'nik* ("cymbal player"), *gusel'nik* ("*gusli* player"), and *poteshnik* ("entertainer").[107]

An appropriate subtitle for this chapter might have been "The Golden Age of the *Skomorokhi*." While the church's verbal abuse of the *skomorokhi* continued unabated, especially in the northeast, the lot of the Russian minstrel seemed to improve considerably with passing time. One must remember, however, that it was largely the nonitinerant *skomorokhi* whom we have been discussing here, and these were by no means the only representatives of the minstrel's art in medieval Russia. It was the itinerant minstrel-entertainers who continued to bear the brunt of the church's harshest criticism. The *skomorokhi* who eventually settled in the north did find there a new and better life, as the cadastres and related sources show; they found the opportunity not only to integrate themselves socially and economically into the life of the community but also, in the process, to gain a new measure of respectability for their profession. Unfortunately their time, like that of Lord Novgorod the Great, soon ran out: first, Ivan IV uprooted many, and then the church, allied with Aleksei, gained final victory over them, after a prolonged and bitter struggle spanning some 650 years.

3
Decline
and
Dispersal

The Soviet historian A. A. Zimin recently observed that even as late as the mid-sixteenth century a significant proportion of the *skomorokhi* continued to lead a peripatetic existence, as indeed they had for over 500 years.[1] The emphasis of the last chapter was on the settled, or registered, minstrel-entertainers. Before attempting to trace the declining fortunes of the *skomorokhi*, and indeed as a necessary prologue to that attempt, I would like to focus specifically on the itinerant minstrels, who in many respects can be regarded as a class unto themselves.

One of the clearest indications of the sharp legal distinction made between the itinerant and nonitinerant *skomorokhi* can be found in the *Sudebnik* of 1589 (drafted in two versions, a short and a long, the latter for use in northern Russia).[2] In the shorter version of this Muscovite legal code there are, in Article 7, three clauses dealing with *skomorokhi*.[3] Mentioned first are the sovereign's, or court, minstrels, and the registered (*opisnye*) *skomorokhi*. If one of these is dishonored or abused, he is to receive compensation in the amount of two rubles, and his wife double that amount. Next come the unregistered (*neopisnye*) *skomorokhi* and their wives. If the same offense is perpetrated against one of these, the compensation is set at one *grivna* (two for a wife), or one-twentieth of the amount prescribed for a registered *skomorokh*. Finally, if the offended *skomorokh* is an unregistered military (*pokhodnyi*) minstrel, he is entitled to a payment of two *dengi* (four for a wife), or one-hundredth of what his registered counterpart could expect.

In the longer version of the 1589 *Sudebnik*, the court minstrels are included in the registered category under Article 65, while the military *skomorokhi* are somewhat upgraded to the level of the regular unregistered minstrels (in Article 66).[4] The rates of compensation remain at two rubles for the registered and one *grivna* for the unregistered. Strangely, in the longer version the wife of a registered *skomorokh* is no longer entitled to any compensation; the unregistered minstrel's wife, on the other hand, continues to receive payment at twice the rate of her husband. One is at a loss to explain this apparent downgrading of the registered *skomorokh's* wife.[5]

A word of clarification is in order regarding the use of the terms "registered" (*opisnye*) and "unregistered" (*neopisnye*) in the *Sudebnik* of 1589. Those *skomorokhi* who had settled down and established permanent residence in some town or rural community eventually found their way into one of the periodic fiscal surveys discussed in the last chapter. In effect, these nontraveling *skomorokhi* became, like almost everyone else of the lower class, registered taxpayers, or *tiaglye liudi*. On the other hand, minstrels who chose to make their living as itinerant entertainers and thus did not stay long enough in any one place to have their names entered on the local tax rolls remained unregistered.

Using the *Sudebnik* of 1589 as a normative standard, one must conclude that there was a clear distinction in the eyes of the authorities between the itinerant and nonitinerant *skomorokhi*. Surprisingly, both had legal rights, but they were by no means equal under the law: the social worth of the registered minstrel was twenty times greater than that of his unregistered counterpart. Revealing also is the high social standing of the registered *skomorokhi* relative to other segments of the population. A middle-class burgher, if dishonored, was entitled to the same compensation of two rubles as a registered *skomorokh*.[6] A *sotskii*, an elected civil official who performed police service and sometimes served as chief administrator and judge in the rural districts of the north, was also on an equal legal footing with the registered *skomorokh*.[7]

Other documents are equally explicit in drawing the distinction between the two classes of *skomorokhi*. A charter issued by the Trinity–Saint Sergius Monastery on 31 October 1555 for the Prisetskaia *volost'*, over which the monastery exercised both ecclesiastical and civil authority, addresses itself both to the itinerant and nonitinerant *skomorokhi*.[8] It states that the latter are henceforth prohibited from taking up permanent residence in the region. Those already in residence are to be seized and beaten, their belongings and property are to be confiscated, and they themselves summarily evicted. Furthermore, the *sotskii* in whose jurisdiction a *skomorokh* has been living is required to pay a fine or surety of ten rubles, which he is to collect from among his constituents. Next, the charter focuses briefly on the *prokhozhie,* or itinerant minstrel-entertainers, forbidding them even to set foot in any town or village under the jurisdiction of the monastery. The distinction here between itinerant and nonitinerant is the more significant since it appears in a document drafted by ecclesiastical authorities. Evidently even within the ranks of the church, where traditionally all *skomorokhi* had been equally despised and persecuted, there was some attempt made to distinguish between the two classes of minstrels.

The importance of distinguishing between the registered and the unregistered *skomorokhi* will become more readily apparent after we have examined some of the evidence that bears directly on the history of the latter. A revealing source in this regard is the *Stoglav* of 1551, a document that embodies the decisions of a church council, the so-called Council of the Hundred Chapters, convened in the reign of Ivan IV as a response to certain abuses and irregularities that had become commonplace in the Russian Orthodox Church. The *skomorokhi* are discussed in three places and mentioned in another, a graphic reminder of the church's continuing concern over the influence of the minstrel-entertainers in Muscovite society and culture.[9] In chapter 41, question 16, they are vehemently condemned for their involvement in wedding ceremonies, where, it is said, they often take precedence over the priest. In question 23 of the same chapter, and again in chapter 93, they are denounced for their intimate association with such traditional pagan festivals as the *Rusaliia*.[10] Finally, in question 19 of chapter 41 they are described as follows: "The *skomorokhi* wander about in distant parts in bands of up to sixty, seventy, or one hundred men, and they forcibly take food and drink from the peasants in the villages; they steal animals from barns and engage in brigandage along the roads." Allowing for the possibility that the figures "sixty, seventy, or one hundred" are exaggerations for shock value, one can draw two conclusions about the itinerant minstrels from this description: they apparently traveled about in large groups, and they had a reputation for lawlessness. Both of these general conclusions are borne out by other sources.

Although the number of *skomorokhi* traveling together was by no means fixed, it usually ranged from a minimum of two to as many as eight to a troupe. The customs duty records from Ustiug Velikii, for example, show that on 29 April 1635 two traveling *skomorokhi* paid a joint tax of eight *dengi* upon entering the town, while on 3 March of the same year a group of five minstrel-entertainers were assessed a duty or head tax of four *dengi* each.[11] The Dutch traveler Adam Olearius has left a vivid description of a performance by a troupe of four itinerant minstrels, which he witnessed in or near Moscow in 1636.[12] An accompanying illustration shows a one-man puppet theater, two musicians (one playing an oval *gusli*, the other a *gudok*), and a dancing bear with his trainer.[13] There is also at least one recorded instance of a troupe of *skomorokhi* that numbered eight performers. They arrived in Turinsk (located some 900 miles east of Moscow, near Tobolsk) on 17 December 1655. Upon entering the town they paid a collective head tax of five *altyny*, two *dengi*, and in addition, they were assessed a duty of two *altyny* on their cart and four *altyny* on their trained bear.[14] (This reference is noteworthy for another reason: it demonstrates that even after their official proscription by Aleksei in 1648, the wandering minstrels, at whom the proscription was primarily aimed, continued to practice their time-honored profession largely unmolested, if only in the more remote areas of Muscovy.)

The *Stoglav's* allegation that the itinerant *skomorokhi* engaged in widespread lawlessness can be substantiated from other sources, as we shall see below. However, just as inflated figures ("sixty, seventy, or one hundred") were cited in the *Stoglav* to focus attention on the potential menace to the peace posed by the roving bands of *skomorokhi*, the blanket condemnation of itinerant minstrels for banditry was apparently calculated to discredit the profession as a whole because of the actions of a few. The charges against the traveling minstrels included the stealing of animals from barns, brigandage along the highways, and forcible appropriation of food and drink from the people. One cannot help but wonder whether these thefts were motivated by malice and greed or were simply the acts of desperate men trying to keep body and soul together. After all, these were among the poorest members of society, and they could rarely eke out an existence on their meager professional earnings. Many, as we have seen, were classified as paupers and lived as wards of the church in hovels provided by the parishes. With no homes, land, or personal possessions to speak of, they scarcely fit the stereotype of the hardened criminal or daring highwayman enriching himself at the expense of others—the *Stoglav's* strong language notwithstanding. Indeed, one has but to recall Sigismund von Herberstein's description of the unfortunate minstrels he chanced upon in the winter of 1526 to fully appreciate their plight.[15]

While it is not until the mid-sixteenth century that specific charges of banditry are first leveled against them, there is evidence that there was concern in some quarters over the conduct of traveling minstrels by the second half of the fifteenth century. A charter of immunity granted by Prince Iurii Vasilievich of Dmitrov to the Trinity–Saint Sergius Monastery in 1470 specifically prohibits minstrels from entertaining in the villages and hamlets belonging to the monastery.[16] Since this was a charter granted to an ecclesiastical petitioner, it might be argued that it only confirms the traditional attitude of the church toward the *skomorokhi*. There were, however, identical charters granted to nonecclesiastical petitioners. In several of these, the more extreme examples to be sure, *skomorokhi* are forbidden to enter designated towns, villages, and hamlets.[17] In other instances they are allowed entry provided they refrain from loud or boisterous entertainment, that is, such as may create a commotion or bring about a disturbance of the peace.[18]

Further evidence that some of the traveling minstrels conducted themselves less than honorably, and even on occasion resorted to force, can perhaps be found in certain folk songs attributed to them, the so-called brigand songs, or *razboinichi pesni*. Among the best known of these is "Usy, udaly molodtsy" (often just "Usy" or "Usishcha").[19] According to most scholars this folk song bears the unmistakable imprint of the *skomorokhi* in both content and form.[20] It describes a band of brigands who visit the home of a wealthy peasant and take advantage not only of his hospitality, but of his life's savings as well. The leader of the band, Grishka Muryshka, was a historical person who achieved notoriety through his daring exploits along the Volga in the 1640s. Grishka, along with his brother Vas'ka, is mentioned by name in a *gramota* issued by the tsar on 28 May 1645.[21] Vas'ka eventually aspired to bigger and better things; in the 1660s he became a forerunner of the legendary Stenka Razin when he led a movement of protest against the government among the upstream Cossacks, and by 1670 he had become one of Razin's chief lieutenants.[22]

"Usy" is permeated with the spirit of the *skomorokhi*. It contains several obvious traces of their workmanship, particularly in its heavy reliance on humor and parody.[23] An excellent example of its strong humorous undercurrent can be found in the closing lines, which introduce the idiot, or fool, as one of the protagonists of the song,[24] and in Muryshka's lengthy speech before the assembled Usy, a convincing parody of an ataman's address to his host frequently found in seventeenth-century historical songs.[25] For all its apparent historicity, however, "Usy" is basically an autobiographical account of the exploits of a band of *skomorokhi* in the early seventeenth century, probably composed as a veiled tribute to their resourcefulness and cleverness in exploiting the unwary with allusions to historical persons and places introduced primarily as camouflage. The song has about it an air of bravado, bordering on arrogance, which only superficially conceals the wretched condition of many of the itinerant minstrels ("those homeless, half-starved masters of merrymaking and laughter"[26]) following the political and social upheavals of the Time of Troubles (1598–1613).

In the village of Likovo, some twenty miles from Moscow, there circulated well into the nineteenth century a story about a band of *skomorokhi* who once came to the village to give a performance. While the villagers were assembled, enjoying themselves and listening to some of the minstrels, other minstrels were busy elsewhere rounding up all the sheep in the village. To add insult to injury, the performing *skomorokhi* repeatedly sang before their unsuspecting audience, "O, mother Likova,/Sew your sleeve to your coat!"—an appropriate bit of folk wisdom.[28] According to Beliaev, old-timers tell many similar stories of how the *skomorokhi* would come into a village in groups, and some would entertain and divert the villagers while others ransacked their homes, barns, and animal pens, making off with whatever they could easily carry. The performing minstrels would frequently allude in song or proverb to the mischief their unseen comrades were engaged in, but no one was the wiser until it was too late.[28]

Whether one dismisses the lawless behavior of some of the *skomorokhi* as mere mischief or condemns it as criminal, one thing is certain—ultimately, the reputation of all the minstrels suffered. Although Aleksei's *gramota* of 1648 was intended to curb the unlawful activities of a few, its effect was to outlaw all of the *skomorokhi*. The distinction between the majority of minstrels, who had become integrated into the social and cultural life of the community, and the few transient *skomorokhi*-brigands, who had not, was lost on Aleksei and conveniently ignored by his ecclesiastical advisers. The latter were mainly interested in eradicating the "pagan" culture that the *skomorokhi* had typified and disseminated among the people for so long, and they seized their opportunity in 1648.

Supposing for the moment that the weak and ineffectual Aleksei had not been prevailed upon by the ecclesiastical authorities to officially denounce the *skomorokhi* in 1648, it is more than likely that he would have done so on his own initiative, for political rather than religious considerations. In May of that year Moscow found itself on the brink of political and social disaster as the discontent of the masses, which had for so long simmered, burst forth into furious mob violence.[29] The Moscow burghers, or *posad* folk, had for some time borne the brunt of the onerous taxes that the government, in constant need of money, continued to levy. Especially hated were the "fifth money," a special assessment imposed on merchants and artisans, and the salt tax. In 1648 the salt tax, which was high to begin with, was suddenly quadrupled. The people petitioned the tsar to reduce the tax, but their entreaties fell on deaf ears. Convinced that influential boyars like Boris Morozov and Prince Iliia Miloslavskii and their corrupt and unscrupulous proteges and appointees had conspired against them, the exasperated Muscovites took to the streets. First, they sacked the houses of many foreigners living in Moscow and then those of the boyars and merchants. They set fires throughout the city, so that eventually half of Moscow lay in ashes. While Morozov and Miloslavskii, the two closest and most visible advisers of Aleksei, escaped with their lives, several other officials were not as fortunate; a few of the more visible offenders were ordered executed by the tsar himself as a concession to the outraged mob. To add to the general confusion, the *strel'tsy*, who were called out to restore order, looked the other way, implicitly lending support to the rampaging crowd.

Taking their cue from the burghers of Moscow, other towns staged similar revolts, protesting against the government's insensitivity to the abuses of its officials. Even the normally conservative and peaceful communities of the north, such as Ustiug, Sol'vychegodsk, Iaroslavl, and the distant Siberian town of Tomsk (where an attempt was made in 1648 to establish an independent Cossack republic), were infected with the spirit of rebellion.[30] Ultimately the violence spread to Novgorod and Pskov. All of these risings were eventually put down, but not before they had made an indelible impression on the young Aleksei. He became much more disposed to listen to the people and, at their behest, to take measures to alleviate some of the conditions that had given rise to the widespread popular discontent. Among these measures was the summoning of the important *zemskii sobor* of 1648–49, which was charged by Aleksei with revising the legal code of the land, something not attempted since 1550. A commission headed by N. I. Odoevskii was promptly set to work on the new code, and it was formally promulgated in April of 1649.[31]

Having satisfied some of the more immediate demands of the people, Aleksei took steps to minimize the possibility of future disturbances. One step was the drafting of a *gramota* in December of 1648 entitled, "On the Righting of Morals and the Abolition of Superstition," which, while ostensibly nonpolitical in tone and content, was not without political motivation. Its primary target was the *skomorokhi*, whose reputation for lawlessness had not escaped the tsar's attention. His close ecclesiastical advisers saw in the crisis of 1648 a splendid opportunity to rid the country of the "pagan menace"; by outlawing the *skomorokhi*, they counseled, the tsar would also be eliminating a potentially disruptive element in Russian society. As Morozov has rightly observed, the attack on the *skomorokhi* by the government in 1648 was but one manifestation of a much wider effort on the part of the tsar and his servitors to deal with the popular unrest that engulfed them.[32]

While the *skomorokhi* themselves, or at least the unruly ones, must bear some of the responsibility for Aleksei's proscriptive *gramota* of 1648, there were factors conspiring against them over which they had little control. These can be traced back to the mid-fifteenth century and synthesized as follows: the fortunes of the *skomorokhi* were intimately bound up with those of Novgorod. When it became a victim of Muscovite aggression and centralization and began to decline, politically as well as culturally, so did the fortunes of the *skomorokhi*. Novgorod's political disintegration began in earnest in 1456 with the imposition by Vasilii II of a treaty that sharply curtailed its independence, though it left its traditional liberties intact. In 1478, with the abolition of both the *veche* and the office of elected *posadnik*, as well as the removal to Moscow of the *veche* bell (symbolic of the city's ancient liberties), Novgorod's independent political life was extinguished and its future securely bound to that of Muscovy. The final blow was administered by Ivan IV in the early 1570s, during the height of the *oprichnina*, when Novgorod's social and cultural elite was decimated and scattered. As for the *skomorokhi*, they shared a common fate with many other skilled craftsmen and artisans forced to leave Novgorod for Moscow on orders of the tsar.

Without a doubt, Ivan IV and his *oprichnina* marked a turning point in the history of the *skomorokhi*.[33] The devastating social and economic effect of the reign of terror in Novgorod is reflected to some degree in the post-*oprichnina* history of the *skomorokhi*, even though the Novgorod minstrels themselves were not a target of Ivan's wrath. Some of the surviving cadastres compiled in Novgorod a decade or so after Ivan's attack on the city offer a graphic illustration of this. A cadastre from 1583–84, for example, contains the following entries: on Dobrynia Street (a traditional haven of the Novgorod minstrels), an empty taxable homestead once owned jointly by Tret'iakov, a *skomorokh*, and Grishinskoi, a *strelnik*, both of whom went begging and disappeared without a trace in 1572; on the same street, another empty taxable homestead formerly belonging to Kharia Semenov, a *skomorokh* who was taken to Moscow by the tsar in 1572; a third vacant, taxable homestead on Dobrynia Street, left by Efimenko, a *skomorokh* who apparently perished in the midst of the turbulence of 1570.[34] This same cadastre also records an empty taxable homestead belonging to the *veselyi* Lobanov, who was taken to Moscow by the tsar, and one-third of another empty homestead abandoned by the *skomorokh* Sozonov, both located on Variazheskaia Street.[35] On Rostkina Street there was a deserted taxable homestead once jointly owned by the furrier Mikhalko and the *skomorokh* Vorob'ia. Mikhalko died in 1571, while Vorob'ia went begging.[36] The same sorry fate befell the *medvednik* Ivashko, who abandoned his taxable homestead on Ianeva Street and turned beggar.[37]

Another Novgorod cadastre, compiled in 1585–86, contains similar entries. It mentions two abandoned, taxable homesteads, one on Korzhova, the other on Proboina Street, formerly owned by *skomorokhi*. One of the minstrels died, while the other "disappeared without a trace" in 1571.[38] This cadastre also provides some revealing information about the plight of other craftsmen and artisans in Novgorod, who were in one way or another affected by the *oprichnina*. A lengthy entry for Bol'shaia Street describes an empty taxable homestead once owned by two shoemakers, Ivanko Kuzmin and Vasiuk Ivanov, and a painter by the name of Tret'iashko Fedorov. Tret'iashko, we are told, turned beggar. One of the shoemakers, Ivanko, was taken to Moscow, while the other became a wandering bear tamer (*medvednik*). Their homestead was turned over to an *oprichnik* from Moscow, a *diak*, or secretary, by the name of Fedorov.[39]

It is clear from these cadastral entries that, intentionally or not, Ivan IV contributed to the decline of the *skomorokhi* by his attack on Novgorod in 1570. What Ivan did, in effect, was to precipitate the first great dispersal of the minstrel-entertainers, a dispersal that involved the most talented of the *skomorokhi*, and one from which they would never recover. Their ranks had already been thinned by the plague that hit Novgorod in the 1560s.[40] Now, in the early 1570s, as a result of the *oprichnina*, many of them lost what little economic security they had and were forced to go on the road as traveling entertainers or virtual beggars. Others were forcibly uprooted and taken en masse to Moscow for the pleasure of Ivan and his court in September 1572. According to the Novgorod chronicle, the order had gone out from the tsar to round up all of the *veselye liudi* in Novgorod and the surrounding communities and to enlist them in the service of the sovereign.

Accordingly, on the twenty-first of that month a large number of *skomorokhi*, together with their trained bears, were loaded onto carts. Accompanied by the *diak* Subota, they left Novgorod for Moscow.[41]

One might ask what motivated this mass transfer of *skomorokhi*. In light of the avowed purpose of the *oprichnina*—to wipe out treason—was this a politically motivated step aimed at the *skomorokhi* as a class or the whim of a fun-loving, indulgent tsar? Surely it was the latter. Ivan IV, as we shall see below, had an intense interest in worldly amusements. He was also aware of the long-standing reputation for excellence enjoyed by the Novgorod minstrel-entertainers; during his month-long stay in Novgorod in 1570 he had probably been entertained by some of them. Furthermore, the fact that the chronicle specifically mentions trained bears suggests that Ivan was particularly fond of this form of entertainment, and that he found the Novgorod bear tamers superior to those of Moscow. As the *Stoglav* of 1551 reminds us, there was no dearth of native *skomorokhi* in Moscow in the sixteenth century, but Ivan, a connoisseur, apparently preferred those of Novgorod to all others. For several reasons, the Novgorod *skomorokhi* may have been artistically superior. To begin with, they were geographically removed from the political and economical instability that characterized the Muscovite lands in the wake of the Mongol invasion; Lord Novgorod the Great had been spared this destructive and disruptive interlude. Unlike their Muscovite counterparts, the Novgorod minstrels enjoyed considerable freedom to evolve professionally because they were subject to far less harassment from church and state, a fact graphically illustrated by the series of miniatures discussed in the previous chapter. Finally, one cannot overlook the basically cosmopolitan atmosphere of Novgorod, which fostered and encouraged secular entertainment.

Although the majority of the Novgorod *skomorokhi* found themselves impoverished as a result of the political chaos of the early 1570s—many of them being forced to join the ranks of the traditionally poorer itinerant class—some of those taken to Moscow by the tsar ultimately fared quite well. The most talented became virtual court minstrels, or, as they are referred to in some sources, sovereign's *skomorokhi*. With this new status came both economic and social rewards. A striking illustration of this can be found in a recently discovered list of names and salaries of *oprichniki* attached to Ivan's household in 1573.[42] Of the 188 persons listed under the general heading of the Order of the Bedchamber (*Postel'nyi prikaz*), which had responsibility for the day-to-day management of the tsar's private estate, two were *skomorokhi.* The two, Pafom and Grasnukha Sergeev, were brothers serving the tsar as *oprichniki.* Their annual rate of pay exceeded that of any other craftsman or artisan in the *Postel'nyi prikaz*: a flat salary of ten rubles, with additional allowances for cloth (forty-eight *altyny*), grain, meat, and salt.[43] The rate of pay for all others in the *prikaz* was a salary of between one and three rubles, with allowances for cloth, grain, meat, and salt scaled down to one-half or one-third that of the two *skomorokhi,* or less.[44]

The comparatively high rate of pay for the two *skomorokhi-oprichniki* is probably indicative of their superior talents as well as their high standing at Ivan's court. While obviously favored by the tsar, they were not the only *skomorokhi* upon whom Ivan called for entertainment. Robert Best, the interpreter for Osepp Napea, the Russian ambassador in London, describes a state dinner given by the tsar at which six *skomorokhi*-singers were brought in to entertain the guests during the meal.[45] Sir Jerome Horsey, an agent of the Russia Company in Moscow between 1575 and 1591, tells of Ivan's custom of bathing daily at three in the afternoon and then solacing himself "with pleasant songs."[46] When the tsar was in an exceptionally good mood, he would have songs about the fall of Kazan and Astrakhan recited to him by *skomorokhi.*[47]

In addition to using the *skomorokhi* quite regularly for his public and private amusement, on occasion Ivan himself took part in their entertainments. Prince A. M. Kurbskii, refers to the *skomorokhi* twice in his biography of Ivan. In discussing .the first, or good, part of Ivan's reign, Kurbskii notes that there were none of these "evil and cunning parasites" around to distract the young tsar and lead him astray.[48] In fact, Ivan had been prevailed upon in 1551 by Metropolitan Ioasaf to include stronger strictures against the *skomorokhi* in the *Stoglav.*[49] But, according to Kurbskii, during the second half of his reign, beginning in 1560, Ivan gave himself up to loose living. He was frequently drunk, and in that state he would don a mask and dance "together with the *skomorokhi,* and so did those who were feasting with him."[50] Ivan was also known to employ *skomorokhi* to mock and heap scorn upon his enemies. He sent Archbishop Pimen of Novgorod, whom he had accused of plotting to betray the city to Poland, back to Moscow in 1570, and had him placed upon a white mare and paraded about the streets in the company of performing *skomorokhi.*[51]

Ivan IV's successor, Fedor I, appears to have enjoyed the performances of the *skomorokhi* as much as his father, though he never took an active part in the merrymaking. Giles Fletcher, the

English ambassador in Moscow, writes of Fedor: "After his sleep he goeth to evensong, called *vechernia,* and, thence returning, for the most part recreateth himself with the Empress till suppertime with jesters and dwarfs, men and women that tumble before him and sing many songs after the Rus manner. This is his common recreation betwixt meals that he most delights in."[52] (Fools and dwarfs, generally referred to as *shuty,* were common at the Muscovite court from the early sixteenth century, and both Ivan IV and Fedor I were very fond of them. Zabelin notes that the court fools, because of their predominantly foreign origin, were frequently called *Spielmen* and that they were distinct from the *skomorokhi.*[53])

During the reign of Fedor I the court *skomorokhi* continued to enjoy a certain degree of social status and to be accorded preferential treatment, perhaps even more than in the reign of Ivan IV. This is obvious, for example, from the 1589 *Sudebnik,* where the designation "sovereign's *skomorokhi*" appears for the first time. As was already pointed out, the minstrels so designated were entitled to a much higher rate of compensation for injury than their socially inferior brethren. The designation, and presumably the privileges that went with it, endured well into the seventeenth century. The Moscow census of 1638, for example, lists two households on Bol'shaia Street belonging to the *skomorokhi* Fedor Tiutchev and Ondrei Shalkov respectively, both of whom are described as "sovereign's entertainers."[54]

Michael Romanov also proved to be an enthusiastic patron of the *skomorokhi.* He made extensive use of the so-called *poteshnaia palata,* or entertainment hall, where *skomorokhi* and other entertainers performed,[55] and at his wedding in 1626, he engaged three *skomorokhi,* Andriushka Fedorov, Vas'ka Stepanov, and Putiata, to mingle with and entertain the guests.[56] Furthermore, it was during Michael's reign that the *skomorokhi* attempted, for the first and last time, to make petitions of grievances directly to the tsar. In May of 1633, four minstrels belonging to Prince Ivan Shuiskii and two attached to the estate of Prince Dmitrii Pozharskii complained to the tsar of having been unlawfully seized and detained by the nobleman Kriukov, who also took from them the rather substantial sum of thirty-seven rubles, their cumulative earnings.[57] What action, if any, was taken by the tsar is not known.

Even the church seems to have softened its traditionally strident attacks on the *skomorokhi* during Michael Romanov's reign. A report issued in 1636 on the spiritual condition of the church in Moscow singles out the *skomorokhi,* particularly the bear tamers, as being in part responsible for distracting Muscovite

Christians from their spiritual obligations.[58] But aside from this general statement of fact, there is no condemnation of the minstrel-entertainers, nor are the faithful forbidden to patronize their performances. This was, however, only the calm before the storm, for the death of Michael Romanov in 1645 ushered in a new and bleak era for the minstrels.

Michael's successor, Aleksei, was by temperament and inclination very different from his father. Early in life he had come under the strong influence of ecclesiastical tutors who provided him with an essentially spiritual *Weltanschauung*, one accurately reflected in his nickname, *Tishaishii* ("the Quietest One"). Throughout his long reign (1645–76) he continued to be a dedicated and informed Orthodox Christian, meticulously observing all prescribed fasts and rituals. Piety and sobriety permeated his private life as well. Rather than amuse himself with sundry entertainers in the *poteshnaia palata*, he preferred the outdoors and, in particular, hunting. In fact, very early in his reign he banned all but the *bakhari* from the entertainment hall, and even these venerable storytellers (now more accurately referred to as *kaleki*) were no longer called upon to recite secular folktales, or *skazki*, but rather religious verse, or *dukhovnye stikhi*.[59]

Aleksei's first marriage, in 1648, provides a striking contrast between the *tishaishii* tsar and his immediate predecessors. Traditionally the joyous event called for much gaiety and merrymaking at court, with the *skomorokhi* and other entertainers taking a leading part. On this occasion, however, the entertainment—if such it can be called—was quite different. For the duration of the three-day wedding feast, fifteen church cantors (*diaki*) were charged with chanting religious verse, *stikhi* taken largely from the *Triod*. On the third and last day of the nuptials, the tsar himself went among the guests and distributed fruit to all present. According to a contemporary account, the entire celebration was marked by peace, joy, and piety.[60]

The first years of Aleksei's reign, plagued with political upheavals such as the Moscow rising of 1648, also witnessed the church's effort to rejuvenate itself spiritually and to eradicate all vestiges of paganism among the people.[61] A series of official pronouncements from this period demonstrate the nature and scope of this effort at spiritual reform. Spearheading the movement was the remarkable band of Zealots of Piety, led by the tsar's confessor, Stefan Vonifat'ev. The Patriarch of Moscow, Iosif, fully supported the efforts of the reformers. In 1646, a year after Aleksei's accession to the throne, he sent a circular pastoral letter to all the clergy, urging them to see to it that the faithful keep the prescribed fasts and behave properly in church; that they enter the House of the Lord with fear and trepidation; and that they refrain not only from talking or whispering, but even from thinking mundane thoughts during the Liturgy and other services.[62]

A year later the Metropolitan of Rostov-Iaroslavl, Varlaam, sent a *gramota* to Antonii, the abbot of the Kirillo-Belozerskii Monastery, in which he paraphrased the words of the Patriarch Iosif, urging the clergy to maintain a vigilant eye over the faithful, especially with respect to keeping holy the Lord's Day. The patriarch and the metropolitan were especially concerned about the commercial activity carried on in the town and village market places on the eve of the Lord's Day. After likening the people who engaged in such unholy activity to Jews, the *gramota* urged the closing of all market stalls on Saturday afternoons and prescribed attendance at vespers as a fitting substitute. All physical labor was likewise to end by three o'clock on Saturday.[63]

The capstone of this movement of spiritual reform came in December of 1648. In that month Aleksei issued two *gramoty* addressed to the question of church discipline and to the whole range of pagan practices common among the people. While some historians find Aleksei's *gramoty* of December 1648 somewhat startling, in reality they are quite consistent both with the character of the young tsar and with the movement launched by the Zealots of Piety. They represent the official confirmation by the tsar, in stern and uncompromising language, of the church's effort at reform. For the *skomorokhi*, who are singled out and harshly censured in these documents, a long tradition of entertainment, in village square as well as at court, finally comes to an end.

While the formal proscription of the *skomorokhi* did not come until December of 1648, it appears that the church, no doubt with the tsar's explicit or implicit concurrence, had even earlier taken formal steps to curb their influence among the people. In the 1647 version of the *Trebnik*, which prescribed the liturgical rite for administering certain sacraments, including secret confession, the clergy was charged with asking all penitents a series of questions: "Did you seek out the games of the *skomorokhi*? Did you seek out Satanic games, look upon these, or yourself take part in them?" If the response to any of these was affirmative, the penitent was required to beg pardon for his sins in the following manner: "I have sinned, I delighted in hearing the sound of the *gusli* and the *organon*, of horns, and all manner of *skomoroshestvo*, of Satanic sayings, and for this I also paid them [that is, the minstrels]."[64]

As the church and state were orchestrating their official

campaign against the *skomorokhi,* some of the lower clergy were beginning to take the law into their own hands. Two such instances have been recorded, one in Nizhnii Novgorod around 1646, the other in the village of Lopatishch (not far from Nizhnii Novgorod) in 1648. Ironically, in both cases the clergymen involved eventually gained fame as spokesmen for the dissident Old Believer movement—the Archpriest Avvakum and his close friend and teacher Ivan (Grigorii, after his religious profession) Neronov, one of the leaders of the Zealots of Piety.

In Neronov's biography, written by one of his followers shortly after his death in 1670, there is an interesting account of the activities of the *skomorokhi* in Nizhnii Novgorod in the mid-1640s. There were a number of minstrels in Nizhnii Novgorod at this time;[65] one encountered them frequently going through the streets of the town with their trained bears, playing musical instruments and giving "shameful" performances on street corners and in the market place. On one such occasion Neronov, a parish priest in the town and an outspoken antagonist of the *skomorokhi,*[66] fell upon the performers and seized their musical instruments and destroyed them. The highhandedness of the priest angered the minstrels, who beat him severely. Neronov remained undaunted, however. Henceforth he and some of his students (presumably the most able-bodied) patrolled the streets of the town during the major festival periods such as *Koliada* in order to discourage the *skomorokhi* from performing. But, says the author, even this proved ineffectual and hazardous, as both Ivan and his students "received not a few wounds at the hands of the *skomorokhi,* those servants of the devil, and they bore these bodily wounds with joy as they returned to their homes, bloodied but alive."[67] This is the only recorded instance of violence involving the *skomorokhi.*

The *skomorokhi* against whom Neronov waged this relentless campaign were permanent residents of the town, members in good standing of the community. In fact, according to the seventeenth-century cadastre from Nizhnii Novgorod cited in the previous chapter, of the thirteen *skomorokhi* living in or near the town in 1621, several were relatively well to do.[68] No doubt this is why Neronov met with little success in his attempt to drive the local minstrels from the town, and why they reacted so boldly and violently to the vigilante tactics of the priest and his students.

Avvakum's encounter with the *skomorokhi,* which he records in his autobiography, was similar in some respects to that of Neronov, though it involved itinerant, rather than resident, minstrels and for that reason was not as violent. It occurred in 1648, several months before Aleksei issued the first of his two *gramoty*.[69] At the time Avvakum was a priest in the village of Lopatishch, east of Moscow. One day, he tells us, entertainers with dancing bears and various musical instruments came into the village. Avvakum acted swiftly and resolutely: "I, a sinner, being zealous in the service of Christ, drove them out and destroyed their masks and drums, one against many in the open field, and I took two great bears from them—one I killed but he later revived, the other I set free in the open field."[70] These itinerant entertainers did not have the same legal rights as their registered counterparts in Nizhnii Novgorod, which presumably explains why they offered no resistance to Avvakum and why he, unlike Neronov, escaped without being physically assaulted.

Both incidents also merit examination for the clues they offer regarding the repertoire of the *skomorokhi*, both itinerant and non-itinerant, in the first half of the seventeenth century. They show that both the trained bear act and music were integral parts of a *skomorokh* entertainment, and more significantly, they seem to confirm the fact that the *skomorokhi* continued to stage crude theatrical performances, complete with masks, as they had done for hundreds of years. It was these performances, with their ribald and lewd dialogue, that Neronov apparently found most objectionable.[71]

Because of their importance to the history of the *skomorokhi* and the phenomenon of *dvoeverie*, or residual paganism, in the mid-seventeenth century, Aleksei's *gramoty* of December 1648 deserve close scrutiny. The earlier is dated 6 December 1648.[72] It is addressed specifically to the *voevoda* of Belgorod, Timofei Fedorovich Buturlin; a note at the end of the *gramota*, however, says that it is also to be dispatched to every town in Russia.[73] The title of this lengthy *gramota* is brief and to the point: "On the Righting of Morals and the Abolition of Superstition." In it the tsar lashes out at all the popular pastimes and amusements that he feels are sapping the moral and religious strength of the country. The *skomorokhi*, not surprisingly, are singled out as perhaps the most nefarious of the evil, pagan influences diverting the Orthodox Christian from the path of virtue.

Aleksei begins by stating that it has been brought to his attention that attendance at church on Sundays and holydays is poor and that among the chief reasons for this are drunkenness and the devilish amusements of the *skomorokhi*. The people, he says, have become oblivious of their Orthodox faith and of God and have instead turned to the minstrel-entertainers: they gather with them in the evenings on the streets and in the open fields to watch their all-night performances and listen to their irreverent and scandalous songs; they watch their puppet shows and delight in their trained bears and dogs; they invite them, with their sundry musical instruments and limitless repertoire of devilish songs, to entertain at their weddings; and they frequently imitate them by donning masks and costumes, especially during Christmastide.

The period from Christmas Eve to the Epiphany, with its ancient customs and rituals going back to pre-Christian times, is accorded a special place in the *gramota*. It is characterized as particularly odious in the eyes of the church because of the spirit of paganism that permeates all of the festivities associated with it. Men and women shamelessly gather together during these days and engage in a variety of fiendish games and rituals. They invoke the plow both in song and gesture (a reference no doubt to carolers' taking a plow with them as they make their rounds on Christmas Eve and New Year's Eve), reciting appropriate verses and incantations to procure for each household a good harvest during the coming year.[74]

A host of other allegedly pagan practices enumerated and condemned may be lumped together under the general heading of witchcraft—such customs as the healing of the sick and infants by widowed old women, omen reading, dream analysis, bathing in a river or lake during a thunderstorm, and washing oneself with silver coins. Some popular amusements are also singled out for censure. Boxing, a favorite sport among both town and country folk, is banned, as are the enormous swings, or roundabouts, which, it is said, cause many deaths. Dice, chess, and card playing round out the list of proscribed amusements.

To curb and ultimately eradicate all these vestiges of paganism, Aleksei proposed drastic measures: all musical instruments connected with *skomorokh* entertainments were to be confiscated and burned,[75] and all persons engaged in any of these activities, including of course the *skomorokhi* and their audiences, were henceforth subject to severe penalties. First and second offenders were to be knouted; those apprehended for the third or fourth time were to be exiled to the border regions.

The second *gramota* is dated 24 December 1648. It is addressed to the *voevoda* of Shuia, Semen Il'ich Zmeev, but directed also to other Muscovite towns and their suburbs, and it carries the title "Concerning *Koliada, Usen'*, and Other Popular Games."[76] Unlike the earlier document, this *gramota* is narrow in scope, focusing primarily on the pagan rituals associated with Christmas and New Year's Day. It begins with some general references to keeping holy the Lord's Day and admonitions to shun such activities as firing up the *bania* (sauna) and doing laundry, shaving, or engaging in commercial activity on Sundays and holydays. It decries the activities of the *skomorokhi*, who are described as wandering about with their musical instruments and trained bears and profaning God's daily bread by roasting and eating all manner of wild and domestic animals and birds. As its title implies, Aleksei's main concern in this *gramota* is with the strong pagan overtones and general dissipation that had come to characterize the winter festivities at Christmastide, a subject to which he had addressed himself briefly in the earlier *gramota*. On Christmas Day and on the Epiphany, people gather for Satanic games; priests and monks wander about the streets in drunken stupor; and swearing, arguing, and fighting fill the streets. More despicable than this is the continuing widespread custom of invoking the plow, *koliada*, and *Usen'* in song and verse on Christmas Eve and the Eve of the Epiphany. The involvement of the *skomorokhi* in these festivities is implicitly denounced. All who persist in the pagan practices enumerated are to be looked upon as disgraced in the eyes of the tsar and punished, though the punishment is not spelled out as it was in the earlier *gramota*.

With the two *gramoty*, the history of the Russian minstrels comes full circle. Surely it is no mere coincidence that in the very first historical reference that we have to the *skomorokhi*, from the mid-eleventh century, they are denounced for their paganism, as they are in the last official references in the seventeenth century. The image of the *skomorokhi* had not changed appreciably in the course of their long history, and consequently their demise appears inevitable—so long as they were closely identified with Russia's pagan past in the eyes of the people and, more importantly, of the church, they would be hounded and persecuted by the authorities. While this persecution varied in intensity from age to age, it reached a climax in the mid-seventeenth century as a result of a combination of factors that conspired against the minstrels and played into the hands of their perennial nemesis, the church.

These factors, as was noted above, can be traced back to Ivan IV and the sack of Novgorod in 1571. By uprooting many of the most talented of the minstrels and removing them to Moscow, Ivan brought about a fundamental shift in the geographic center of their activity. Some of the transplanted *skomorokhi* fared well at the Muscovite court; others, the majority, were eventually forced to join the ranks of the impoverished, half-starved itinerant entertainers. This increased the number of unregistered *skomorokhi* roaming the countryside, and it was these rootless individuals who contributed to the lawlessness that ultimately gave the entire profession an unsavory reputation. The process of disintegration from within was thus set in motion by Ivan IV himself, who, ironically, was one of their most enthusiastic patrons.

The reigns of Fedor and Michael witnessed no significant deterioration in the condition of the *skomorokhi*, though the Time of Troubles certainly contributed to their growing impoverishment, as it did to that of many others in the early seventeenth century. Then the young and pious Aleksei, the Quietest One, ascended the throne in 1645, and the mood of the Muscovite court changed drastically overnight. Educated by clergymen in his youth, Aleksei continued, upon becoming tsar, to be strongly influenced by ecclesiastical advisers. Prominent among these was Iosif, the Patriarch of Moscow, who was responsible for launching the all-out campaign to eradicate vestiges of paganism among the people.

The straw that broke the camel's back, however, was the series of political upheavals in Moscow and elsewhere in 1648, which seemed to convince the young tsar that the largely itinerant and reputedly unruly minstrel-entertainers were a potentially disruptive element in society and had to be neutralized. Consequently, in December of 1648 Aleksei issued two famous *gramoty* outlawing the *skomorokhi*, along with a host of other "pagan" traditions and practices. The long and colorful history of the Russian minstrels was thus officially brought to an end. The *coup de grace* came in 1657 when the church added its voice to the official ban by declaring the *skomorokhi* excommunicated.[77]

Just how effective was Aleksei's ban on the *skomorokhi?* It would be naive to assume that the tsar could, by official fiat, wipe out a social and cultural institution of several hundred years' standing; the country was simply too vast and the rural population too dispersed to permit adequate enforcement of such a ban. No doubt in the larger cities and towns the activities of the *skomorkhi* were sharply curtailed. There are, for example, noticeably fewer references to them in cadastres, censuses, and customs duty records after 1648; in fact only three such references have been found. One, cited earlier in this chapter, appears in the customs duty records from Turinsk for 1655, where eight itinerant *skomorokhi* and their trained bear are recorded;[78] the other two occur in the Iaroslavl census of 1668, where two *skomorokhi*, one a musician, the other a bear tamer, are registered.[79]

In the countryside, particularly in the northern and eastern provinces, Aleksei's ban on the *skomorokhi* seems to have had little or no immediate effect.[80] This is borne out, for example, by the fact that in 1649 and again in 1657 the original *gramota* of 5 December 1648 had to be reissued to combat the continuing popularity and influence of the minstrels in these outlying regions.[81] Underscoring the ineffectiveness of the 1648 ban is the fact that the tsar found it necessary to include condemnations of the *skomorokhi* in subsequent pronouncements dealing with matters other than superstition and paganism. Thus, in a *gramota* of 16 August 1653 addressed to the inhabitants of the villages along the Mologa River north of Moscow, there is a lengthy discussion of state regulation of the production and sale of liquor, tavern ownership, and related matters.[82] Then quite unexpectedly the focus shifts to the *skomorokhi*: they are prohibited from appearing in the region covered by the *gramota*, with stiff penalties for those who are caught entertaining here.[83] Interestingly, this *gramota* mentions that small trained dogs, in addition to bears, were featured in the entertainment of some *skomorokhi*.

Other evidence also suggests that the *skomorokhi* did not completely disappear following Aleksei's proscription of 1648. There is, first of all, a 1681 *gramota* of Fedor II in which the tsar addresses himself to civil disturbances in the village of Lyskovo (located east of Moscow). Mentioned among the factors contributing to the disorders are the *skomorokhi*, who are described as making frequent appearances at the local village tavern with their trained bears and all manner of Satanic entertainment.[84] A few years later an anonymous foreign writer describing Muscovy in the late seventeenth century observed, "Many among them [that is, the Muscovites] support themselves by leading around to different villages their trained dancing bears."[85] As late as the mid-eighteenth century, according to one surviving document, a *skomorokh* could still be found who was engaged in the reading of "palms of women, young girls, and children."[86] A century or so after Aleksei's ban went into effect, there were apparently *skomorokhi* who had not only survived the purges but continued to practice skills that linked them intimately to their own and Russia's pagan past.[87]

There is also the testimony of the Russian historian V. N. Tatishchev, who commented in a footnote to the first volume of his *Istoriia rossiiskaia*, "Formerly, I used to listen to *skomorokhi* sing ancient songs about Prince Vladimir, in which his wives were enumerated; also songs about famous heroes such as Ilia Muromets, Alesha Popovich, Solovei Razboinik, Diuk Stefanovich, and others."[88] Since Tatishchev was born in 1685, it is more than likely that he was introduced to the poetic art of the *skomorokhi* in the late seventeenth century when he was still a child or early adolescent.

The songs and heroes to which Tatishchev refers belong, of course, to the Kievan cycle *byliny*. It is fairly certain that these continued to be sung by the few surviving professional minstrels well into the eighteenth century. Kirsha Danilov recorded the songs for his *Sbornik* from some of them, as a letter from P. A. Demidov to G. F. Miller, dated 22 September 1768, suggests. Demidov, a wealthy mill owner in the Urals who had, according to some scholars, commissioned Kirsha Danilov to compile his well-known collection of *byliny* and historical songs,[89] sent Miller two folk songs with a brief covering letter: "I came upon these by way of some Siberian people, since they send here all manner of intelligent fools who sing aloud about past history. . . ."[90] In his 5 December 1648 *gramota* Aleksei stipulated that the punishment for recalcitrant *skomorokhi*, those caught in the act for the third or fourth time, was banishment to the border regions, and this policy evidently continued in force through the mid-eighteenth century. It would appear that the designated place of exile for many of the *skomorokhi* was western Siberia, just beyond the Urals.[91]

After 1768 there are no further references to *skomorokhi* in the extant sources. All indications are that the profession simply died out in the latter part of the eighteenth century.[92] The second great dispersal of the *skomorokhi*, set in motion by Aleksei in 1648, did indeed prove fatal to the Russian minstrels. It was, to be sure, the culmination of the process of disintegration from within begun by Ivan IV in 1571, and no doubt aided by two factors that distinguished eighteenth-century imperial Russia from its medieval Muscovite past: creeping civilization and Western cultural influence. Both had begun to make inroads not only in the urban centers like Saint Petersburg and Moscow, but in the more remote parts of the empire as well. Both brought with them changes which could not but alter traditional patterns of social and cultural life, even in the countryside.

Though the profession died out, the legacy of the *skomorokhi* endured. To this day one cannot help but note their pervasive influence in many areas of Russian culture, even in an age of radio, television, films, and the like. It is manifest, for example, in the delightful antics of the trained bears of the Moscow Circus and has been carried the world over by Sergei Obraztsov and his celebrated troupe of marionettes. Precisely what that legacy was is the subject of the next two chapters.

An artist's reconstruction of the
Kievan Sophia staircase frescoes.
(From A. Nicoll, Masks, Mimes
and Miracles [New York, 1931].
Reprinted by permission of George
G. Harrap & Company Ltd.

An artist's reconstruction of the recently restored left section of the staircase frescoes. (From S. A. Vysotskii and I. F. Totskaia, "Novoe o freske 'skomorokhi' v Sofii Kievskoi," in Kul'tura i iskusstvo drevnei Rusi: sbornik statei v chest' professora M. K. Kargera *[Leningrad, 1967])*

A tenth-century Byzantine pneumatic organ. (From S. A. Vysotskii and I. F. Totskaia, "Novoe o freske 'skomorkhi' v Sofii Kievskoi")

Initial **T** *from Pskovian Psalter,*
late thirteenth or early fourteenth
century. (From V. V. Stasov,
Slavianskii i vostochnyi ornament
po rukopisiam drevniago i novago
vremeni *[St. Petersburg, 1887])*

Two mid-fourteenth-century Novgorod initials (Ä) from a Psalter (left) and a Liturgicon (right). (From V. V. Stasov, Slavianskii i vostochnyi ornament)

Initials **Р** *and* **Б** *(left and center)*
showing animal tamers, from the
1323 Evangelie nedel'noe *from*
Novgorod. *On the right, initial* **Б**,
from the 1355 edition of the
Evangelie nedel'noe *(Novgorod).*
(From V. V. Stasov, Slavianskii i
vostochnyi ornament)

73

A dancing musician. Initial Р from the Novgorod Evangelie nedel'noe *of 1358. (From V. V. Stasov,* Slavianskii i vostochnyi ornament)

A juggler **(Ч)** *and two actors* **(ДИ)**,
initials from the 1544 edition of the
Evangelie nedel'noe *from Riazan.*
(From V. V. Stasov, Slavianskii i
vostochnyi ornament*)*

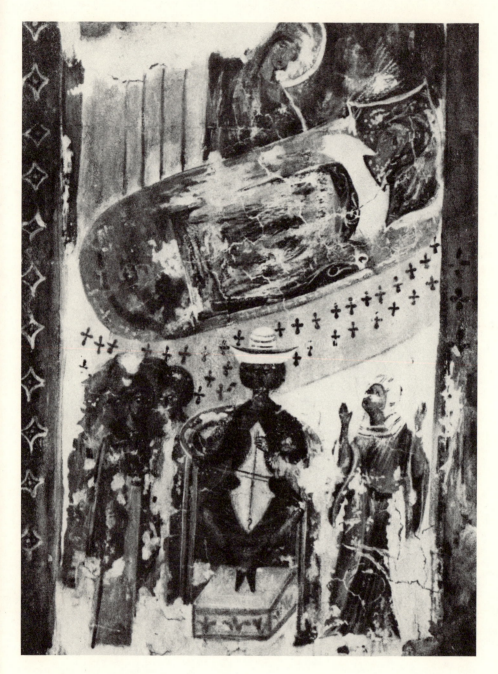

Meletovo fresco. The words **ЯНТЬ СКОМОРОХ**, *barely visible, touch the brim of the musician's hat on both sides. (From N. N. Rozov, "Eshche raz ob izobrazhenii skomorokha na freske v Meletove. K voprosu o sviazakh monumental'noi zhivopisi s miniatiuroi i ornamentom," in* Drevne-russkoe iskusstvo: khudozhestvennaia kul'tura Pskova *[Moscow, 1968])*

An early Votjak kantele reminiscent of the oval gusli-psaltery. National Museum of Finland

A four-sided, seventeenth-century Finnish kantele similar to the traditional Russian gusli. National Museum of Finland

77

Two skomorokhi *singing the praises of Michael Romanov while two others dance (Ladoga, 1634). (From Adam Olearius,* Vermehrte newe Beschreibung Der Muscowitischen und Persichen Reyse *[Schlesswig, 1656])*

LADOGA

A skomorokh *entertainment in the 1630s. The unique one-man puppet show is pictured in the center. (From Adam Olearius,* Vermehrte newe Beschreibung Der Muscowitischen und Persichen Reyse)

4
Contribution
to Oral
Literature

It is generally acknowledged that the *skomorokhi* have had an impact on four areas of Russian culture—oral literature, secular music, theater, and dance. While not always adequately appreciated, their contribution to the last three is readily apparent and has seldom been questioned. In the area of oral literature, where they have left their most indelible imprint, unanswered questions remain. The most persistent of these have to do with the role of the *skomorokhi* in the composition, preservation, and dissemination of oral tradition, particularly the two genres known as *byliny* (heroic tales) and *istoricheskie pesni* (historical songs). To a lesser degree these same questions apply to other genres of Russian folk literature, including folktales, incantations, seasonal and wedding songs, and proverbs, where the imprint of the *skomorokhi* can also be discerned.

Byliny and historical songs hold a unique place in the history of Russian literature, representing a literature that has survived for hundreds of years in oral form only. Not until the mid-nineteenth century was an effort made to systematically collect and publish this large body of oral tradition, which has, in the case of *byliny*, been traced back to Kievan times. Although much has been written about this literature and scholars have come to grips with the question of its origin, a certain vagueness about its relationship to the *skomorokhi* persists.

Tatishchev's remark about listening to *skomorokhi* sing *byliny* in the late seventeenth century, together with what we know about the involvement of the *skomorokhi* in the recitation and composition of historical songs in the reigns of Ivan IV and Michael Romanov,[1] makes it fairly certain that, at least from the second half of the sixteenth century, the Russia minstrels regarded oral tradition as part of their professional repertoire. Less certain is their relationship to this literature in an earlier age, during the Kievan and early Muscovite periods. Nowhere in the historical sources, for example, are the *skomorokhi* directly associated with the recitation of narrative heroic poetry. What has given rise to the widespread notion that the *skomorokhi* were in some way connected with the *byliny* in their formative stage is the internal evidence of some of the heroic tales themselves. To illustrate, let us take a close look at the *bylina* "Dobrynia v ot'ezde."[2]

The hero, Dobrynia Nikitich, has been absent from his home and his wife, Nastasia, for twelve years. Alesha Popovich, his sworn brother, brings the wife false tidings of her husband's death and then proceeds to woo and marry her. While the three-day marriage feast is in progress, Dobrynia returns to Kiev, having been told what happened by his faithful steed and then by his mother. Enraged, he resolves to go to the marriage banquet unannounced and incognito.

> They brought him his *skomorokh* attire,
> They brought him his *gusli* of maple-wood,
> The youth dressed himself as a *skomorokh*,
> And went to the splendid, honorable feast.[3]

Without stopping to ask leave of the gatekeepers, Dobrynia makes his way into the banquet hall.

> "Tell me which is the *skomorokh's* place for me?"
> Vladimir of royal Kiev replied in anger:
> "That is the *skomorokh's* place for you,
> On that glazed oven there,
> On the glazed oven behind the stove."
> Hastily he jumped onto the place indicated,
> Onto the glazed oven;
> He tightened his silken strings,
> His golden chords,
> And began to wander over the strings;
> He began to sing snatches of song,
> He played a tune from Tsargrad,
> And in his song he recounted all that had taken
>   place in Kiev,
> Both of old and young.[4]

Dobrynia's playing pleases Vladimir, and the prince rewards the *skomorokh* by asking him to come down from the glazed oven and to sit at the head table with him and the guests of honor, the newly-weds. Dobrynia finally makes his true identity known and reclaims his wife from Alesha, whom he beats severely for his perfidy.

V. F. Miller and other scholars regard this *bylina* and Dobrynia's role in it as indicative of the participation of the *skomorokhi* in Kievan court life and entertainment.[5] Miller goes a step further and suggests that the *skomorokhi* not only sang *byliny* but also composed them.[6] One must agree with Miller that Dobrynia's song, in which "he recounted all that had taken place in Kiev, both of old and young," was indeed a *bylina*. In the light of convincing evidence to the contrary, however, one has to disagree with his second premise, namely, that the *skomorokhi* were the equivalent of court minstrels, or bards, in Kievan Rus'. What we know of the early *skomorokhi* from historical and other sources shows that they were a distinctly lower-class phenomenon, emerging from among the peasants and restricting their activities largely to that class. It would thus have been extremely difficult for them to gain access to the inner precincts of the princely court, as Dobrynia seems to have done. Furthermore, in at least two other folk songs in which the *skomorokhi* play an active primary role,[7] and one in which they are mentioned in passing,[8] they evince an insouciant earthiness that is both wholly consistent with their traditional character and totally incompatible with the seriousness of a court bard.

It is conceivable that in the original version of "Dobrynia v ot'ezde," the hero could have employed the disguise of a court minstrel to gain entry into Vladimir's banquet hall. His disguise might have resembled the costume worn by the figure on the twelfth-century Kievan bracelet, which Rybakov has described as a *gusli* player. The bracelet figure is wearing a pointed cap and a loose-fitting, ankle-length shirt, attire which differs radically from that worn by the flamboyant *skomorokhi* as they are depicted, for example, in the fourteenth-century Novgorod miniatures. He is playing a five-sided *gusli* with both hands while holding what appears to be a crude version of a bagpipe in his mouth.[9] Dobrynia, therefore, probably assumed the role of a *gusliar* and not a *skomorokh*. It is entirely possible that the name *skomorokh* was introduced into the *bylina* at a later date when the Russian minstrel had become synonymous in the popular mind with entertainment and merrymaking.

Existing evidence suggests that it was not the *skomorokhi* but rather the *gusliari*, or *gusli* players, who served as court minstrels and were the original bearers of the Kievan heroic tradition. Evidence for a tradition of heroic poetry in early Rus' can be found in several historical and literary sources.[10] The *Ipatievskaia letopis'*, for example, mentions at least three court minstrels, one of them the illustrious bard Mitus, who was taken prisoner by Prince Daniil of Galich in 1241.[11] Another early chronicle relates that after his victory over the German knights in 1242, Alexander Nevskii had songs of praise sung in his honor in Pskov.[12] Finally, there is that most famous of all Kievan singers, Boian, whom the *Slovo o polku Igoreve* describes as chanting the praises of Iaroslav the Wise (d. 1054), Mstislav of Tmutorokan (d. 1036), and Roman Sviatoslavich (d. 1079).[13] Unfortunately, except for a few lines attributed to him and quoted in the *Slovo*, nothing of Boian's poetic genius has survived.

In addition to the named and unnamed court minstrels mentioned in historical sources, there were no doubt others whose fame has not survived but whose anonymous art has been preserved to this day, if only in much altered form, in the *byliny*. It is to these *gusliari* that one must look for the origins of the Kievan heroic tradition.

With the passing of the Kievan heroic age and the patronage of the Kievan princes with it, the *gusliari* gradually disappeared. They were replaced by the newly emerging popular entertainers, the *skomorokhi*, who became the heirs of the oral tradition nurtured by the court bards; eventually they would bring this wealth of new oral literature to Novgorod and Muscovy. The circumstances surrounding this transfer of the *byliny* from the Kievan lands to the remote parts of northern Russia have been the object of considerable controversy.

In the mid-1850s, several years before the appearance of the first truly comprehensive compilation of *byliny* and prior to the inception of serious scholarly research into this newly uncovered field of Russian literature, M. P. Pogodin had already raised a fundamental question of the relationship of *byliny* to their place of origin. In the course of his prolonged dispute with M. A. Maksimovich over the antiquity of the Ukrainian language, Pogodin at one point advanced the following argument: "The Little Russians [Ukrainians] are a song-loving people. Why then have there not been preserved among them any songs about our ancient past, especially since songs about Vladimir and his retinue are sung in most other places—in Arkhangel'sk and Vladimir, Kostroma and Siberia. One can only conclude from this that at the time of Vladimir's reign there lived in Kiev not Little Russians but Great Russians who carried these songs with them to all parts of Russia."[14] The Ukrainians, Pogodin continues, had come into the Kievan area from the Carpathian mountain region only after the Mongol invasions of the 1240s, at which time the native Great Russian population migrated northward, taking the *byliny* with them.[15] When he originally conceived this argument, Pogodin was primarily interested in strengthening his own position on the place of the Great Russians in the history of the Kievan state. Little did he realize that his casual remark about the absence of a *byliny* tradition among the Ukrainian people would usher in a new era of productive scholarly research into the disappearance of the *byliny* from Kievan territory.

Among the first to respond to Pogodin's challenge was P. Kulish. In 1857 he published a Ukrainian fairy tale entitled "Skazka o Solov'e Razboinike i o slepom tsareviche," which, he pointed out, could be compared in some respects to the byliny dealing with Ilia Muromets and Solovei Razboinik.[16] A few years later P. A. Bezsonov, in his introduction to the fourth volume of Kireevskii's *Pesni*, reproduced a Ukrainian *duma* describing a storm on the Black Sea in which Oleksij Popovych Pyriatynskij appears as the main character and hero.[17] This *duma*, according to Bezsonov, bears a striking resemblance to the *byliny* about Alesha Popovich and Sadko, and raises the possibility of a direct relationship between some of the Ukrainian *dumy* and Russian *byliny*.[18] It is obvious that both Kulish and Bezsonov were intent on demonstrating that Ukrainian folk literature had retained echoes of Kievan *bogatyr* epos.

O. F. Miller provided additional impetus to the controversy about the disappearance of the *byliny* from Kiev and their relationship to Ukrainian *dumy* with his important paper, "Velikorusskiia *byliny* i malorusskiia *dumy*," presented to the Third Archeological Congress held in Kiev in 1874.[19] Taking his cue, as he admits, from Bezsonov,[20] and relying primarily on the newly published anthology of Ukrainian *dumy* compiled by Dragomanov and Antonovich,[21] Miller compares several of the recently published *dumy* with selected *byliny* and shows the extent and nature of the similarities between the two. For example, he compares Prince Dmytrii Vyshnevetskij (Bajda), a central figure in some of the early *dumy*, to the *byliny* hero Mikhailo Potyk, and sees many parallels between incidents in the Bajda cycle *dumy* and those in some of the *byliny*. In addition to Oleksij Popovych Pyriatynskij, whom Miller likens to Alesha Popovich, Sadko, and Vasilii Buslaev, such other *dumy* heroes as Samijlo Kishka, Holota, and Zhurilo, according to Miller, either have their direct counterparts in the *byliny* or at least exhibit qualities common to the Kievan *bogatyri*. Miller sums up his argument in the best Pan-Slavic tradition by pointing out that the *byliny* can be compared to a great tree: the *dumy* are but one branch of this mighty tree, which has roots deep in All-Russian soil.[22]

In the discussion that followed Miller's paper, M. P. Dragomanov took strong exception to his argument that traces of the *byliny* can be found primarily in the *dumy*. In an open letter to Miller published in *Drevniaia i novaia Rossiia*, Dragomanov argued that if echoes of the *byliny* are to be found anywhere, they must be sought in Ukrainian fairy tales (*skazky*) and ceremonial songs (*koliadky, vesnianky*, and so forth) rather than in the *dumy*.[23]

Not long after the appearance of the letter, N. I. Petrov published an article in which he set out to test Dragomanov's hypothesis that Ukrainian fairy tales and ceremonial songs, more than the *dumy*, contained elements reminiscent of the *byliny*.[24] Petrov's effort resulted in some interesting, if inconclusive, observations. He showed, for example, that Ukrainian *koliadky* and *shchedrivky* abound in references and allusions to the plow and to the sowing of grain. In one such *koliadka*, Christ himself is pictured as the plowman and the Virgin as the bearer of the seed, which, according to Petrov, resembles the *byliny* about Mikula Selianinovich, "the good plowman."[25] Petrov also pointed out some close parallels between the customs and traditions surrounding the feast of Saint George (*Iurij den'*) and the *byliny* about Sviatogor. In Ukrainian folk tradition Iurij is the keeper of the key that unlocks the regenerative forces of the earth and makes it fruitful. Similar powers are sometimes attributed to the superhuman giant Sviatogor. Even Sviatogor's unusual death is vividly reflected, according to Petrov, in the Ukrainian fairy tale "Nastasia prekrasnaia."[26] Two other *byliny* were singled out by Petrov for comparison with Ukrainian folktales. The hero of the first, Ilia Muromets, is shown to bear a resemblance to such legendary Ukrainian favorites as Chobotko and Kyrylo Kozhumiaka, while the theme of the *byliny* about Dunai is found to recur in several Ukrainian *koliadky*.[27]

While Petrov, Miller, Bezsonov, and other scholars were trying to uncover traces of the *byliny* in Ukrainian folklore to prove that these had never totally disappeared from the Kievan lands, some scholars were intent on finding an explanation for the seemingly mysterious transfer of the *byliny* from the south to the north of Russia. In 1862 the Ukrainian literary journal *Osnova* published an article that explored for the first time the question of the disappearance of the *byliny* from Kiev.[28] The article emphasized, among other things, the alleged propensity of the Ukrainian people to forget their old tales and heroes rather easily because of the continuing influence upon them of new historical forces. Somewhat more vaguely, it argued that conditions for preserving the *byliny* were much more favorable in the north than in the south.

It was N. I. Kostomarov, however, who, ten years after the

appearance of the *Osnova* article, advanced a much more refined explanation for the absence of a *byliny* tradition among the Ukrainian people.[29] His basic premise was that a people are inclined to retain from their past whatever they can readily identify with and whatever is relevant in their own time and age. In the course of the sixteenth and seventeenth centuries, during the so-called Cossack era, events of extraordinary dimensions shook the consciousness of the Ukrainian people and became indelibly etched on their minds. Their vision of the future was so optimistic that they preferred not to look back to their past; understandably, whatever songs and heroes they had had were quickly forgotten and replaced by new ones. The result was the displacement of the *byliny* by the totally new oral tradition embodied in the *dumy*.[30]

Unfortunately Kostomarov addressed himself to only half the problem, offering a reasonably plausible explanation for the virtual absence of *byliny* in the geographic area where they had originally developed and flourished, but saying nothing about how this body of oral literature came to be deposited in the northern parts of European Russia (Arkhangel'sk and Olonets provinces), to be preserved intact for hundreds of years. L. N. Maikov had touched upon this question briefly in 1863 when he proposed his migration theory of *byliny* transfer. He argued that as early as the tenth century, and certainly by the twelfth century, there was a steady northward flow of Kievan settlers who brought many of the *byliny* with them.[31] In the 1880s M. Khalanskii refined and modified Maikov's theory of migration by proposing that it was primarily the merchants, pilgrims, and warriors of Kievan Rus' who carried the heroic tales from tribe to tribe and region to region, depositing them eventually in the north.[32]

Strangely, in all the speculation about the disappearance of the *byliny* from Kiev and their reappearance in northern Russia, scarcely a handful of scholars seriously considered the *skomorokhi* as perhaps the most logical link between the heroic tradition of Kievan Rus' and the *byliny* of the north, for, even though scholars had isolated what were purported to be traces of the *byliny* in Ukrainian folklore, there remained the inescapable fact that they had not explained the disappearance of an entire body of oral literature from one area and its preservation for centuries in another hundreds of miles away. Furthermore, even these alleged traces might be the result of much later influence, perhaps even literary influence, and thus they did not constitute evidence of the direct linear evolution of one folk epos from another.

What apparently happened is this. As ecclesiastical pressure mounted and political instability became widespread, the *skomorokhi* began to leave the Kievan lands for the north, particularly Novgorod. With them they took their recently acquired store of oral heroic tradition. Meanwhile, during the twelfth century, Novgorod began to colonize the northwest region. This colonization came in waves, ending in the 1470s after the defeat of the proud city-state by Ivan III. In the course of the extension of Novgorodian rule to the northwest, the *skomorokhi* deposited the *byliny* in the general area of Lake Ladoga, Lake Onega, and the White Sea region. The extent of *skomorokh* penetration into the White Sea region has recently been underscored by A. A. Morozov, who has found evidence that suggests that by the mid-sixteenth century a number of minstrels were supplementing their professional earnings by working in the local saltworks; in fact, one of the saltworks in Nenoksa, located on the Letnyi Coast of the White Sea, was called Skomoroshitsa.[33]

In a paper read before the Ninth International Congress of Anthropological and Ethnological Sciences in Chicago (August–September 1973), S. I. Dmitrieva demonstrated conclusively that the spread of the *byliny* in northern Russia can best be explained in association with Novgorod colonization.[34] Citing the most recent findings of A. N. Nasonov and M. D. Vitov, Dmitrieva observed that the distribution of *byliny* is confined to a distinct area that does not, as some have claimed, encompass all of northern Russia, but only the northwest; that even within this area there are regional differences in the *bylina* tradition, reflecting, no doubt, different stages in the colonization of the north; and, finally, that these patterns of colonization help to explain both the affinity between certain epic traditions of the north and the dominance of heroic *byliny* in such districts as the Zimnii Coast of the White Sea, the Kuloi, Mezen, and Pechora.

Noteworthy in this regard is the experience of A. D. Grigor'ev, who made an expedition into the White Sea region in 1899–1901 in search of folklore material. He found here not only numerous examples of *byliny*, which he had recited for him by local *skaziteli*, or narrators, but also convincing evidence of the role of the *skomorokhi* in the preservation and dissemination of this ancient Kievan heroic tradition. Among the *skaziteli* who recited *byliny* for Grigor'ev was Matrena Skomorokhova, a young woman of twenty-five or thirty. She was from the village of Shotogorka on the Pinega River and was reputed to know at least fifteen *byliny*, although Grigor'ev was able to persuade her to recite only one, "Kniaz Dmitrii i ego nevesta Domna."[35] Grigor'ev writes that there were several other families with the surname Skomorokh in Shotogorka.[36]

The *byliny* that have been recorded in the northwest are, with few exceptions, of a superior quality, reflecting the superb artistry of the minstrels who brought them there. As Morozov has rightly observed, these *byliny* represent the Kievan heroic tradition at its best, and this tradition owes its preservation to the highly skilled minstrel-entertainers of Novgorod, the direct descendants of the Kievan *skomorokhi.*[37]

As one might expect, the *byliny* were not appropriated by the *skomorokhi* and brought north without considerable editing and revising: after all, these heroic tales were no longer recited in the banquet halls of princes, but in the village huts of peasants. They had to be reworked and modified, frequently through the addition of humorous or fantastic elements, to accomodate the taste of the noncourtly audience for which they were now intended. Even the tunes to which they were sung, once tranquil and stately, gradually acquired a swifter and gayer air. One of the classic examples of *skomorokh* editing occurs in a version of the song about Dobrynia's prolonged absence from home and his wife's remarriage to Alesha Popovich.[38] While in most *byliny* Prince Vladimir is treated with the utmost respect and affection, this song depicts him as a foolish old man, who is told to stuff his mouth with an old shoe-rag, for his part in arranging the marriage.[39] Clearly when this *bylina* was originally performed at court, it would not have contained such an uncomplimentary portrait of the Sun of Kiev, Prince Vladimir the Great. But the audience had changed, and so the song had to be tailored to fit the mood of its listeners.

Even more obvious is the imprint of the *skomorokhi* on the *bylina* "Vasilii p'ianitsa," a song dating from the early Mongol period that describes the liberation of Kiev from Batu Khan and his horde by the hero Vasilii.[40] Originally this song was serious and heroic,[41] but in the hands of the *skomorokhi* it became mock-heroic and frivolous; the hero, Vasilii, is transformed into a common drunkard, while the mighty Prince Vladimir is once more characterized as undignified and foolish. Kiev is besieged by the Tartars, while Vasilii, who represents the last hope for the city, lies in drunken stupor in a local tavern. Prince Vladimir hastily puts on his coat and boots (over his bare feet) and runs to the tavern in search of the hero. He finds him, wakes him, and bids him to come to the "feast" for the Khan. Vasilii tells Vladimir first, that he is so drunk he can barely stand, and secondly, that he has neither horse nor weapons, since he has bartered everything to the tavern owner for drink. Vladimir urges Vasilii to have yet another drink of green wine to sober himself, and the two proceed to the "feast." Upon arrival at the palace, the Prince asks his trusted *bogatyr* Dobrynia to go to the tavern and buy back Vasilii's horse and weapons. He does so, and, returning, joins Vasilii and Alesha Popovich in turning back the Khan and his horde from Kiev. The song concludes with a grateful Prince Vladimir assuring Vasilii that he is welcome to make his home in the palace and imbibe to his heart's content to the end of his days.

Like the Kievan *byliny*, those of Novgorod were subject to considerable editing at the hands of the *skomorokhi*. Originally they too were composed by professional minstrels and sung for and about the wealthy merchant class of the city. Their heroes, notably Sadko and Vasilii Buslaev, stand apart from the *bogatyr* heroes of Kiev, no doubt reflecting the basic difference in the social and political ethos of the two cities. The one, Kiev, was concerned with national defense, and thus its *byliny* are permeated with the military ideals of bravery and strength. The other, Novgorod, boasted a vigorous spirit of commercial enterprise and fierce individualism, both of which found vivid expression in the songs about Sadko and Vasilii Buslaev.[42]

In the Novgorod cycle *byliny* one encounters a liberal sprinkling of the fantastic and mythical, added by the *skomorokhi* to make these basically bourgeois tales more appealing to the masses. Nowhere is this more apparent than in the songs about Sadko. Sadko, frequently cast in the dual role of wealthy merchant and accomplished musician, owes his good fortune to the Tsar of the Sea, whom he charms with his *gusli* of maple wood. The *byliny* about Sadko have a fairytale quality about them, as the following lines show.

> Sadko slumbered on the blue sea,
> On the blue sea, at the very bottom.
> He could see the crimson sun burning through the water,
> The evening star, the morning star.
> Sadko noticed, in the blue sea
> A white stone palace standing;
> Sadko entered this white stone palace:
> There in the palace sat the Tsar of the Sea,
> His head resembling a large stack of hay.
>
> As Sadko began playing his *gusli* of maple wood,
> The tsar began to dance in the blue sea,
> The Tsar of the Sea danced in earnest.
> Sadko played around the clock, and then some,
> Sadko even played for a third straight day,
> While the Tsar danced continuously in the blue sea.

The water in the blue sea grew turbulent,
It became murky with yellow sand,
Many ships were wrecked on the blue sea,
Many valuables were lost,
Many righteous souls drowned:
So the people began praying to Saint Nicholas.[43]

In addition to humor and fantasy, the *skomorokhi* used
other stylistic devices to transform courtly literature into popular
entertainment. The most common are *zachiny* ("beginnings") and
iskhody ("exodes"), basically stock introductory and closing verses
that are meant to reflect the lives of the minstrels.[44] In some introductory verses one finds an enumeration of places visited by a
group of itinerant *skomorokhi*, and perhaps also some brief, play-
ful allusion to the virtues and vices associated with each. Typical,
though somewhat longer than usual, are the introductory verses
from the *bylina* "Vasilii Ignat'evich i Batyga."

Oh, there is open country around Pskov,
And there are broad open spaces around Kiev,
And high hills at Sorochinsk,
And church buildings in Moscow, the city of stone,
And the ringing of bells in Novgorod.
Oh, there are cunning rogues in the Valdai Hills,
Oh, there are fine fellows and dandies in the city of
    Iaroslavl,
And easy kisses in the region of Beloozero,
And sweet drinks in Petersburg,
And mosses and swamps by the blue sea,
And skirts with wide hems in Pudoga.
Oh, the sarafans are tanned with the wool inside along the
    Onega River,
And the women of Leshmozersk are fruitful,
And the women of Pozheresk have bulging eyes.
Oh, the Danube, the Danube, the Danube,
And beyond that I know of no more regions to sing.[45]

The exodes, too, are often frivolous and comical, sometimes in stark contrast to the rest of the *bylina*; they may even be
totally unrelated to the song to which they are appended. Frequently they hint at the reward or payment expected by the performers for their effort.

Such is the *starina*,[46] such the deeds—
As if for the calming of the blue sea,

And for the swift rivers glory till they reach the sea,
As if for good people to hear,
For young fellows to imitate,
And for us, *veselye molodtsy* [i.e., *skomorokhi*] for a diversion,
Sitting quietly in conversation,
Drinking down mead and green wine;
And where we drink beer, there also we render honor
To that great *boyar*,
And to our gracious host.[47]

One can also detect the hand of the *skomorokhi* in the *byliny* about Staver and Solovei Budimirovich, not to mention some versions of the songs about Dobrynia and Sadko where the minstrel himself assumes an important part in the tale. Here he is invariably depicted in the most sympathetic fashion, which probably reflects the concern of the *skomorokhi* with their public image. As is obvious from the historical sources, the church never ceased to vilify "that devil's brood, the *skomorokhi*" from the beginning of their professional existence in the early eleventh century. In the *byliny* they apparently found an appropriate forum to try to counteract the negative image conjured up by persistent attacks, and at the same time an opportunity to render their profession more respectable in the eyes of their new audience.

In addition to the heroic *byliny* there are some songs which, though frequently referred to as *byliny*, must be considered in a class by themselves—the so-called *byliny-skomoroshiny* (or simply *skomoroshiny*), which, as their name implies, are intimately identified with the *skomorokhi*.[48] Essentially nonheroic, these tales are somewhat reminiscent of the French fabliaux. They date from the post-Mongol period and are generally assumed to have been composed entirely by the *skomorokhi*. Among the best known are "Vavilo i skomorokhi" and "Terentii muzh Danil'evich" (also called "Gost' Terent'ishche"). The protagonists of both songs are the minstrels themselves, and both, (but particularly "Vavilo i skomorokhi") idealize and glorify the profession of the minstrel-entertainers.

"Terentii muzh Danil'evich" is set in Novgorod, probably in the late fifteenth or early sixteenth century.[49] Its plot revolves around Terentii's young wife, Avdotia, who lies bedridden, suffering, apparently, from a bad case of ennui. At her urging, Terentii takes a hundred rubles and goes in search of doctors to cure her. He encounters a troupe of *skomorokhi* and tells them about his wife's illness. They nod to each other knowingly and then offer to cure her. First, however, they purchase a sack of silk and two wooden clubs. They place Terentii in the sack and proceed to his house. Seeing the *veselye molodtsy* approaching, Avdotia asks their purpose and hastens to tell them that the master of the house is not in. They reply that they come at the request of her husband, who unfortunately has met with a fatal accident. On hearing this Avdotia invites the minstrels in and asks them to play on their *gusli* and sing her a song about "that old son of a whore/ by the name of Terentii,/ that I may never lay eyes on him again in this house!"[50] The *skomorokhi* address their song to Terentii, urging him to come out of the sack and "cure" his wife of her not-so-mysterious illness. He rushes out and administers the "cure" with his two clubs. Then he gratefully rewards the minstrels with an additional hundred rubles for helping the truth to prevail.

"Vavilo i skomorokhi" deserves special consideration, as it is a truly unique apologia for the art of the *skomorokhi*. It was first recorded at the turn of the century by Grigor'ev from the peasant woman Mar'ia Dmitrievna Krivopolenova in the village of Shotogorka, in the White Sea region.[51] Only one variant of this *bylina* is known to exist. Its decasyllabic meter, considered to be the most ancient Slavic verse type, sets it apart from other *byliny*.

The story is set in Muscovy, most probably in the second half of the seventeenth century, during the reign of Aleksei.[52] (While one cannot be absolutely certain, it is reasonable to assume that the frequent references in the song to Tsar Sobaka—literally "that dog of a tsar"—are veiled allusions to Aleksei.)[53] A troupe of *skomorokhi* paying a visit to the widow Nenila, whose son, Vavilo, is in the fields hard at work plowing and sowing to provide for himself and his mother. The *skomorokhi* ask Vavilo whether he would not like to join them. They are on their way to challenge (artistically and politically, as it turns out) Tsar Sobaka. Vavilo explains that he can neither sing nor play a musical instrument. At this two of the *skomorokhi*, named Cosmas and Damian after the traditional patron saints of the Russian minstrel-entertainers, insist that Vavilo try to play the *gudok*. He does so and, much to his amazement, plays extremely well. The crowd of onlookers, impressed with Vavilo's miraculous virtuosity, conclude that these are no mere mortals before them. Following the spectacular transformation of Vavilo, the *skomorokhi* return to Nenila's house, where Vavilo and his companions once more demonstrate their supernatural powers, this time in order to persuade the widow to give her only son up to the worthy profession of *skomoroshestvo*. Nenila gives Vavilo her blessing, convinced that "these are no ordinary people, but saints."[54] Leaving her house, the *skomorokhi* resume their journey to Tsar Sobaka's court. On the way they meet first a farmer and then a tinker, who scorn the minstrels and wish them ill in their forthcoming musical confrontation with the tsar. In both encounters Vavilo is asked by his companions to play his *gudok,* and its marvelous music causes considerable mischief for the farmer and the tinker; a flock of pigeons descend upon the farmer's peas and peck at them, while the tinker's pots and pans mysteriously fly out of his wagon, leaving him with only some small crocks. Astonished at what they have seen, both men acknowledge that they have sinned grievously against the saintly minstrels and that they should have prayed for them rather than ridiculed them. As they near their destination the *skomorokhi* encounter a beautiful young girl, who, like the farmer and tinker, inquires about their journey and its purpose. Learning of their intention to deal with Tsar Sobaka, she wishes them good luck and Godspeed. At this Vavilo plays his magical *gudok* once more. The girl's plain clothes are instantly transformed into fine silk, as she is rewarded for her kindness. The denouement follows swiftly. Upon reaching the court, the *skomorokhi* are greeted by Tsar Sobaka playing his *gudok,* whose music causes the waters to rise and threatens to drown them. But Vavilo comes to the rescue; he plays his own *gudok* and causes a herd of buffaloes to appear and drink up the rising waters. As he continues to play, Sobaka's kingdom is enveloped in flames and totally destroyed. Vavilo the *skomorokh* is now proclaimed tsar. The *bylina* concludes with Vavilo's bringing his mother to live happily with him at court.

While one must be careful not to read too much into these two *byliny,* the portrait of the *skomorokhi* that they paint is a revealing one, one that was no doubt intended to arouse popular sympathy and respect for them and their profession at a time when they were hard pressed by both church and state. One of the more interesting features of the second *bylina* is the fusion in the person of the *skomorokhi* of Christian and pagan elements, making the Russian minstrels living examples of *dvoeverie,* or ditheism, that unique feature of early Muscovite culture and religion. They are at the same time presented as saints in the image of 'Cosmos and Damian,[55] and sorcerers capable of magic, which they practice with the aid of their musical instruments. They reward those who show them kindness and punish those who wish them evil; ultimately they even triumph over the tsar who wishes to destroy them.

Related to the *byliny* in style and content is the other epic genre of Russian folk literature, the *istoricheskie pesni* ("historical songs"), though they are of much later origin, dating from the early sixteenth century, and generally of a poorer quality. They deal, as their name implies, with historical persons and events and are thus more factual and less fanciful than their earlier Kievan and Novgorodian counterparts. They are closely linked in their origin with the reign of Ivan IV, and it is important to bear that in mind when considering their relationship to the *skomorokhi*.

The precise role of the *skomorokhi* in the evolution of the historical songs has never been adequately explained. Some have assumed a priori that the *skomorokhi* not only sang but also composed these neoheroic tales; others have maintained that they only sang them. Still others, among them the noted Russian folklorist Iurii Sokolov, have skillfully avoided the question by attributing the historical songs, somewhat vaguely, to that amorphous group known as "the masses." "It may be assumed," writes Sokolov, "that the historical songs had their origin among those who had taken part in the military campaigns of [Ivan] the Terrible, among the masses of the people, who sympathized with his struggle against the Tartars, and shared with the Tsar a distrust and hatred of the treacherous noblemen."[56] This statement, though vague and noncommittal with respect to the *skomorokhi*, does contain one significant point—the suggestion that the historical songs were composed in the ranks of the military, by men who were eyewitnesses to many of the events described in them. Though Sokolov does not identify these military minstrels, it is fairly certain that they were *skomorokhi*. Evidence for this can be found in several cadastres from the sixteenth and seventeenth centuries. In the 1565–68 cadastres from Kazan, whose capture by Ivan IV has been recorded in numerous historical songs, one finds the name of the *skomorokh-strelets* Elka, a military servitor who paid no taxes and lived on Zdvizhenskaia Street.[57] A minstrel living in the Kazan garrison at this time is described as a *domrachei* ("*domra* player"), whose specialty was singing to the accompaniment of a *domra*, a crude prototype of the modern Russian *balalaika*.[58] Another military bard, Ontoshko Petrov is entered in a cadastre from Pskov for 1585.[59] A 1621 cadastre from Nizhnii Novgorod also contains the name of a *skomorokh-strelets*.[60] All of these minstrels were quite handsomely rewarded with land, homesteads, and a taxfree status. They and others like them were called upon to entertain their comrades in arms and were apparently quite common in the military garrisons of such cities as Kazan, Pskov, and Nizhnii Novgorod.

One can only speculate as to the type of entertainment that the *skomorokhi* provided for the troops, but it is reasonable to assume that it embraced heroic narratives about the glories of past campaigns, such as the legendary capture of Kazan by Ivan IV in 1552. Ivan IV himself was fond of reminiscing about his military exploits in this fashion; Salomon Henning, the Baltic chronicler, writes that when Ivan was in a particularly good mood he would have songs about the taking of Kazan and Astrakhan recited to him.[61] Although Henning does not say who sang for and about Ivan, it was presumably the *skomorokhi*. They had always enjoyed a special place at Ivan's court, as Prince Kurbskii reminds us in his biography. Furthermore, the *skomorokhi*, who had for centuries preserved and perpetuated the ancient heroic tradition of Kiev, were clearly the best qualified to compose and recite such neoheroic historical songs.

Additional evidence linking the *skomorokhi* to the historical songs is provided by the Dutch traveler Adam Olearius and by P. A. Demidov, the eighteenth-century Siberian mill owner who commissioned Kirsha Danilov to compile his famous *Sbornik*. Olearius describes a dinner in Ladoga in 1634 at which he and his companions were entertained by two musicians, one with a *gusli*, the other with a *gudok*, who "played and sang about the Great Sovereign and Tsar, Mikhail Feodorovich."[62] It is clear from Olearius's description that the two musicians were singing historical songs about the reigning tsar, Michael Romanov. Demidov is even more explicit in attributing the historical songs to the *skomorokhi*—in his letter to G. F. Miller, cited earlier, he describes them as "narrating past history in song."[63]

Unlike the *byliny*, the historical songs contain no specific references to the *skomorokhi* or to their profession. With the passing of the Kievan heroic age the bard had become obsolete and was no longer a part of the courtly scene, as Dobrynia (in disguise) once was at Vladimir's court. Furthermore, the heroic narrative itself was taken out of the traditional banquet hall and was now set on the field of battle or some other public arena. From the standpoint of the *skomorokhi* themselves, they had found in Ivan IV and his immediate successors willing, generous, and, in Ivan's case, demanding patrons who made it possible for them to enjoy an unprecedented degree of popularity and freedom. This apparently obviated the necessity to interpolate into their songs justificatory references to themselves and their profession.

An interesting development with respect to the historical song is that by the sixteenth century the profession of minstrel-entertainer had undergone a considerable degree of specialization, so that apparently only a talented few of the *skomorokhi* were engaged in the composition and singing of this neoheroic epos. Just as in an earlier age it was the *gusliari* who carried on the *byliny* tradition in Kievan Rus', now it was primarily the *domracheii* and *gusel'niki,* or highly skilled musicians, who sang the praises of the tsars to the accompaniment of the *domra* and the *gusli.*

Like the *byliny,* the historical songs show some evidence of editing, which can be attributed either to the *skomorokhi* or the more recent peasant *skaziteli* of the north, who inherited this body of oral tradition from the professional minstrels. It is usually difficult to say what constitutes an interpolation by a *skomorokh* or a peasant reciter in a given song. However, the hand of the *skomorokhi* is quite apparent in the series of historical songs and fragments of songs about Ivan IV's taking of Kazan, published by V. F. Miller in 1915.[64] The generally lighthearted tone and emasculated plot of many of the surviving Kazan songs indicate that they are but a pale reflection of the original (or originals) in which Ivan IV delighted. By and large they paint a rather uncomplimentary portrait of the tsar, and it is not Ivan, but rather a young gunner whom Ivan in a fit of anger threatens to execute for incompetence, who emerges as the real hero of the songs. This is indeed an improbable turn of events in songs that were originally intended as a panegyric to the Dread Tsar. As Carl Stief has observed, "From being a eulogy and a paean the [Kazan] song has been reduced to a mere anecdote."[65]

The songs about the capture of Kazan can be traced to two basic variants, a long and a short one, with basically the same plot. The longer, with which we will not be concerned here, appeared first in Kirsha Danilov's *Sbornik.* Its bookish vocabulary and political sophistication (for example, references to Ivan at the beginning of the song as grand duke of Muscovy and at the end, after the fall of Kazan, as tsar) have raised questions about its authenticity as oral tradition.[66] Unlike the shorter version, it contains a prologue and an epilogue in which the tsar of Kazan, Simeon [Ediger], and his wife are introduced as passive actors. Its author was probably a bookman familiar with the chronicle account of the Kazan campaign.

The shorter variant of the Kazan song, of which there are at least twenty-three versions, is characterized by coarse humor, frequent use of stock introductory refrains, or *zapevy,* and occasional nonsense rhymes. Illustrative of the coarse humor that permeates many of the Kazan songs are the following lines:

> The Tartar women of Kazan stood on the walls [of the city],
> They stood on the walls and bared their a————! [*sic*][67]

Of the many different *zapevy* used to introduce the song, the most interesting contains an indirect reference to the *skomorokhi* themselves.

Good people, lend an ear,
As we, fine lads, begin to tell
About the dread tsar Ivan Vasil'evich.[68]

"Fine lads" (*malye rebiata*) is a well-known epithet of the *skomorokhi*. When Ivan flies into a rage over his inability to breach the walls of the city, he threatens to execute all of his gunners, who are enumerated in this curious fashion: "Strizhka, iaryzhka and the son of Fedorych."[69] This last is an obvious example of the occasional nonsense rhymes introduced by the minstrels into some of the songs. Taken together, these characteristics point to the *skomorokhi* as probable editors of these originally stately and serious historical songs.

There is one other genre of Russian oral literature in which the influence of the *skomorokhi* is readily apparent and lends itself to analysis—the *skazki*, or folktales. These have been the object of considerable scholarly attention from the early nineteenth century to the present. In recent years both the folktale and the *bylina* have been subjected to detailed comparative analysis to determine whether or not these genres developed independently, and, if not, what influence was exerted by one upon the other.[70] The consensus among scholars seems to be that the folktale is older than the *bylina* and probably influenced it to some degree.[71] The question of the relationship of the *bylina* to the folktale was raised above in the discussion of the disappearance of the *byliny* from Kievan territory.

The earliest reference we have to Russian folktales dates back to the eleventh century.[72] Here, as in all subsequent references down to the seventeenth century, they appear under the name *basni* (singular *basnia*) and are condemned by the church as vigorously as other aspects of Russian native culture.[73] A twelfth-century account of a rich man preparing to retire for the night gives an interesting description of one of the primary functions of the folktale in medieval Russia. When he lies down and cannot fall asleep, his friends "rub his feet, others stroke his hips, others scratch him across the shoulders, others play [a tune], others tell folktales."[74] Similarly, Ivan IV customarily had three old blind men, or *bakhari* as they eventually became known, recite folktales in his bedchamber to help him fall asleep.[75] In the early seventeenth century Vasilii Shuiskii owned a *bakhar* by the name of Ivan, while Michael Romanov kept several of these storytellers in his chambers.[76] Whether these professional folktale reciters were in fact *skomorokhi* is difficult to say. Zabelin seems to feel that they were, noting that the functions of the *bakhar* and the *domrachei* were often interchangeable at this time.[77]

What was the relationship of the *skomorokhi* to the folk-tale? A cursory glance at some of the *skazki* reveals that they abound in such static literary devices as stock beginning and ending lines, a variety of constant epithets, and numerous formulaic details. This has led L. N. Brodskii to conclude that the Russian folktales were originally the creation of professional singers or reciters, whom he identifies with the *skomorokhi*.[78] More recently V. P. Adrianova-Peretts has expressed a similar view, contending that the *skomorokhi* were indeed directly involved in the composition of folktales, as well as other genres of oral literature.[79]

Among the folktales Brodskii cites to illustrate the involvement of the *skomorokhi* in their composition is one from Afanas'ev's monumental collection of the mid-nineteenth century. Its closing lines are:

> Whoever is rich but miserly: does not brew beer,
> To us, young lads, he gives neither food or drink.
> To him God will give a cat's breathing,
> A dog's gasping.
> To the poor but generous man,
> Who brews beer, and treats us, young lads, to it,
> God will grant fertility in the fields,
> Abundance on the threshing floor,
> Success in the kneading of bread,
> Plenty on the table.
> Of his beer the muzhik drank his fill,
> He drank his fill, then lay down in the shed,
> About his mouth enough crumbs to fill a cap and a half.[80]

The reference to "young lads" (*molodtsy*) is probably to the *skomorokhi*, who were frequently referred to, in both literary and historical sources, as *veselye molodtsy, dobrye molodtsy*, or simply *molodtsy*. The well-known storyteller from the Samara region, Abram Novopol'tsev (whose repertoire fills the better part of Sadovnikov's collection), used to end all of his folktales with the formula:

> Here the tale ends,
> A young lad told it,
> And for us, young lads, a small glass of beer,
> At the end of the tale a small glass of wine.[81]

These lines, according to Brodskii, clearly demonstrate that the *skomorokhi* had a direct hand in the composition of the folktales Novopol'tsev recited.[82]

While the internal evidence linking the *skomorokhi* to the folktale is suggestive, it is by no means conclusive. The formulaic devices and interpolations that Brodskii attributes to the *skomorokhi* may simply be an indication of editing and no more. After all, one can find similar evidence of *skomorokh* editing in the *byliny*, where the authorship must be attributed to the *gusliari* of the Kievan heroic age. I believe that a far stronger link between the *skomorokhi* and the folktale can be established by going back to the origins of the Russian minstrels, which reach far back into the pagan past of the Eastern Slavs, to an age when myth and reality merged in the minds of the people; when the phenomena and mysteries of nature were personified as malevolent beings that had to be appeased lest they wreak havoc on mankind; when the people turned to their spiritual leaders, the *skomorokhi*-priests, for an explanation of what was beyond their ken. It seems logical to assume, as many scholars have, that in these explanations lie the roots of the Russian folktale, and, by extension, that the *skomorokhi*, as spiritual leaders of the people, may have played some role in the creation of the folktale. The high esteem in which the people once held the *skomorokhi*-priests as teachers and philosophers is reflected in a popular tale that describes a debate between a learned Jewish philosopher named Taraska and a lowly *skomorokh*. The debate centers on the relative merits of the religions of the antagonists, Judaism and Christianity. The *skomorokh*, of course, easily triumphs over his opponent and is handsomely rewarded by the Christian prince.[83] How ironic that the people should choose a *skomorokh*, the personification of Russia's pagan past, as the defender of their Christian faith!

What has been said about the relationship of the *skomorokhi* to the folktale might be applied to such other genres of Russian oral tradition as ritual seasonal songs and incantations. In Chapter 1 we discussed the presiding role of the *skomorokhi* in such seasonal festivals as the *Rusaliia* and *Koliada*. After the introduction of Christianity their role was gradually reduced to that of merrymakers or masters of ceremony, but in pre-Christian times it probably carried with it important sacerdotal responsibilities. It is in the context of their former priestly functions that one might attribute to the *skomorokhi* a role in the creation of the large body of ritual songs for these annual celebrations. Some of the surviving *koliadki* do in fact vividly reflect the creative input of the *skomorokhi*: not only are these Christmas and New Year songs characterized by coarse humor and a generally bawdy tone, but they frequently also refer to the *skomorokhi* by name.[84]

Turning, briefly, to the genre of oral literature that can be described loosely as charms (*zaklinaniia*), we are brought once again face to face with the *skomorokhi* as former priests, or, more appropriately, warlocks. In addition to presiding over the many cyclic festivals that punctuated the calendar year, the *skomorokhi* were called upon to use their magical priestly powers to ward off evil, affect cures, divine the future, and perform a myriad of other supernatural functions. They were frequently asked to keep evil spirits away from the wedding party and, through the use of prophylactic and productive magic, to insure a fruitful and happy marriage for the couple. They were able, through the use of charms, to cast evil spells on their own and, on request, other people's, enemies; this power was retained and used by some of the descendants of the early *skomorokhi* as late as the mid-seventeenth century.[85] These and other occult practices embraced a rich oral tradition of incantations to which the *skomorokhi* had not only been privy, but to which they had also in no small measure contributed.

There is, finally, another genre of Russian oral literature to which the *skomorokhi* bear a peculiar relationship—the proverb, or aphorism. There are no fewer than seventeen proverbs about the *skomorokhi* and their profession preserved in various compilations dating back to the late eighteenth century.[86] They range in content from the pedestrian to the profound, from statements of simple fact to comments on the verities of life. "Anyone can dance, but not like a *skomorokh*." "The wife of a *skomorokh* is always merry."[87] "Even a *skomorokh* weeps sometimes."[88] Some of the proverbs are not altogether complimentary. "God gave the priest; the devil, the *skomorokh*."[89] "A *skomorokh's* entertainment is the devil's joy."[90] "A *skomorokh* can tune his voice to a *gudok*, but his own life he cannot keep tuned."[91] The last three probably originated in ecclesiastical circles and were perhaps intended to detract from the widespread popularity of the *skomorokhi*. It is impossible to say how many of these and other proverbs are the creation of the *skomorokhi* themselves, and how many are simply the product of accumulated folk wisdom. Whichever is the case, they are but another example of the enduring legacy of the Russian minstrels among the people.

5
Contribution
to Music, Dance,
and Theater

Because oral tradition and the *skomorokhi* both have deep native roots, it is not difficult to see a direct relationship between them. There is, in addition, considerable literary and other evidence to confirm the important contribution that the *skomorokhi* have made in this area of Russian culture. In the case of the performing arts—music, dance, and theater—however, the legacy of the Russian minstrels is not so readily apparent. There are two reasons for this. First, there is the widely held notion that all three of the performing arts are either foreign in origin or closely patterned after Western models; lacking native roots, they are naturally thought of as having very little in common with native art forms. Second, it is assumed that because modern Russian music, dance (or ballet), and theater did not take shape until the late eighteenth and early nineteenth centuries, and the *skomorokhi* had ceased to function as a professional class one hundred and fifty years earlier, the link between them had long been severed.

No art form can be transplanted into a cultural vacuum, however. It must be grafted onto an already thriving and vigorous tree, which in this instance had been cultivated for centuries by the native minstrel-entertainers. As for the assumption that there is an unbridgeable chronological gap between the medieval *skomo-rokhi* and the performing arts of modern Russia, the fact is that though the *skomorokhi* as a class had become extinct by the late seventeenth century, much of their art survived intact even to our own day. It was deposited among the peasants of northern Russia, where it awaited the genius of Glinka and others, who would give it wide currency and establish it once and for all as an integral part of Russia's cultural heritage.

Music

The Eastern Slavs have from time immemorial been a song-loving people, as the volume and variety of folksongs collected among them attest. Some of these folksongs have been traced back to pre-Christian times and are evidence for the existence of an indigenous musical tradition among the Kievan Slavs prior to the introduction of Christianity and Byzantine liturgical music in the late tenth century. Much of this pre-Christian Kievan music was of a sacred variety, including both ritualistic songs of worship, with solo and congregational singing, and seasonal songs associated with the cyclic festivals such as *Koliada* and *Rusaliia*.[1] It was characterized by a simple melodic structure, a free rhythmical style, and the repetition of short melodies, verse after verse. Its range of melodies was that of thirds, fourths, and fifths, and it was basically diatonic in progression.[2]

With the advent of Christianity some native religious music was suppressed outright, some, like the seasonal songs, was incorporated into the church's liturgical calendar, and some even found its way into the new *znamenny* chant. This last may seem surprising, since it has always been assumed that Byzantine influence was all-pervasive in liturgical matters in Kievan Rus'. However, as recently as 1955 the Soviet antiquarian Vladimir Malyshev chanced upon an old collection of eleven Gospel canticles attributed to Fedor the Christian, which, when deciphered by Maksim Brainikov, "were found to be suffused in a folk-song idiom, leaving far behind all that we had theretofore associated with *znamenny* chant and showing that in the earlier stages the two great bodies of Russian music—the religious and the secular—may have been united by the closest common ties."[3] Given the intimate relationship of the early *skomorokhi* to the pagan cult of ancient Rus' and their continuing identification with surviving pagan ritual and song among the people, it is reasonable to assume that they had, in no small way, contributed to the preservation and perpetuation of native folk music, and thus indirectly to the evolution of the new liturgical chant as well.

In addition to sacred music there was a flourishing secular musical tradition, both vocal and instrumental, in Kievan Rus'.[4] Major events in a person's life—his wedding, for example—were celebrated to the accompaniment of music and song, and many of these ancient songs, and the rites associated with them, have survived to our own day. Music was also a part of Kievan court life and a favorite pastime of the aristocracy. Nestor's vivid account of Feodosii Pecherskii's visit to the court of Sviatoslav II of Kiev in 1073 bears this out: the saintly monk witnessed both musicians and singers performing before the prince.[5] References in the *Slovo o polku Igoreve* to the illustrious bard Boian and in the chronicles to Mitus and other court poets confirm the existence and continuing popularity of the professional courtly singers, or *gusliari*.

It is also evident from the early sources that instrumental music was popular in Kievan times. Three basic types of musical instruments were known to the early Slavs: stringed instruments, referred to generically in the early sources as *gusli*; wind instruments, which included a variety of wooden horns, pipes, and trumpets; and percussion instruments, notably the tambourine and cymbals. The tambourine (*bubny*) and certain wooden pipes and horns were indispensable to the military band.[6] Both the horn and the *gusli* were once closely associated with the pagan cult of ancient Rus', where they were widely used in the practice of medicine, magic, and related occult arts;[7] as was noted earlier, it was because of their medico-religious functions that they were closely identified with the *skomorokhi*.

In the course of their long history one musical instrument— the *gusli*—became a trademark of the *skomorokhi*. The term *gusli* itself is quite broad in meaning. Among the Eastern Slavs it ultimately acquired the meaning of "horizontal harp."[8] In the early Russian sources it was used to denote strings and the sound that they made; a musical instrument in general; and a stringed musical instrument, as distinct from a percussion or wind instrument.[9] (A comparable term in the West might be *cithara*.[10]) Not until the first half of the sixteenth century did *gusli* acquire the meaning it has today. Evidence from the *byliny* suggests that the *gusli* the early *skomorokhi* carried was probably a small, light instrument of maple wood, resembling a four-sided horizontal harp. It had three or more strings of woven horse hair and was always played with the hand or fingers, never a bow. Prior to the eighteenth century it was used primarily to provide accompaniment for the singer. There are no extant examples of early *gusli*, though Famintsyn has tried to reconstruct the instrument on the model of the earliest surviving Finnish *kantele*.[11]

By the thirteenth century the oval or half-moon *gusli*-psaltery had become popular among the Eastern Slavs, especially in the northwest. This instrument, though frequently thought of as a variant of the traditional *gusli*, did not derive from it but was probably borrowed by the northern Slavs from the Balto-Finns, as

I. Tõnurist has convincingly demonstrated.[12] In the so-called Radziwill, or Königsberg, Chronicle from the late fourteenth or early fifteenth century, there is an illustration accompanying the narration of the temptation of Saint Antonius in which one of the devil-tempters is playing a five-string oval *gusli*.[13] Kondakov, who has made a thorough study of the chronicle's illustrations, maintains that they are copies of late thirteenth-century originals, and that while many are patterned after Byzantine miniatures, the temptation of Saint Antonius is of native origin.[14] As the oval *gusli*-psaltery was gaining in popularity, a triangular version of the instrument also came into vogue; late thirteenth- and early fourteenth-century miniatures from Pskov and Novgorod bear this out. Like its oval counterpart, the triangular *gusli*-psaltery was probably of Balto-Finnic origin.

The *skomorokhi* began very early to favor the versatile *gusli*-psaltery, both oval and triangular, over the traditional four-sided version; in fact, this is the instrument depicted in all of the extant illustrations of *skomorokhi* playing the *gusli*, including the famous Olearius woodcut from the early seventeenth century. Its popularity can be explained by the simple fact that the traditional *gusli*, like the Finnish *kantele*, must be played in a sitting position, with the instrument resting on one's lap or on a table. The *gusli*-psaltery, on the other hand, can be played either sitting or standing (with the instrument propped up against one's chest), giving the performer much greater freedom of movement and even enabling him to dance while playing. The miniature from the 1358 collection of Sunday Gospels and another one from a fourteenth-century Novgorod Liturgicon show how this can be done.[15]

Ironically, as the fortunes of the *skomorokhi* declined in the seventeenth century, the *gusli*, with a host of other musical instruments, was also threatened with extinction. On more than one occasion Tsar Aleksei ordered the confiscation and destruction of all musical instruments, whether they were used by the minstrels or not. That the tsar's orders were taken seriously is attested to by Olearius: "two years ago he ordered the destruction of any tavern musicians' [that is, *skomorokhi*] instruments seen in the streets. Then he banned instrumental music altogether and ordered the seizure of musical instruments in the houses; once, five wagon loads were sent across the Moscow River and burned there."[16] Fortunately the *gusli* fared much better in the face of official persecution than did the *skomorokhi*. It not only survived Aleksei's wrath but went on to enjoy unprecedented popularity in the late eighteenth and early nineteenth centuries.[17]

For hundreds of years the Russian minstrels had been

closely identified with the *gusli* and had contributed much to its evolution and development. Their legacy to secular music is thus bound up with the instrument; to quote one scholar: "The instrument and its literature interests us not only because of its antiquity or its role as the direct historical predecessor to Russian piano music, but because it occupied a position of great importance in the whole evolution of Russian national musical culture."[18]

The other stringed instrument with which the *skomorokhi* are frequently identified is the *gudok*; both the fifteenth-century Meletovo fresco and the Olearius illustration picture *skomorokhi* playing it. This instrument, which resembles the modern cello, made its appearance very early in Russia, apparently imported from central Asia.[19] Onion-shaped, with three strings, the *gudok* was held in a vertical position and played with a bow. Two of its strings were tuned in unison; the third, a fifth higher.

During the sixteenth century, and perhaps even earlier, the *skomorokhi* are known to have used several other musical instruments: the *domra*, which eventually gave birth to the modern Russian *balalaika*, the drum, the fiddle, the flute, and the horn. None of these, however, approached the *gusli* and *gudok* in popularity. With the exception of the *domra*, they seem to have been used primarily to provide musical accompaniment for dancing.

Dance

The dance has been described as one of the most ancient manifestations of man's spiritual and emotional being in the primeval stage of cultural development. Among the Eastern Slavs, as among other peoples, it was a native art form, distinctive in character, with roots deep in antiquity: evidence from the Trypilia settlement in the Kiev region suggests that some form of dance existed here as early as the third millenium B.C. In its earliest form it was probably associated with man's need to express his deepest feelings and emotions outwardly through rhythmic movement. It also served as a means of communication between primitive man and nature, and as such played an important part in his cult conceptions and ceremonies. On the more practical level, dance provided a basically agricultural people with a rhythmical pattern for seasonal tasks. These patterns are frequently referred to as dance-games, and some have survived to quite recent times.[20]

In an agricultural society the sun and the seasons are the focus of the economic, social, and spiritual life of the people. In spring they plant and sow; in summer they watch over and rejoice in their forthcoming harvest; in fall they reap; in winter they rest and await the return of the sun's warming rays. With their very survival dependent on the beneficence of nature and the success of the harvest, nothing could be left to chance. A continuous cycle of rites and ceremonies had to be performed to placate and ward off malevolent spirits and to invoke the aid of benevolent ones. For the most part these cyclic rites, which involved the entire community, found expression in the circle dance, or *khorovod*. In its earliest stage of development the *khorovod* was actually a dance-game. Its basic form, the circle, was associated with the cult of the sun, source of all life-giving power. As the community grew, so did the *khorovod*, and gradually solo performers, coryphaei or actors, emerged. These never numbered more than three in a *khorovod*, and their function was to act out the lyrics of the songs performed by the dancing chorus. According to Vsevolodskii-Gerngross, these early "actors" were apparently the forerunners of the *skomorokhi*.[21]

With the coming of Christianity the *khorovod* gradually lost much of its religious, though not its artistic and ritualistic, appeal. It continued to dominate the cultural and social life of the community, with the *skomorokhi* quite naturally assuming the role of dance-masters, or coryphaei. In this capacity they continued to act out dance-games well into the seventeenth century, as Aleksei reminds us in his first 1648 *gramota*. Unfortunately, we know next to nothing about the form and content of these early dance-games. Apparently they involved the use of masks and costumes and, like the *koliada* skit described earlier, retained certain features linking them to a primitive fertility cult.

Histories of Russian ballet frequently single out the two squatting musicians depicted in the eleventh-century staircase frescoes of the Kievan Sophia as the earliest examples of dancing *skomorokhi*.[22] In light of recent findings (discussed in Chapter 1), one must reject this conclusion and look elsewhere for early evidence of *skomorokh* involvement in the dance. The earliest written records linking the *skomorokhi* directly to the dance, or specifically, to dance-games, date from the late twelfth century.[23]

Like other aspects of secular culture, dancing was looked upon as pagan and sinful by the church, especially when engaged in by women. A graphic illustration of this can be found in a popular tale from the sixteenth century. There was a young woman who was so fond of dancing that she would dance even on holydays. One day she returned home from her frolic late at night and went to sleep. As she slept she was taken bodily down to the depths of hell, where her beautiful hair was badly singed and her face terribly disfigured. When she awoke she was in great pain. Her mother summoned a priest, who heard her confession and found her to be blameless but for one grave sin—dancing.[24]

Besides the written record, which, as the above parable illustrates, is largely denunciatory or didactic, we are fortunate to have several pictorial representations of dancing *skomorokhi*. Two are quite early, dating from the mid-fourteenth century, while the third dates from the mid-seventeenth. The earlier two are miniatures depicting the Old Slavonic letters Р and Д, and show flamboyantly dressed minstrels playing the *gusli* and simultaneously dancing.[25] The *skomorokh* depicted in the initial Д has been described by some as dancing in the traditional Russian fashion, *vprisiadku*.[26]

More revealing as far as the history of Russian dance is concerned is the seventeenth-century illustration from Olearius, which shows two *skomorokhi* playing musical instruments and singing the praises of the tsar (Michael Romanov), and two others dancing.[27] Regarding the dancers, Olearius writes: "Observing that we liked their performance, they added some amusing dances and demonstrated various styles of dancing practiced by both men and women. Unlike the Germans, the Russians do not join hands while dancing, but each one dances by himself. Their dances consist chiefly of movements of the hands, feet, shoulders, and hips. The dancers, particularly the women, hold varicolored embroidered handkerchiefs, which they wave about while dancing although they themselves remain in place almost all the time."[28] The reference to "various styles of dancing" seems to indicate that by the seventeenth century the *skomorokhi* had achieved a degree of professionalism in their dancing and could boast a diversified repertoire. Olearius's further comment that solo performances were quite common and his description of these in terms of controlled body movement in place suggest that he was witnessing the rudiments of ballet dancing in a nontheatrical setting.[29]

Theater

According to the noted Soviet scholar B. V. Varneke, the man who must be credited with the idea of organizing a theatrical troupe in Moscow and, more significantly, with the cultivation of the legitimate theater in Russia, is Tsar Aleksei himself.[30] How ironic that the tsar who tried to suppress not only the *skomorokhi*, but all popular secular entertainment, should be hailed as one of the first official patrons of the Russian performing arts.[31] Aleksei had evidently mellowed with age since the publication of the *gramota* of 1648, or there were, perhaps, other reasons for his change of heart which are open to conjecture. Some point to his travel abroad and exposure to Western culture, especially the theater, as a possible catalyst; others attribute the change in attitude to the influence of favorites, such as the boyar Artaman Sergeevich Matveev, a cultured and thoroughly Westernized man, in whose household Aleksei's second wife, Natal'ia Naryshkin, was reared and educated.[32] Or perhaps it was the influence of Natal'ia, who, after her marriage to Aleksei in 1672, brought a breath of fresh air into the austere Muscovite court. Whatever the source of Aleksei's secularization or Westernization, it had a far-reaching effect upon the history of the Russian theater.

Yet one must not lose sight of the fact that the dramatic urge was by no means absent in Russia before Aleksei's reign. Traditional folk drama, theater in its less-structured popular form, flourished among the Eastern Slavs in antiquity and manifested itself in the whole range of cyclic festivals and rituals. Luka Zhidiata, the eleventh-century bishop of Novgorod, was no doubt alluding to this rudimentary drama when he warned his flock to shun *moskoludstvo*, or games characterized by the wearing of masks.[33] The twelfth-century author of the "Life of Saint Nifont" must also have had it in mind when he described the *Rusaliia* festival in his time; among those participating in the festival were *skomorokhi* who donned masks and "made sport of man."[34] One wonders whether these *skomorokhi* were not in fact acting out a fable or bestiary—so popular in medieval Europe—and, if so, why nothing of this satiric drama has survived. Distinct echoes of this primitive drama can be heard in some of the ancient Ukrainian *koliadki* with mythological themes that focus on the goat-grain as a fertility symbol. The relationship of the *skomorokhi* to these has already been discussed at some length in Chapter 1.

Nowhere is the dramatic urge of the Eastern Slavs more apparent than in their wedding customs. It is no exaggeration to say that the elaborate ceremonies connected with the Russian wedding at one time constituted a play in several acts performed before the entire community, with an unwritten script that was strictly adhered to and roles assigned not only to the principals— the bride, bridegroom, and their attendants—but to members of the couple's families as well. Scene followed scene in predictable fashion, with most of the action taking place at the home of the bride. A chorus of the bride's close friends provided a running commentary on the action and gave it continuity. Directing the performance from beginning to end was the best man or groomsman, usually a *skomorokh*, as most of the early sources seem to indicate, whose close identification with magic and the occult qualified him to perform the duties of this important office.[35] It was his responsibility to protect the couple from evil and to insure their future good fortune.

In addition to cyclic ritual drama and that associated with the wedding, there was a purely secular theater that the *skomorokhi* helped to popularize by improvising comic dialogues for the people's amusement. Through repeated usage and oral tradition these improvisations became fixed and eventually developed a life of their own as independent folk comedies. In the seventeenth and eighteenth centuries, they came under considerable influence from scholastic and court drama, which resulted ultimately in the creation of such legitimate folk plays as "Tsar' Maksimilian."[36]

O. E. Ozarovskaia calls attention to another indication of the involvement of the *skomorokhi* in early secular drama in her recent collection of Russian folk literature. She has appended a brief note to the *bylina* "Gost' Terent'ische," which she recorded from the peasant woman Elena Ol'kina in the Pinega region. To distinguish between the various characters in the song, she writes, the singer would change the tone and quality of her voice, explaining simply that "this is how it is sung." Ozarovskaia speculates that perhaps in earlier times this *bylina* was acted out by several people, and that Ol'kina's unique rendering reflected a once-flourishing popular dramatic tradition.[37] How many other *byliny*, historical songs, *khorovody*, or similar genres of Russian oral literature were acted out by troupes of *skomorokhi* is a tantalizing but unanswerable question.

Any discussion of the contribution of the *skomorokhi* to Russian theater must include the trained bear act and the puppet theater. Both were once an integral part of a *skomorokh* entertainment, as the illustration from Olearius shows, and both can be said to represent the most direct and enduring legacy of the *skomorokhi* to Russian popular culture. In the West trained bears have generally been regarded as merely a foreign curiosity. Interestingly, it was the *skomorokhi* who, according to A. N. Veselovskii, introduced the performing bear into Germany and Italy in the early sixteenth century.[38] In Russia itself they have enjoyed continuous popularity from medieval times and to this day are one of the main attractions of the Moscow Circus.

The earliest reference that we have to trained bears, used for omen reading rather than entertainment, appears in the *Kormchaia kniga* of 1282;[39] as was indicated above, there is evidence that the *skomorokhi*-priests may have used the bear in pre-Christian times primarily for divination. As late as the sixteenth century, according to Waliszewskii, "pregnant women gave bread to the bears led about in troops by wandering jugglers (*skomo-rokhy*) [*sic*], and judged the sex of the unborn child according to the creatures' growls."[40] As a form of entertainment, performing bears were already quite popular by the early fifteenth century,[41] and by the early sixteenth century, references to *skomorokhi-medvedniki*, or bear tamers, are numerous, particularly in the cadastres and census books. As was true of the *skomorokhi* in general, the best bear tamers came from Novgorod, as Ivan IV's mass transfer of *veselye liudi* and their trained bears from Novgorod to Moscow in 1572 attests.[42]

P. N. Berkov has recently attempted to reconstruct what he describes as a typical "bear comedy."[43] It includes sundry short skits in which the bear mimics a young girl prettying herself before a mirror, a young boy stealing peas from a garden, a priest saying vespers, an old woman clumsily burning her hand while baking *blintsy*, a drunk, a lecherous old man, and so forth. The bear might also dance, by himself or with his trainer, and play some musical instrument; sometimes he would even wrestle with his master. At the conclusion of the act he goes around with hat in hand, soliciting donations from the audience.

Perhaps the single most unique contribution of the *skomo-rokhi* to Russian culture—one, however, for which they have never received just credit—is the puppet theater, *kukol'nyi teatr*, or Petrushka. This delightful, highly refined form of Russian non-legitimate theater is not well known in the West. There are passing references to it in popular histories of puppetry and the like, but unfortunately these are more often confusing than enlightening. Perhaps even more unfortunately, Petrushka has been neglected by native scholars as well. Their failure to deal seriously with the origins of the Russian puppet theater has been particularly glaring, and they have also largely ignored its early history; most have, in fact, been content to view as a *terra incognita* the entire period prior to the 1630s, when Adam Olearius's famous illustrated description of a performing Russian puppeteer appeared.[44]

The few scholars who have studied the early history of Russian puppetry have generally sought its roots in one of three foreign cultures: the Italian, the Byzantine, or the Chinese. Most maintain that the Russian puppet theater was borrowed from the West, specifically, from Italy. They argue that the prototype of the Russian puppet hero Petrushka is the Italian Pulcinella, who was brought to Russia from Italy, via Germany, in the early seventeenth century by the *skomorokhi*; in essence the close similarity between Petrushka and Pulcinella is regarded as proof of the Italian, or Western, origin of the Russian *kukol'nyi teatr*.[45] Less widely accepted is the hypothesis that the puppet theater had its roots in Byzantium and was brought to Kievan Rus' by visiting mimes as early as the tenth or eleventh century.[46] The proponents of this argument point to the staircase frescoes of the Kievan Saint Sophia, whose extreme left section was thought until recently to represent a troupe of Byzantine puppeteers preparing to give a performance,[47] and to the strong cultural influence exerted by Byzantium on the Eastern Slavs, which makes Constantinople a logical place to seek the origin of the Russian puppet theater. Finally, some have raised the possibility that it was brought to Russia from the Far East, from China by way of the Mongols; after all, the Mongols transmitted their knowledge of Chinese lantern pictures, or shadow puppetry, to the Turks.[48] Could they not have done the same for the Russians?

Each of these explanations has serious drawbacks. Petrushka's striking resemblance to the Italian puppet hero Pulcinella is indisputable, but he also resembles the English Punch, the French Pulichinelle, the German Hanswurst, the Czech Kašpárek, the Hungarian Vitez Laszko, and the Turkish Karagöz, among others. Rather than prove his Italian or Western origin, the similarity between Petrushka and the other puppet heroes seems to point up the universality of the character. Veselovskii's contention that a section of the Saint Sophia frescoes represents a group of Byzantine puppeteers appeared until recently to have considerable merit; however, as was pointed out in Chapter 1, Vysotskii and Totskaia have demonstrated quite conclusively that what some have taken to be a Byzantine puppet theater is in fact a Byzantine pneumatic organ.[49] Nor can the possibility of tracing the origins of the Russian puppet theater to China through the intermediacy of the Mongols be dismissed out of hand. The main difficulty here, however, is to reconcile the Chinese technique of shadow puppetry, or lantern pictures, with the Russian hand and string puppets. In Turkey the lantern technique, which we know was introduced by the Mongols, has survived to this day, but in Russia, with one questionable exception, there is no evidence of its ever being used. This exception, which is indeed intriguing, arises from Baird's speculation that the Scythians, as well as some of the nomadic peoples of Central Asia, could have been familiar with shadow puppetry as early as 500 B.C. "It is known," he writes, "that the Scythians of the third and fourth centuries B.C. made handsome silhouettes of leather. And in the burial grounds among the Altai Mountains near Outer Mongolia, along the old trade route between China and Russia, there have been found cutout leather animals, one a moose that could well have been a shadow figure."[50]

One is more inclined, however, to agree with Karl Jettmar, who describes similar leather silhouettes as appliqué decorations, quite common among the nomadic peoples of this area; some have been found, for example, in the Altai region of Central Asia adorning the exterior of a wooden sarcophagus and a saddle dating from the Scythian era.[51]

Despite their weaknesses, the three hypotheses must be acknowledged to have some merits, particularly the arguments on behalf of the Western or Italian origin of Petrushka. The *kukol'nyi teatr*, even in its early stage, was subject to considerable foreign influence. Those persons most closely identified with the early history of puppetry, in Russia and elsewhere, were by nature widely traveled. There is evidence not only that the *skomorokhi* had visited Germany and Italy as early as the sixteenth century, but that German *Spielleute* and Byzantine mimes had even earlier (certainly no later than the thirteenth century) made their way into Kievan Rus' and Muscovite Russia. Surely there was some exchange of technique and method, if not repertoire, among these troupes of entertainers. But one should not confuse influence with origins, and it is here precisely that I take issue with the traditional interpretations.

By blurring the distinction between influence and origins, scholars have inadvertently overlooked many centuries of indigenous East Slavic sociocultural development, especially in popular mythology and folk ritual, and lost sight of the elemental fact that puppetry, like drama, had its genesis in religion and religious ceremony.[52] As Professor Vernadsky, writing about the *Maslenitsa* festival, has recently observed: "Companies of itinerant actors and musicians (*skomorokhi*) performed short plays, some of them remnants of the old sacred drama of the heathen times. . . . An outgrowth of these shows was the puppet-threatre (Petrushka)."[53]

The masks and anthropomorphic images that once constituted the essential trappings of many primitive religions were, with time and the impact of civilization and Christianity, gradually cast aside, becoming the tools of the trade for the early puppeteer. Precisely how this transformation from religious idol to secular puppet occurred in a given society is as difficult to explain as the unique transformation of Greek ritual to Greek drama. This difficulty should not, however, deter one from examining the evidence in support of the indigenous origins of the Russian puppet theater.

Although little evidence survives regarding official public worship among the pagan ancestors of the Eastern Slavs, certain traditional rituals, as we have seen, have been preserved to our own day. The best known is the cycle of rites with the theme of bidding farewell to winter and ushering in spring and summer.[54] The winter part of the cycle includes the two festival periods of *Koliada* (Christmas–New Year) and *Maslenitsa* (pre-Lenten, or Mardi gras); the spring part of the cycle includes the *Rusaliia* (Trinity Sunday) and *Kupalo* (Feast of Saint John the Baptist, or Midsummer). In pre-Christian times the two winter festivals corresponded more or less to the winter solstice and spring equinox respectively, while the spring festival was observed around the time of the summer solstice.

Among the most ancient of the customs associated with *Koliada* and *Maslenitsa* was the wearing of masks and costumes. The masks were almost exclusively of animals, the most favored being the goat, the aurochs, the horse, the bear, and the wolf. Though in recent times these two festivals have acquired a far less serious tone, they once served a magical, semireligious purpose, as they were intended to secure a good harvest for the coming year. Like the Mardi gras and Carnival in the West, to which it has frequently been compared, *Maslenitsa* is celebrated the week before the beginning of Lent.[55] Since it was formerly celebrated around the spring equinox, the *Maslenitsa* has often been described as a ritual of bidding farewell to winter, and it has preserved certain ancient features that link it closely with Russia's pagan past. It culminates in the carrying in procession and eventual destruction (by drowning, burning, or burial) of Winter, represented by an image, or puppet, of straw or wood, called variously Iarilo, Chuchilo, or Chudo.[56] The religious overtones of this ceremony are obvious: the god of darkness and death, symbolizing winter and represented here by the puppet, is physically annihilated to make way for spring, the harbinger of new life and plenty.

Rusaliia and *Kupalo*, the two festivals dominating the spring cycle, were originally celebrated as one, at the time of the summer solstice in June. Both bear a close resemblance to *Maslenitsa* in that puppet-like straw images provide the focal point for their rites. Much circle dancing and choral singing (performed simultaneously as *khorovody*) take place at the *Rusaliia* festival. This culminates in a tug of war in the open fields over the *rusalka* puppet, which is eventually torn and scattered to the four winds, making the world safe for yet another year from these menacing female spirits.[57] In some regions the straw puppet is burned or drowned.[58]

In the ceremonies surrounding *Kupalo*, music, dance, fortune telling and leaping through open bonfires by young unmarried couples are the most characteristic diversions. A male puppet and numerous female straw puppets are made for the occasion; because the young men repeatedly "abduct" the female puppet, the girls must make new ones to replace her. Eventually the puppet couple, Kupalo and Marena, are either torn and scattered or drowned.[59]

Clearly, puppets and masks played an integral part in many of these religious rituals. Furthermore, it is no accident that the *skomorokhi*, whose origins, as we have seen, can be traced back to the popular pagan cult of ancient Rus', were also the first Russian puppet masters. Together with the *volkhvy*, the *skomorokhi* were intimately involved in the cult of the people, with its wealth and diversity of ritual. As former priests or cult leaders they were the logical inheritors of the cult images, or puppets, which, after the introduction of Christianity in 988, became, like the *skomorokhi* themselves, anathema to the church.

Veselovskii has suggested another link between the *skomorokhi* and puppetry. As he has meticulously demonstrated, the modern Russian word for puppet, *kukla*,[60] did not always refer to a marionette;[61] in fact, as late as the nineteenth century it had attached to it in certain regions, notably the provinces of Orlovsk and Pskov, the connotation of sorcery or witchcraft.[62] It may be that the *kukla* was originally used by the *skomorokhi* in their role as warlocks as a medium for inflicting harm on their enemies (that is, as a voodoo doll).

We have traced the progression from pagan religious rite to secular marionette that occurred among the Eastern Slavs as it did, according to Baird, in other early societies.[63] The question that remains is *when* the *skomorokhi* began to use puppets for non-ritualistic, entertainment purposes. Was it, as some have suggested, in the late sixteenth or early seventeenth century, shortly before Olearius chanced upon the *skomorokh*-puppeteer he described in his *Travels*? I believe it was much earlier.

In 1733 there appeared in the *Sankt-Peterburgskie vedomosti* an anonymous article entitled "O pozorishchnykh igrakh, ili komediakh i tragediakh," which discussed in print for the first time in Russia the characteristics of the *kukol'nyi teatr*.[64] It is significant that the author used a relatively modern Russian word for puppet, *kukla*, to describe one of the theatrical arts included under the general heading of *pozorishche* (sometimes *pozor*).[65] "Among the *pozorishchnyi igry*," he wrote, "one must also include the *kukol'nye igry*, in which the performances are not given by live actors but rather by puppets." A brief description of the potential scope of puppets as actors follows.

One will therefore probably search in vain to find early

references to the Russian puppet theater under its modern names, *kukol'nyi teatr* or *kukla*,[66] as is further demonstrated by two seventeenth-century documents. In his *gramota* of 1648, Aleksei condemned the *skomorokhi* for a multitude of alleged evils, including "*pozorishche* on the streets and in the open fields,"[67] but nowhere in this lengthy and exhaustive enumeration of their professional activities is the *kukol'nyi teatr* or *kukla* mentioned. Yet before 1648, as Olearius's illustration proves, the puppet theater was an important part of a *skomorokh* entertainment. Is it not safe to assume that the reference in Aleksei's *gramota* to *pozorishche* is in fact a reference to the puppet shows of the *skomorokhi*?

In an earlier seventeenth-century document, an *ukaz* of the Patriarch Filaret from 1628, there is a stern denunciation of all surviving folk games and festivals with pagan overtones, and among the practices condemned is one that can be translated literally as "going about with mares."[68] Of some twenty-three surviving original episodes involving the puppet hero Petrushka, twenty describe him as bargaining with a gypsy over a mare.[69] The Olearius illustration pictures a mare on the portable stage the puppeteer has raised over his head; Olearius has evidently reproduced one of these popular episodes from "Petrushka."[70] Filaret's reference to "going about with mares" can be only interpreted as an allusion to the puppet shows of the *skomorokhi*. Again, there is no reference here to *kukol'nyi teatr* or *kukla*.

I have tried to show that as late as the mid-eighteenth century, the term commonly used to refer to puppetry in Russia was *pozorishche*. Between the eleventh and thirteenth centuries, *pozorishche* was used exclusively to render the Greek word for "theater" or "theatrical performance" ($\theta\acute{\epsilon}\alpha\tau\rho o\nu$).[71] By 1284 it was no longer used simply for translation but appeared independently in the *Kormchaia kniga Riazanskaia,* a collection of ecclesiastical law from Riazan, still retaining its original meaning of "theater" or "theatrical performance."[72] However, here we find *pozorishche* listed along with *igrishche*, long regarded by scholars as the Old Russian term for a dramatic performance, usually one involving real actors.[73] A distinction between *pozorishche* and *igrishche* is obviously intended. According to Vsevolodskii-Gerngross, the common people have always looked upon these two terms as distinct, regarding *pozorishche* as the forerunner of the modern word for "theater" (in the sense of "performance" or "spectacle") and *igrishche* as the early equivalent of "drama."[74]

Sources such as the *Povest' vremennykh let* contain frequent references to *igrishcha* in the context of ritual games associated with the pagan cult of the ancient Slavs.[75] As in ancient Greece, these games represent the earliest stage in the evolution of drama in Russia. To this day the popular Russian expression for a wedding (a thoroughly dramatic affair, as described above) is *igrat' svad'bu*.

In light of this evidence, is it not possible that the reference in the *Kormchaia kniga Riazanskaia* to *pozorishche* is in fact an allusion to a nondramatic theatrical performance, one differing from the *igrishche* not only in tone and content, but also in its reliance on puppets rather than live actors as *dramatis personae*? And would this not place the origins of the Russian puppet theater sometime in the late thirteenth century, rather than in the early seventeenth century as many have alleged?

The early history of the Russian puppet theater is bound up with the history of the *skomorokhi*. By the early seventeenth century the puppet show was already an established tradition among the *skomorokhi* and an integral part of their entertainment. According to Olearius, "[The Russian] dancing-bear impresarios have comedians with them, who, among other things, arrange farces employing puppets. These comedians tie a blanket around their bodies and spread it above their heads, thus creating a port-able stage with which they can run about the streets, and on top of which they can give puppet shows."[76] The illustration accom-panying this description shows a dancing bear with his trainer, two musicians, one playing an oval *gusli*, the other a *gudok*, and a puppeteer giving a performance. The puppeteer's portable stage was made by tying a blanket at the waist, and, with the help of two wooden poles, raising it over his head; this left both his hands free to manipulate the hand puppets.[77] This kind of one-man portable puppet stage seems to be unique to Russia, and not only does it demonstrate the ingenuity of the *skomorokhi*, but it also implicitly confirms a long tradition of puppetry among them.

The scene depicted on Olearius's stage is taken from an early version of "Petrushka." The hero, Petrushka, is shown bar-gaining vigorously with the gypsy over a mare while his wife looks on. As was noted above, twenty versions of this scene have sur-vived.[78] It is impossible to say what other plays, besides the num-erous adventures of Petrushka, were included in the repertoire of the *skomorokhi*-puppeteers, since much of their original repertoire was, like the *byliny* and historical songs they recited, transmitted orally and never written down. It is safe to assume, however, that because of the itinerant nature of the productions, the repertoire was limited by the amount of equipment that could be carried.

Shortly after Olearius had witnessed his first *skomorokh* entertainment and puppet show, the fortunes of the Russian minstrel-entertainers took a decided turn for the worse. Aleksei's *gramota* of 1648 outlawed the *skomorokhi* and their entertainments as well, and the *skomorokhi* never recovered from this blow. The Russian puppet theater, on the other hand, not only survived but found new life in Aleksei's own lifetime, and prospered even more in the reigns of Peter the Great and his successors. Like so many other aspects of Russian society and culture, however, it was subjected to progressively stronger foreign influence and came to lose much of its native character. One learns, for example, that in 1660 a certain Ivan Hebdon [Gebdon], an English merchant living at court to whom the tsar frequently turned for foreign goods and services, was commissioned by Aleksei to bring from Germany to Moscow an unspecified number of puppet masters.[79] In 1699 a Russian puppeteer (no longer called a *skomorokh*, but rather a *komediant*, a term obviously borrowed from the West) by the name of Ivan Antonovyi was buying his puppets from Denmark; he ordered thirty of them from Gottfried Kaulitz, who delivered only six, for which breach of contract he was severely beaten by Ivan.[80] A year later Peter the Great himself dispatched (for reasons which are not clear) a trio of Prussian puppeteers to tour and give performances in selected Ukrainian towns.[81] In fact, by the mid-eighteenth century, touring German, Italian, and French companies had become common, not only in Moscow and Saint Petersburg, but in smaller Russian towns as well.[82]

If Petrushka was not totally forgotten during this period, he was certainly eclipsed by the foreign heroes and their exploits. Some of the surviving playbills from the period bear this out. In 1733 in Saint Petersburg, for example, the touring puppet company of Johann Christofor Zigmund was showing, among other pieces: "Adam and Eve" (a comedy), "The Crucifixion of Christ," "The Life and Death of Don Juan," "King Agasfer and Queen Esfir," "King Admet and the Strength of the Mighty Hercules," and "Princess Florian and the Beautiful Bancefori."[83] To what extent native Russian puppeteers, or *komedianti*, the spiritual successors of the *skomorokhi*, continued to bring Petrushka's adventures to country people during this period is difficult to say. That they did is certain, however, since Petrushka not only survived this foreign intrusion but, even more importantly, remained untainted by it; the twenty-three Petrushka episodes that have come down to us in manuscript form from the nineteenth century attest to that.[84] His very name, like that of Punch in England, has become so closely identified with puppetry in Russia that today the two are synonymous—to his countrymen Petrushka was and is the Russian puppet theater.

This chapter has described the vigorous native tradition of secular music, dance, and theater in Russia prior to the influx of Western forms in the eighteenth century. It is obvious not only that the *skomorokhi* were an integral part of that tradition, but that the tradition owed much of its vitality, even its survival, to them. Like many other aspects of Russian native, pre-Christian culture, the early performing arts were considered pagan by the church, and they would probably have withered and died had not the minstrel-entertainers nurtured them in their embryonic state.

Conclusion

In the foregoing pages I have traced the origins and history of the *skomorokhi* up to their dispersal in the seventeenth century and assessed their influence on Russian music, dance, theater, and oral tradition. The task has not been easy, since the Russian minstrels are an elusive breed. To compensate for the dearth of material evidence it has been necessary to make use of a wide range of ancillary sources—literary, documentary, folkloric, toponymic, and artistic—and to subject the evidence to close scrutiny. I believe the portrait that emerges, though at times sketchy, does achieve the main objective of this study—to rescue the Russian minstrels from the historical obscurity to which they have been relegated.

Scholars will no doubt continue to reinterpret the existing facts, as Belkin has recently done, to support their own theories regarding the place of the *skomorokhi* in Russian history. But unless some startling new evidence is brought to light in the future, the historian's task is done. Much more can, and no doubt will, be done by the folklorist, the musicologist, and the student of Muscovite literature. In the area of folklore, S. I. Dmitrieva has recently suggested some fruitful new lines of research by focusing attention on the distribution of heroic *byliny* in northern Russia and on the relationship between certain epic traditions in the north. Important work is also being done by ethnomusicologists, notably I. Tõnurist, on the origins and early history of the *gusli*. Their efforts will perhaps yield some new clues regarding the musical legacy of the Russian minstrels. Equally promising is the research of such scholars as Richard H. Marshall of the University of Toronto, whose interest in the transition from oral to written literature that occurred in the seventeenth century has prompted him to look to the *skomorokhi* as a possible bridge between these two literary traditions. Finally, as S. A. Vysotskii and I. F. Totskaia have recently demonstrated, one cannot exclude the possibility that even the role of the *skomorokhi* in the evolution of Russian dance and theater—for which the evidence is much less tangible—may undergo some fundamental reevaluation as a result of new archeological or other findings.

To fully appreciate the cultural heritage of the Russian people one must first come to know the *skomorokhi*. Not only did they exert a preponderant influence on secular folk culture, but they also played a vital role in the religious life of the people. Their close ties to Russian paganism made the *skomorokhi* a ready target when the church and the state launched their vigorous campaign against superstition in the seventeenth century; yet, those ties also made them in a very real sense the embodiment of *dvoeverie*, that unique fusion of pagan and Christian elements that gave Russian spirituality its distinctive character.

Notes

Introduction

1. Most of this literature can be found listed in the two major bibliographic guides to Russian folklore: N. L. Brodskii, N. A. Gusev, and N. P. Sidorov, comps., *Russkaia ustnaia slovestnost'* (Leningrad, 1924), pp. 11–12; and M. Ia. Mel'ts, comp., *Russkii fol'klor: bibliograficheskii ukazatel'*, vol. 1: *1917–1944* (Leningrad, 1966), pp. 384–89; vol. 2: *1945–1959* (Leningrad, 1961), pp. 215–19; vol. 3: *1960–1965* (Leningrad, 1967), pp. 218–20.

2. A. A. Belkin, *Russkie skomorokhi* (Moscow, 1975), pp. 3–29, 110–63.

3. In a recently published essay, A. A. Morozov expresses scepticism about the attribution of the roles of political activists and leaders of popular rebellion to the *skomorokhi*. "K voprosu ob istoricheskoi roli i znachenii skomorokhov," *Russkii fol'klor* 16 (1976): 62.

4. N. Findeizen, *Ocherki po istorii muzyki v Rossii*, vol. 1 (Moscow-Leningrad, 1928), pp. 45–170.

5. A representative bibliography relating to this controversy can be found in M. Vasmer, *Russisches Etymologisches Wörterbuch*, vol. 3 (Heidelberg, 1955), pp. 643–44.

6. R. Zguta, "*Skomorokhi*: The Russian Minstrel-Entertainers," *Slavic Review* 31 (1972): 297–313; H. M. Chadwick and N. K. Chadwick, *The Growth of Literature*, vol. 2, pt. 1: *Russian Oral Literature* (Cambridge, 1936), pp. 261–69.

7. Iu. M. Sokolov, *Russian Folklore*, trans. C. R. Smith (New York, 1950), p. 298.

8. R. N. Leonard, *A History of Russian Music* (New York, 1957), p. 23.

9. J. Spiegelman, "Style Formation in Early Russian Keyboard Music,"

in *The Eighteenth Century in Russia*, ed. J. G. Garrard (Oxford, 1973), p. 312.

10. N. Roslavleva, *Era of the Russian Ballet* (New York, 1966), p. 19.

Chapter 1

1. A. S. Famintsyn, *Skomorokhi na Rusi* (St. Petersburg, 1889), p. 1.

2. A good bibliographic guide to the literature on the origins of the *skomorokhi* can be found in Vasmer, *Russisches Etymologisches Wörterbuch*, 3: 643–44.

3. P. I. Safarik, *Slavianskiia drevnosti*, vol. 1, bk. 2 (Moscow, 1837), p. 240; G. A. Il'inskii, "Slavianskiia etimologii, XXXVI–LXX," *Izvestiia otdeleniia russkago iazyka i slovesnosti Rossiiskoi Akademii Nauk* 23, bk. 2 (1918): 243–45.

4. I. Beliaev, "O skomorokhakh," *Vremennik Imperatorskago obshchestva istorii i drevnostei rossiiskikh* 2 (1854): 70.

5. A. Afanas'ev, *Poeticheskiia vozzreniia slavian na prirodu*, vol. 1 (Moscow, 1865), pp. 336–49.

6. A. I. Kirpichnikov, "K voprosu o drevnerusskikh skomorokhakh," *Sbornik otdeleniia russkago iazyka i slovesnosti Imperatorskoi Akademii Nauk* 52, no. 5 (1891); A. Sobolevskii, "K voprosu drevne-russkikh skomorokhakh, A. I. Kirpichnikova," *Zhivaia starina* 3 (1893): 255.

7. A. I. Ponomarev, "K poucheniiam o raznykh istinakh very i zhizni," in *Pamiatniki drevne-russkoi tserkovno-uchitel'noi literatury*, vol. 3 (St. Petersburg, 1897), p. 298.

8. D. Tschizewskij, ed., *Die Nestor-Chronik* (Wiesbaden, 1969), p. 166. English translation by S. H. Cross and O. P. Sherbowitz-Wetzor, *The Russian Primary Chronicle* (Cambridge, Mass., 1953), p. 147.

9. Tschizewskij, *Die Nestor-Chronik*, pp. 163, 165; Cross, *The Russian Primary Chronicle*, pp. 146, 147, and p. 265, n. 209.

10. Tschizewskij, *Die Nestor-Chronik*, p. 187; Cross, *The Russian Primary Chronicle*, p. 161.

11. Findeizen, *Ocherki po istorii muzyki v Rossii*, 1: 59–60.

12. On early Slavonic music see G. Vernadsky, *The Origins of Russia* (Oxford, 1959), pp. 154–61.

13. F. Buslaev, *O vliianii Khristianstva na slavianskii iazyk* (Moscow, 1848), pp. 109, 113. According to F. Slawski (*Slownik etymologiczny iezyka polskiego*, vol. 1 [Cracow, 1952–56], p. 379), *gusla* in Old Polish meant "divination" (fortune telling) or "superstition." A dialectical variant, *guslic*, meant (by the fifteenth century) "to bewitch" or "to tell fortunes."

14. K. W. Wojcicki, *Historya literatury polskiej w zarysach*, vol. 1 (Warsaw, 1859), p. 4. The anonymous Polish chronicler, "Gallus," describes the social upheaval in Poland directed against the church, which allegedly followed the death of Boleslaw I in 1025. Gallus, however, does not implicate pagan priests in this violent popular reaction; "Galli Chronicon," *Monumenta Poloniae Historica* (henceforth cited as *MPH*), vol. 1 (Warsaw, 1960), pp. 415–17. An entry in the Primary

Chronicle for the year 1030 reveals that following the death of Boleslaw the Great, there was considerable unrest in Poland, as the people rose up against their bishops, priests, and boyars, killing many of them. There is no suggestion here that pagan priests instigated the political upheaval (Tschiżewskij, *Die Nestor-Chronik*, p. 146). Both Gallus and the Primary Chronicle quite erroneously associate the social disorders with the death of Boleslaw I in 1025, when in fact it was the death of Mieszko II in 1034 that seems to have signaled the beginning of the pagan reaction in Poland. *The Cambridge Histry of Poland*, vol. 1 (Cambridge, 1950), pp. 35–36.

15. Wojcicki, *Historya literatury polskiej w zarysach*, 1: 35.

16. Findeizen, *Ocherki po istorii muzyki v Rossii*, 1: 30.

17. Buslaev, *O vliianii Khristianstva na slavianskii iazyk*, p. 70.

18. N. D. Chechulin, *Goroda moskovskago gosudarstva v XVI veke* (St. Petersburg, 1889), pp. 163, n. 1; 181–82, n. 2; 197–98, n. 1; 253–54, n. 1.

19. *Entsiklopedicheskii slovar'*, vol. 27 (St. Petersburg, 1899), pp. 294–95. An excellent account of the spread of this commemorative feast among the Slavs is given by F. Miklosich in his "Die Rusalien," *Sitzungsberichte der Kaiserlichen Akademie der Wissenchaften* (Philosophisch-Historische Classe) 46 (1864): 386–405.

20. B. A. Rybakov, "Kalendar' IV veka iz zemli Polian," *Sovetskaia arkheologiia* 4 (1962): 66–89.

21. P. P. Chubinskii, ed., *Trudy etnografichesko-statisticheskoi ekspeditsii v zapadno-russkii krai*, vol. 3 (St. Petersburg, 1872), pp. 187–92; P. V. Shein, comp. and ed., *Velikoruss v svoikh pesniakh, obriadakh, obychaiahk, verovaniiakh, skazkakh, legendakh i t. p.*, vol. 1, pt. 1 (St. Petersburg, 1898), pp. 344–45 and 349–66.

22. One scholar does take issue with the purported close identification between the *skomorokhi* and the *Rusalii*, maintaining that with the single exception of the *Azbukovnik* (in which one finds *"rusaliia = igry skomorosheskiia"*), whenever the two appear in a series they are simply being enumerated and not identified. N. I. Korobka, "K izucheniu malorusskikh koliadok," *Izvestiia otdeleniia russkago iazyka i slovesnosti Imperatorskoi Akademii Nauk* 8, no. 3 (1902): 265–66.

23. A. N. Veselovskii, "Genvarskiia rusalii i gotskiia igry v Vizantii," *Zhurnal ministerstva narodnago prosveshcheniia* 9 (1885): 13.

24. Ibid. See also P. A. Lavrovskii, "Opisanie semi rukopisei Imperatorskoi S.-Petergsburgskoi Publichnoi Biblioteke," *Chteniia v Imperatorskom obshchestve istorii i drevnostei rossiiskikh pri Moskovskom universitete* 4 (1858): pt. 3, p. 22.

25. *Zapiski Imperatorskago moskovskago arkheologicheskago instituta imeni Imperatora Nikolaia II* 18 (1913): 267. The "Life of St. Nifont" circulated widely in Kievan Rus' prior to the Mongol conquest. The "Slovo" dealing with *Rusalii* became separated from the "Life" sometime in the late fourteenth or early fifteenth century and has survived independently since.

26. A. N. Veselovskii, *Razyskaniia v oblasti russkago dukhovnago*

stikha, pts. VI–X in *Sbornik otdeleniia russkago iazyka i slovesnosti Imperatorskoi Akademii Nauk* 32, no. 4 (1883): 205.

27. Tschiżewskij, *Die Nestor-Chronik*, p. 77; Cross, *The Russian Primary Chronicle*, p. 93.

28. The *volkhvy* have received little attention from Russian scholars. No comprehensive study of the pagan priesthood of Kievan Rus' has ever been made. They are discussed briefly by Vernadsky, *The Origins of Russia*, pp. 124–27, and passim. See also E. E. Golubinskii, *Istoriia russkoi tserkvi*, vol. 1, pt. 1, 2d ed. (Moscow, 1901), pp. 177, 211–14; and G. P. Fedotov, *The Russian Religious Mind: Kievan Christianity, the Tenth to the Thirteenth Centuries* (New York, 1960), pp. 344–47.

29. Vernadsky, *The Origins of Russia*, pp. 293–95, 125, 191.

30. Tschiżewskij, *Die Nestor-Chronik*, pp. 37–38; Cross, *The Russian Primary Chronicle*, p. 69.

31. Tschiżewskij, *Die Nestor-Chronik*, pp. 144, 170–71, 175; Cross, *The Russian Primary Chronicle*, pp. 134, 150–54.

32. Tschiżewskij, *Die Nestor-Chronik*, pp. 172–73; Cross, *The Russian Primary Chronicle*, p. 151–52.

33. A. S. Orlov, V. P. Adrianova-Peretts, and N. K. Gudzii, eds., *Istoriia russkoi literatury*, vol. 1 (Moscow-Leningrad, 1941), pp. 83–86. On Bogomilism in Russia see D. Obolensky, *The Bogomils* (Cambridge, 1948), pp. 277–83.

34. Vernadsky, *The Origins of Russia*, p. 311.

35. Ibid., pp. 310–11.

36. On the phenomenon of *dvoeverie*, or the coexistence of paganism and Christianity during the Kievan period, see E. Anichkov, *Iazychestvo i drevniaia Rus'* (St. Petersburg, 1914); also N. M. Gal'kovskii, *Borba khristianstva s ostatkami iazychestva v drevnei Rusi*, vol. 1 (Kharkov, 1916).

37. A. S. Pavlov, ed., "Pamiatniki drevne-russkago kanonicheskago prava," *Russkaia istoricheskaia biblioteka* 6 (1908): 18.

38. Y. Arbatsky, *Etiudy po istorii russkoi muzyki* (New York, 1956), p. 136; Vernadsky, *The Origins of Russia*, p. 156.

39. K. M. Obolenskii, ed., *Letopisets Pereiaslavlia-Suzdal'skago* (Moscow, 1851), p. 47. For an interpretive analysis of this mysterious passage, which is, in fact, a description of the preparatory or first stage of a Mordvinian communal worship service, see my article "The Pagan Priests of Early Russia: Some New Insights," *Slavic Review* 33 (1974): 259–66.

40. F. Buslaev, ed., *Istoricheskaia khrestomatiia tserkovnoslavianskago i drevne-russkago iazykov* (Moscow, 1861), p. 381.

41. Simon Azarin, *Kniga o chudesakh pr. Sergiia*, ed. S. O. Platonov (St. Petersburg, 1888), pp. 46–47.

42. Shein, *Velikoruss v svoikh pesniakh*, 1: 483.

43. *Stoglav*, chap. 41, ques. 16.

44. A. D. Grigor'ev, comp. and ed., *Arkhangel'skiia byliny i istoricheskiia pesni*, vol. 1 (Moscow, 1904), pp. 376–81.

45. H. Thurston and D. Attwater, eds., *Butler's Lives of the Saints,*

vol. 3 (New York, 1962), pp. 259–60. With respect to the popular legends about the two saints that eventually surfaced in Russia, see A. A. Morozov, "Skomorokhi na severe," in *Sever: al'manakh arkhangel'skogo otdeleniia soiuza sovetskikh pisatelei* (Arkhangel'sk, 1946), pp. 233–34.

46. Chubinskii, *Trudy etnografichesko-statisticheskoi ekspeditsii,* 3: 186–87; special *Rusaliia* songs, pp. 187–92. See also V. Petrov, "The Festival of the Rusalky or Mavky," in *Ukraine: A Concise Encyclopaedia,* vol. 1 (Toronto, 1963), p. 358.

47. *Stoglav,* chap. 41, ques. 23.

48. Veselovskii, *Razyskaniia v oblasti russkago dukhovnago stikha,* p. 207.

49. Even as late as the early twentieth century, fragments of this drama had apparently been preserved in the more remote rural districts of Russia. In the village of Spassk, Tambov Province, N. N. Evreinov witnessed a play called "Parting with the *rusalka,*" which was performed at sunset. Significantly, the play was performed around the time of the *Radunitsa,* or the day set aside for the commemoration of dead ancestors. *Istoriia russkogo teatra s drevneishikh vremen do 1917 goda* (New York, 1955), p. 35.

50. An excellent description of the *Koliada* in its earliest manifestations can be found in V. Petrov, "Koliada: the Koliadky and the Shchedrivky," in *Ukraine: A Concise Encyclopaedia,* 1: 354–57.

51. Shein, *Velikoruss v svoikh pesniakh,* 1: 304–9, 314–27; Chubinskii, *Trudy etnografichesko-statisticheskoi ekspeditsii,* 3: 264 ff.

52. Shein, *Velikoruss v svoikh pesniakh,* 1: 317, No. 1070.

53. Chubinskii, *Trudy etnografichesko-statisticheskoi ekspeditsii,* 3: 427–31, 478–79.

54. Petrov, "Koliada," p. 355; Sokolov, *Russian Folklore,* pp. 180–81.

55. Chubinskii, *Trudy etnografichesko-statisticheskoi ekspeditsii,* 3: 265–66.

56. N. N. Evreinov saw a modern version of this ancient *Koliada* play in December of 1915 in the village of Babino in Belorussia. The part of the *mikhonosha* was played by a *ded,* or grandfather. There was a *mekhonosha,* however, who was entrusted with collecting the donations made by the onlookers at the conclusion of the play and placing these in his sack. A small boy clad in goat skin impersonated the goat, and a chorus of musicians narrated the action. Evreinov, *Istoriia russkogo teatra,* pp. 29–32.

57. Ibid., p. 28.

58. Ibid., pp. 29–30; Vernadsky, *The Origins of Russia,* p. 154; Petrov, "Koliada," p. 356.

59. Veselovskii, *Razyskaniia v oblasti russkago dukhovnago stikha,* p. 210.

60. A. P. Evgen'ev and B. N. Putilov, eds., *Drevnie rossiiskie stikhotvoreniia sobrannye Kirsheiu Danilovym* (Moscow-Leningrad, 1958), pp. 17–22. Veselovskii (*Razyskaniia v oblasti russkago dukhovnago stikha,* p. 216) regards this *skomorokh* song about Gost' Terentii and his ailing wife as a parody of the goat-grain *koliadka.*

61. W. Stscherbakiwskyj, "The Early Ukrainian Social Order As Reflected in Ukrainian Wedding Customs," *Slavonic and East European Review* 31 (1953): 325–52; L. Niederle, *Byt' i kul'tura drevnikh slavian* (Prague, 1924), pp. 28–38; Sokolov, *Russian Folklore*, pp. 203–23.

62. For surviving nineteenth-century wedding customs and songs from Great Russia see Shein, *Velikoruss v svoikh pesniakh*, vol. 1, pt. 2; for Ukrainian wedding customs from the period see Chubinskii, *Trudy etnografichesko-statisticheskoi ekspeditsii*, vol. 4 (St. Petersburg, 1877), pp. 52–696.

63. P. Morozov, "Narodnaia drama," in *Istoriia russkago teatra*, ed. V. V. Kallash and N. E. Yefros, vol. 1. (Moscow, 1914), p. 8.

64. Tschiževskij, *Die Nestor-Chronik*, pp. 12–13; Cross, *The Russian Primary Chronicle*, p. 56. The festival, or games, alluded to here by the chronicler is obviously the *Kupalo*, which is related to the *Rusaliia* and is celebrated on 24 June. *Kupalo*, as Rybakov has demonstrated ("Kalendar' IV veka iz zemli Polian," p. 80) can, like *Rusaliia*, be traced to the fourth century A.D. Even to this day it has preserved some of the sexual overtones for which it was well known and vigorously condemned in Kievan times. See also F. Kuzela, "The Rite of Kupalo," in *Ukraine: A Concise Encyclopaedia*, 1: 330–31.

65. A good description of the magic and its use in the wedding ceremony can be found in Sokolov, *Russian Folklore*, pp. 204–7.

66. According to Elsa Mahler, "Der Družka scheint ein direkter Nachfolger der 'Skomorochi' zu sein." *Die russischen dörflichen Hochzeitsgebräuche* (Berlin, 1960), p. 140.

67. Chap. 41, ques. 16.

68. Shein, *Velikoruss v svoikh pesniakh*, vol. 1, pt. 2, p. 483; examples of prescribed wedding incantations appear on pp. 456–58. See also A. K. Moreeva's informative article on traditional Russian wedding incantations, "Traditsionnye formuly v prigovorakh svadebnykh druzhek," *Khudozhestvennyi fol'klor* 2–3 (1927): 122–29.

69. V. Varentsov, comp., *Sbornik pesen samarskago kraia* (St. Petersburg, 1862), pp. 168–70.

70. Chubinskii, *Trudy etnografichesko-statisticheskoi ekspeditsii*, 4: 465, 580.

71. Niederle, *Byt' i kul'tura drevnikh slavian*, p. 38.

72. Buslaev, *Istoricheskaia khrestomatiia*, pp. 382–83.

73. Tschiževskij, *Die Nestor-Chronik*, pp. 114–16; Cross, *The Russian Primary Chronicle*, pp. 116–17. As was indicated earlier in this chapter, the *volkhvy*, the official spokesmen of this paganism, did not disappear. Some even survived into the thirteenth century; we learn from an entry in the First Novgorod Chronicle that in 1227 four *volkhvy* were burned in the courtyard of the prince's residence for practicing magic in Novgorod. *Polnoe sobranie russkikh letopisei* (hereafter cited as *PSRL*), vol. 3: *Novgorodskaia pervaia letopis'* (St. Petersburg, 1841), p. 42.

74. Most of these negative references to the *skomorokhi* are cited in abbreviated form in I. I. Sreznevskii, *Materialy dlia slovaria drevne-*

russkago iazyka po pis'mennym pamiatnikam, reprint ed., vol. 3 (Graz, 1956), p. 379.

75. These canons had been handed down by the Trullan (Constantinople, 692), and other church councils. J. D. Mansi, ed., *Sacrorum consiliorum nova et amplissima collectio,* vol. 2 (Graz, 1960), canons 51, 61, and 62, pp. 967, 970–71. See also A. Nicoll, *Masks, Mimes and Miracles* (New York, 1931), pp. 145–68.

76. In addition to the noun, the verb *shpil'maniti* and the adjective *shpil'manskyi* occur in the same text. Sreznevskii, *Materialy dlia slovaria drevne-russkago iazyka,* 3: 1598; Vasmer, *Russisches Etymologisches Wörterbuch,* 3: 426. See also I. K. Grot, "O slove 'shpil'man' v starinnykh russkikh pamiatnykakh," *Russkii filologicheskii vestnik* 1, no. 1 (1879): 35–38.

77. A. Kh. Vostokov, *Slovar' tserkovno-slavianskago iazyka,* vol. 2 (St. Petersburg, 1861), p. 576; Veselovskii, *Razyskaniia v oblasti russkago dukhovnago stikha,* p. 177.

78. F. Vogt, *Leben und Dichten der deutschen Spielleute im Mittelalter* (Halle, 1876), p. 7. See also V. F. Miller, *Ocherki russkoi narodnoi slovesnosti,* vol. 1: *Byliny* (Moscow, 1897), p. 53.

79. P. Piper, *Die Spielmannsdichtung,* vol. 1 (Berlin-Stuttgart, 1887), p. 12.

80. On Kiev's relations with the West see G. Vernadsky, *A History of Russia,* vol. 2: *Kievan Russia* (New Haven, 1948), pp. 337–47; also F. Dvornik's *The Making of Central and Eastern Europe* (London, 1949), pp. 236–61. One possible reason why so little is known from native sources about Kiev's relations with medieval Europe is the apparent reluctance on the part of the early chroniclers to write about the Latin West for religious and ideological reasons. M. Ye. Shaitan, "Germaniia i Kiev v XI v.," *Letopis' zaniatii* 34 (1927): 3.

81. For the text of the Raffelstätter customs statute see *Monumenta Germaniae Historica* (hereafter cited as *MGH*), *Leges,* vol. 3 (Stuttgart-Vaduz, 1965), pp. 480–81.

82. V. Vasil'evskii, "Drevniaia torgovlia Kieva s Regensburgom," *Zhurnal ministerstva narodnago prosveshcheniia* 258 (1888): 132.

83. Shaitan, "Germaniia i Kiev v XI v.," p. 4.

84. T. Ediger, *Russlands älteste Beziehungen zu Deutschland, Frankreich und die römische Kurie* (Halle, 1911), pp. 104–7, 110, 112.

85. M. N. Berezhkov, *O torgovle Rusi s Ganzoi do kontsa XV veka* (St. Petersburg, 1879), pp. 78, 86, and passim.

86. A somewhat different interpretation of Olga's 957 visit to Constantinople has recently been advanced by M. Chubatyi, who sees it as first and foremost an attempt on Olga's part to negotiate a marriage alliance between her son Sviatoslav and a Porphyrogenita princess. *Istoriia khrystyianstva na Rusy-Ukrajini,* vol. 1: *Vid pochatku do 1353 r.* (New York, 1965), pp. 180–81.

87. *MGH,* Scriptores, vol. 1 (Hannover, 1826), pp. 624–25; Chubatyi, *Istoriia khrystyianstva na Rusy-Ukrajini,* pp. 182–84.

88. Lambert (Lampert) Hersfeld, *Annales* in *MGH, Scriptores*, vol. 3 (Hannover, 1838), p. 63.

89. Letter to Emperor Henry II of Germany, c. 1008, *MPH*, 1: 224–25.

90. Thietmar of Meresburg, *Chronicon*, ed. F. Kurze (Hannover, 1889), p. 258; Adam of Bremen, *Gesta Hammaburgensis ecclesiae Pontificum*, ed. G. H. P. Pertz (Hannover, 1846), p. 62.

91. Dvornik, *The Making of Central and Eastern Europe*, pp. 242 ff.

92. Obolenskii, *Letopisets Pereiaslavlia-Suzdal'skago*, p. 3.

93. Nicoll, *Masks, Mimes and Miracles*, pp. 143–51. For a graphic description of the genealogy of the Byzantine mime see the foldout chart at the end of H. Reich, *Der Mimus*, vol. 1, pt. 2 (Berlin, 1903).

94. Constantine Porphyrogenitus, *De Ceremoniis Aulae Byzantinae*, in J. P. Migne, *Patrologia Graeca*, vol. 112 (Paris, 1897), p. 1111. See also I. E. Zabelin, *Istoriia russkoi zhizni*, vol. 2 (Moscow, 1912), pp. 187–89.

95. T. T. Rice, *A Concise History of Russian Art* (New York, 1963), p. 25.

96. Nestor, "Zhitie prepodobnago otsa nashego igumena pecherskago, opisannoe prep. Nestorom," *Uchenyia zapiski vtorago otdeleniia Imperatorskoi Akademii Nauk* 2, no. 2 (1856): 178.

97. A. I. Kirpichnikov, "K voprosu o drevnerusskikh skomorokhakh," p. 11.

98. Feodosii Pecherskii, *Sochineniia*, ed. I. I. Sreznevskii in *Uchenyia zapiski vtorago otdeleniia Imperatorskoi Akademii Nauk* 2, no. 2 (1856): 195.

99. H. Frisk, *Griechisches etymologisches Wörterbuch*, vol. 2 (Heidelberg, 1970), pp. 410–11.

100. Recently an opposing view has been expressed by a Soviet scholar who argues that, "An analysis of the architectural composition of the Kievan Sophia leads to the conclusion that the latter was built by Russian masters." N. I. Brunov, "Kievskaia Sofiia—drevneishii pamiatnik russkoi kamennoi arkhitektury," *Vizantiiskii vremennik* 3 (1950): 154–200. See also O. Povstenko, *The Cathedral of St. Sophia in Kiev*, published as vol. 3–4 (1954) of *The Annals of the Ukrainian Academy of Arts and Science in the U.S.*, p. 141.

101. V. N. Lazarev, "Novye dannye o mozaikakh i freskakh Sofii Kievskoi," *Vizantiiskii vremennik* 10 (1956): 163–64.

102. Findeizen, *Ocherki po istorii muzyki v Rossii*, 1: 54. See also A. Voyce, *The Art and Architecture of Medieval Russia* (Norman, Okla., 1967), p. 97.

103. Two of the musicians are female. The other instruments represented are the horn, flute, and cymbals.

104. Veselovskii, *Razyskaniia v oblasti russkago dukhovnago stikha*, p. 188.

105. Nicoll, *Masks, Mimes and Miracles*, p. 160.

106. S. A. Vysotskii and I. F. Totskaia, "Novoe o freske 'skomorokhi' v Sofii Kievskoi," in *Kul'tura i iskusstvo drevnei Rusi: sbornik statei v chest' professora M. K. Kargera* (Leningrad, 1967), pp. 50–57.

107. Ibid., p. 57.

108. F. A. Wright, trans., *The Works of Luitprand of Cremona* (New York, 1930), p. 210.

109. The striking colors of the *krotopolie* worn by the *skomorokhi* can be seen in the fourteenth-century miniatures discussed in Chapter 2.

110. Among the wide twelfth-century silver bracelets found in Kiev are several on which *gusli*-playing minstrels are depicted wearing this costume. B. A. Rybakov, *Remeslo drevnei Rusi* (Moscow, 1948), p. 267 and illus. 61, p. 269.

Chapter 2

1. S. I. Smirnov, ed., *Materialy dlia istorii drevne-russkoi pokaiannoi distsipliny* (Moscow, 1912), p. 54.

2. V. Semenov, ed., *Drevniaia russkaia Pchela po pergamennomu spisku*, in *Sbornik otdeleniia russkago iazyka i slovesnosti Imperatorskoi Akademii Nauk* 54, no. 4 (1893): 361.

3. I. I. Sreznevskii, ed., *Drevnie pamiatniki russkago pisma i iazyka X–XIV vekov* (St. Petersburg, 1882), p. 56.

4. Findeizen, *Ocherki po istorii muzyki v Rossii*, 1: 105.

5. Ibid., map insert following p. 144. Findeizen based his ingenious map showing the villages and hamlets that once bore or still bear the name of the *skomorokhi* on surviving sixteenth- and seventeenth-century cadastres and other historical records.

6. Pskov did not gain political independence from Novgorod until 1348.

7. V. V. Stasov, *Slavianskii i vostochnyi ornament po rukopisiam drevniago i novago vremeni* (St. Petersburg, 1887), plate 61, No. 21.

8. N. N. Rozov, "Eshche raz ob izobrazhenii skomorokha na freske v Meletove. K voprosu o sviazakh monumental'noi zhivopisi s miniatiuroi i ornamentom," in *Drevne-russkoe iskusstvo: khudozhestvennaia kul'tura Pskova* (Moscow, 1968), p. 87.

9. Stasov, *Slavianskii i vostochnyi ornament*, plate 65, Nos. 15, 23 and 16, 17, 24, 25.

10. A. I. Kirpichnikov is of the opinion that the costumes represented in these miniatures resemble closely those worn by the *Spielmänner*. "K voprosu o drevnerusskikh skomorokhakh," p. 13.

11. Stasov, *Slavianskii i vostochnyi ornament*, plate 65, Nos. 33, 35.

12. Ibid., plate 67, No. 2.

13. Ibid., plate 68, Nos. 19, 25.

14. N. D. Uspenskii, *Drevne russkoe pevcheskoe iskusstvo* (Moscow, 1965), p. 52.

15. Rozov, "Eshche raz ob izobrazhenii skomorokha," illus. p. 91.

16. Stasov, *Slavianskii i vostochnyi ornament*, plate 85, Nos. 7, 9, 22.

17. A. I. Nekrasov, *Ocherki iz istorii slavianskogo ornamenta: chelovecheskaia figura v russkom teratologicheskom rukopisnom ornamente XIV v.*, Pamiatniki drevnei pis'mennosti i iskusstva, no. 183 (St. Petersburg, 1914), p. 70; Rozov, "Eshche raz ob izobrazhenii skomorokha," p. 92.

18. In addition to these there are several others which Stasov has reproduced in his book *Slavianskii i vostochnyi ornament* and which are similar to those discussed here. They appear in a fourteenth-century *Evangelie nedel'noe* from Novgorod (plate 69, Nos. 2, 8, 10) and a Novgorodian psalter from this same period (plate 71, No. 3).

19. The *Zlataia tsep*, dating from this same period, is identical in content to the *Zlatoust*. Sreznevskii, *Drevnie pamiatniki russkago pisma i iazyka*, p. 292.

20. *Zlatoust* (Moscow, 1909), pp. 114, 115, 115b.

21. A. Nasonov, *Pskovskie letopisi*, Part 1, Slavica-Reprint no. 2 (The Hague, 1967), pp. 61, 67.

22. Iu. N. Dmitriev, "Melëtovskie freske i ikh znachenie dlia istorii drevnerusskoi literatury," *Trudy otdela drevnerusskoi literatury* 8 (1951): 403–12.

23. Ibid., p. 410; D. S. Likhachev, "Drevneishee russkoe izobrazhenie skomorokha i ego znachenie dlia istorii skomoroshestva," in *Problemy sravnitel'noi filologii: sbornik statei k 70-letiiu V. M. Zhirmunskogo* (Moscow-Leningrad, 1965), p. 462.

24. Dmitriev, "Melëtovskie freske," p. 412.

25. Likhachev, "Drevneishee russkoe izobrazhenie skomorokha," pp. 463–64; see p. 466 for a brief explanation of the origin of *Limonis*. The full Old Slavonic text of the tale is on p. 464.

26. Ibid.

27. According to Rozov ("Eshche raz ob izobrazhenii skomorokha," p. 94) the wide-rimmed hat that he is wearing is not native but Byzantine in origin, and it is similar to that worn by Byzantine clerics during this period.

28. Rozov, "Eshche raz ob izobrazhenii skomorokha," p. 94.

29. Ibid., p. 95, and illus. p. 88, also that following p. 94.

30. Likhachev, "Drevneishee russkoe izobrazhenie skomorokha," p. 466; Rozov, "Eshche raz ob izobrazhenii skomorokha," p. 94.

31. Likhachev, "Drevneishee russkoe izobrazhenie skomorokha," p. 466.

32. In a "poslanie" of Archbishop Gennadii of Novgorod on the occasion of the official condemnation by the church of the Judaizer heresy in 1490, there is reference to the desecration by the heretics of the Virgin Mary's icon. N. A. Kazakova and Ia. S. Lur'e, *Antifeodal' nye ereticheskie dvizheniia na Rusi XIV veka* (Moscow-Leningrad, 1955), p. 380.

33. V. Malinin, *Starets Eleazorova monastyria Filofei i ego poslaniia* (Kiev, 1901), p. 3 of Appendix.

34. N. Andreyev, "Pagan and Christian Elements in Old Russia," *Slavic Review* 21 (1962): 18, n. 7.

35. The full title of this *gramota* is: "Zhalovannaia gramota Dmitrovskago Kniazia Iuriia Vasil' evicha, o tom chtoby v Inobozheskikh selakh Troitskago Sergieva monastyria kniazheskie iezdoki ne stavilis, kromi iedushchikh po podorozhnym, i skomorokhi ne igraly." *Akty, sobrannye v bibliotekakh rossiiskoi imperii arkheograficheskoiu ekspeditsieiu Im-*

peratorskoi Akademii Nauk, vol. 1: *1294–1598* (St. Petersburg, 1836), p. 62.

36. Ibid., pp. 117, 120–22, 139–41, 256–57, 267.

37. Ibid., pp. 153–54, 179–81, 206–7.

38. "Tri sviatitel'skiia poucheniia dukhovenstvu i mirianam, o raznykh predmetakh tserkovnoi distsipliny," *Russkaia istoricheskaia biblioteka* 6 (1908): 925–26.

39. V. F. Rzhiga, "Neizdanye sochineniia Maksima Greka," *Byzantinoslavica* 6 (1935–36): 105–9.

40. V. Zhmakin, *Mitropolit Daniil i ego sochinennia* (Moscow, 1881), p. 21 in Appendix.

41. Sigismund von Herberstein, *Rerum moscoviticarum commentarii* (Antwerp, 1557), p. 65b; *Description of Moscow and Muscovy*, ed. B. Picard, trans. J. B. C. Grundy (New York, 1969), p. 19. Grundy's translation is not very accurate.

42. E. K. Chambers, *The Mediaeval Stage*, vol. 1 (London, 1903), p. 48.

43. Zhmakin, *Mitropolit Daniil i ego sochinennia*, p. 21 in Appendix.

44. Findeizen, *Ocherki po istorii muzyki v Rossii*, 1, insert map following p. 144.

45. V. I. Petukhov, "Svedeniia o skomorokhakh v pistsovykh, perepisnykh i tamozhennykh knigakh XVI–XVII vv.," *Trudy Moskovskogo istoriko-arkhivnogo instituta* 16 (1961): 401–19.

46. H. L. Eaton, "Cadastres and Censuses in Muscovy," *Slavic Review* 21 (1967): 55.

47. E. N. Kolotinskaia, *Pravovye osnovy zemel'nogo kadastra v Rossii* (Moscow, 1968), p. 29; H. L. Eaton, "Early Russian Censuses and the Population of Muscovy, 1550–1650" (Ph.D. diss., University of Illinois, 1970), pp. 12, 15.

48. Ibid., p. 19.

49. A virtually complete list of published sixteenth- and seventeenth-century cadastres and censuses can be found in S. V. Voznesenskii's *Materialy dlia bibliografii po istorii narodov SSSR XVI–XVII vv.*, in *Trudy istoriko-arkheograficheskogo instituta* (1933): 19–23, 190–96.

50. A. I. Iakovlev, ed., *Tamozhennye knigi moskovskogo gosudarstva XVII veka*, 3 vols. (Moscow-Leningrad, 1950–51).

51. Arkheograficheskaia kommissiia, *Novgorodskiia pistsovyia knigi*, vol. 1 (St. Petersburg, 1859), pp. 50, 65, 73, 208; vol. 2 (St. Petersburg, 1862), pp. 446, 474, 476, 499, 581, 631; vol. 4 (St. Petersburg, 1886), pp. 211, 480; vol. 5 (St. Petersburg, 1905), p. 694; vol. 6 (St. Petersburg, 1910), pp. 130, 219, 328, 466, 493.

52. Findeizen, *Ocherki po istorii muzyki v Rossii*, 1, map insert following p. 144.

53. "Pistsovye knigi goroda Kazani 1565–68 gg. i 1646 g.," in *Materialy po istorii narodov SSSR*, vol. 2: *Materialy po istorii tatarskoi ASSR* (Leningrad, 1932), pp. 14, 18, 19 (female *skomorokh*), 23, 24, 33, 36, 43.

54. *Spisok s pistovoi i mezhevoi knigi goroda Sviiazhska i uezda* (Kazan, 1909), pp. 24, 47; K. N. Shchepetev, "Torgovopromyshlennaia

deiatel'nost' i rassloenie krest'ianstva v votchinakh Cherkasskikh v XVII v.," in *K voprosu o pervonachal'nom nakoplenii v Rossii (XVII–XVIII vv.)* (Moscow, 1958), p. 58; N. A. Naidenov, ed., "Dozornaia kniga 1624 g.," in *Tobol'sk: materialy dlia istorii goroda XVII i XVIII stoletei* (Moscow, 1885), pp. 7–8.

55. Petukhov, "Svedenie o skomorokhakh," p. 413.

56. Ibid.

57. *Novgorodskiia pistsovyia knigi*, 1: 152, 156, 219, 238, 658, 756–57, 758, 760, 788, 817; 2: 43, 213, 416, 508, 548, 591, 642, 704, 719, 821, 826–27; 3: 494, 518, 528, 556, 882–83; 4: 117, 291, 379, 401, 402–3; 5: 134, 147, 191, 207, 240, 263. M. A. Obolenskii, ed., *Perepisnaia okladnaia kniga po Novgorodu vot'skoi piatiny, 1500 godu*, in *Vremennik Imperatorskago moskovskago obshchestva istorii i drevnostei rossiiskikh* 11 (1851): 112 in *Materialy*; 12 (1852): 3 in *Materialy*.

58. *Novgorodskiia pistsovyia knigi*, 3: 882–83.

59. Chechulin, *Goroda moskovskago gosudarstva*, p. 51, nn. 1, 2, 3.

60. Ibid., p. 37.

61. Ibid., pp. 67, n. 3 and 68, n. 1.

62. Petukhov, "Svedenie o skomorokhakh," p. 412; Chechulin, *Goroda moskovskago gosudarstva*, pp. 157, 163, n. 1.

63. N. V. Kalachov, ed., *Pistsovyia knigi XVI veka*, vol. 1, pt. 1 (St. Petersburg, 1872), pp. 628, n. 13; 629 n., 632, nn. 1, 8; Chechulin, *Goroda moskovskago gosudarstva*, p. 158.

64. Kalachov, *Pistsovyia knigi XVI veka*, vol. 2 (St. Petersburg, 1877), pp. 1082, 1090; Chechulin, *Goroda moskovskago gosudarstva*, p. 260.

65. "Pistsovye knigi goroda Kazani 1565–68 gg. i 1646 g.," pp. 14, 18, 19, 23, 24, 33, 36, 43.

66. Chechulin, *Goroda moskovskago gosudarstva*, p. 206.

67. The female *skomorokh*, Ovdot'ia by name, is recorded in a cadastre from Kazan from 1565–68. "Pistsovye knigi goroda Kazani 1565–68 gg. i 1646 g.," p. 18. The *skomorokh's* son who became a priest was from Gdov, a suburb of Pskov. V. Nechaev, ed., *Pskov i ego prigorody*, bk. 1, in *Sbornik moskovskago arkhiva ministerstva iustitsii*, vol. 5 (Moscow, 1913), p. 218.

68. Originally a small auxilliary force used chiefly to complement the mounted army of *dvoriane* and *deti boiarskie*, the *strel'tsy* grew in size and influence until by 1632 they outnumbered the mounted army. A series of uprisings in the late 1600s, some with political overtones, ultimately led to the disbanding of the *strel'tsy* by Peter the Great in 1698.

69. "Pistsovye knigi goroda Kazani 1565–68 gg. i 1646 g.," p. 36.

70. One *sazhen'* equals approximately seven feet or 2.133 meters.

71. Nechaev, *Pskov i ego prigorody*, p. 431.

72. Arkheograficheskaia kommissiia, *Pistsovaia i perepisnaia knigi XVII veka po Nizhnemu Novgorodu* (St. Petersburg, 1898), p. 143.

73. Two other *skomorokhi-strel'tsy* appear in a cadastre from Sviiazhsk from 1565–67 (*Spisok s pistsovoi i mezhevoi knigi goroda Sviiazhska i uezda*, pp. 24, 47), and four are recorded in Voronezh in 1615 (*Materialy dlia istorii voronezhskoi gubernii*, vol. 2 [Voronezh, 1891], pp. 5, 12, 13,

14, as cited in Petukhov, "Svedenie o skomorokakh," p. 415). There is one instance in the cadastres of a *skomorokh*-Cossack. These so-called inner Cossacks (not to be confused with the frontier Cossacks) were, like the *strel'tsy*, exempt from taxes and lived in specially designated enclaves of the town (Naidenov, *Tobol'sk*, p. 8). There is also an entry in a 1625 cadastre from Torzhok that describes a tax-exempt household owned by a *skomorokh* who was neither a *strelets* nor a Cossack, but a *pushkar*. The *pushkari*, or gunners, were a military corporation much like the *strel'tsy* ("Pistsovaia kniga g. Torzhka i posada," in *Pamiatnaia knizhka tverskoi gubernii na 1865 god* [Tver, 1865], pt. 4, p. 10).

74. *Spisok s pistsovoi i mezhevoi knigi goroda Sviiazhska i uezda*, p. 47.

75. Nechaev, *Pskov i ego prigorody*, p. 11. Between the fifteenth and the seventeenth century, the *grivna* was equivalent to approximately one-tenth of a ruble.

76. *Pistsovaia i perepisnaia knigi XVII veka po Nizhnemu Novgorodu*, p. 279.

77. *Perepisnaia kniga goroda Moskvy 1638 goda* (Moscow, 1881), p. 244.

78. Iakovlev, *Tamozhennye knigi moskovskogo gosudarstva XVII veka*, 1: 265.

79. S. Shumakov, *Uglicheskii akty (1400–1749)* (Moscow, 1899), pp. 118–25. The document is entitled "Myrovaia po delu o Vesegonskoi tamge 1563 goda."

80. Kalachov, *Pistsovyia knigi XVI veka*, vol. 1, pt. 1, p. 315, n. 10.

81. Ibid., p. 632, nn. 1, 8.

82. Iakovlev, *Tamozhennye knigi moskovskogo gosudarstva XVII veka*, 1: 12; pp. 199 and 299 for additional examples.

83. Ibid., 3: 47.

84. Nechaev, *Pskov i ego prigorody*, p. 19.

85. *Viazemskie pistsovye knigi, 1627 g.*, in *Trudy tul'skoi gubernskoi uchenoi arkhivnoi komissii*, bk. 1 (Tula, 1915), p. 48.

86. N. A. Naidenov, ed., "Pistsovaia kniga 1628 goda" in *Viatka: materialy dlia istorii goroda XVII i XVIII stoletei* (Moscow, 1887), p. 14. There is a reference on the same page to an empty shop, also in "fish row," belonging to a *skomorokh* named Klimka.

87. Serpukhov—P. Simson, *Istoriia Serpukhova* (Moscow, 1880), p. 334 in Appendix, which contains the full text of the "Sotnia serpukhov-skaia kniazia Funikova 1551 g." (pp. 311–34). Riazan—N. A. Naidenov, ed., "Pistsovaia kniga 1626 goda," in *Riazan': materialy dlia istorii goroda XVI–XVIII stoletei* (Moscow, 1884), p. 14. Viatka—Naidenov, *Viatka*, p. 13.

88. A. P. Proshtein, *Velikii Novgorod v XVI v.* (Khar'kov, 1957), pp. 246, 247, 250, as cited in Petukhov, "Svedenie o skomorokhakh," p. 415.

89. *Novgorodskiia pistsovyia knigi*, 3: 882–83.

90. *Pistsovaia i perepisnaia knigi XVII veka po Nizhnemu Novgorodu*, pp. 108–9.

91. N. A. Naidenov, ed., "Sotnia kniga 1630 goda," in *Ustiug Velikii:*

materialy dlia istorii goroda XVII i XVIII stoletei (Moscow, 1883), p. 17; Naidenov, *Riazan'*, p. 20.

92. V. V. Maikov, ed., *Kniga pistsovaia po Novgorodu Velikomu kontsa XVI v.* (St. Petersburg, 1911), p. xxxiii.

93. See especially the *bylina* "Dobrynia v ot'ezde" in A. E. Gruzinskii, ed., *Pesni sobrannyia P. N. Rybnikovym*, 2d ed., vol. 1 (Moscow, 1909), No. 26, pp. 162–72.

94. Naidenov, *Viatka*, p. 8.

95. Naidenov, *Riazan'*, p. 20.

96. S. Bogoiavlenskii, ed., "Sotnitsa s mozhaiskikh pistsovykh knig 1544 g. na slobodki luzhkovskago monastyria," *Chteniia v Imperatorskom obshchestve istorii i drevnostei rossiiskikh pri Moskovskom universitete* 4 (1908): 19 (Smes').

97. *Novgorodskiia pistsovyia knigi*, vol. 2, pt. 2, pp. 238, 508.

98. Moscow—*Perepisnaia kniga goroda Moskvy 1638 goda*, pp. 80, 131. Tula—Kalachov, *Pistsovyia knigi XVI veka*, 2: 1090. Nizhnii Novgorod—*Pistsovaia i perepisnaia knigi XVII veka po Nizhnemu Novgorodu*, p. 140.

99. Tula—Kalachov, *Pistsovyia knigi XVI veka*, 2: 1082; I. S. Beliaev, ed., *Raspisi gorodov Tuly i Krapisvny 7137 [1629] g.*, in *Trudy tul'skoi gubernskoi uchenoi arkhivnoi kommissii*, bk. 1 (Tula, 1915), p. 196. Kolomna—Kalachov, *Pistsovyia knigi XVI veka*, 1: 309, n. 20; 310, nn. 1, 2.

100. *Novgorodskiia pistsovyia knigi*, 4: 379 (landed homestead); 291, 402–3 (landless).

101. "Pistsovye knigi goroda Kazani 1565–68 gg. i 1646 g.," p. 43.

102. *PSRL*, 30: *Novgorodskaia vtoraia (arkhivskaia) letopis'* (Moscow, 1965), p. 189.

103. *Perepisnaia kniga goroda Moskvy 1638 goda*, p. 218.

104. V. A. Borisov, *Opisanie goroda Shui i ego okresnostei* (Moscow, 1851), pp. 451–52.

105. Kalachov, *Pistsovyia knigi XVI veka*, 2: 297, n. 1.

106. Kalachov, *Pistsovyia knigi XVI veka*, 2: 310, n. 1; 342, n. 1; 1090; "Pistsovye knigi goroda Kazani 1565–68 gg. i 1646 g.," pp. 14, 18, 19, 33, 36, 43; Chechulin, *Goroda moskovskago gosudarstva*, p. 198, col. 2.

107. *Pistsovaia i perepisnaia knigi XVII veka po Nizhnemu Novgorodu*, pp. 105, 108, 109, 120, 121, 130, 140, 185; *Perepisnaia kniga goroda Moskvy 1638 goda*, pp. 14, 244.

Chapter 3

1. A. A. Zimin, "Skomorokhi v pamiatnikakh publitsistiki i narodnogo tvorchestva XVI veka," in *Iz istorii russkikh literaturnykh otnoshenii XVIII–XX vekov* (Moscow-Leningrad, 1959), p. 337.

2. The short version contains 56 articles; the long version, 231. Both are drafts of the revised *Sudebnik* of 1550. Only the 1589 versions contain clauses, or articles, dealing with *skomorokhi*. Reference here will be

to the latest Soviet edition of the 1589 draft. Akademiia Nauk SSSR, Institut istorii, *Sudebniki XV–XVI vekov* (Moscow-Leningrad, 1952).

3. *Sudebniki XV–XVI vekov*, p. 353.

4. Ibid., p. 384.

5. In an explanatory note to Articles 65–66, the editors of the 1589 *Sudebnik* maintain that the phrase in Article 65 that reads "and his wife nothing" (*a zhene ego nichego*) is a textual error and that it should in fact read "and his wife twice that amount" (*a zhene ego vdvoe*). *Sudebniki XV–XVI vekov*, p. 473.

6. Ibid., p. 383, Article 53.

7. Ibid., Article 57.

8. *Akty, sobrannye v bibliotekakh i arkhivakh rossiiskoi imperii arkheograficheskoiu ekspeditsieiu Imperatorskoi Akademii Nauk*, 1: 267, No. 244.

9. A possible fifth reference to the *skomorokhi* was evidently omitted from the final draft of the *Stoglav*. The reference in question appears in an anonymous document believed to have been used as a basis for some of the council deliberations in 1551. It describes the *skomorokhi* as transforming themselves, figuratively speaking, into demons at wedding celebrations. N. S. Tikhonranov, "Zametka dlia istorii *Stoglava*," *Letopisi russkoi literatury i drevnostei* 5 (1863): pt. 3, p. 138.

10. In chap. 93 they are only mentioned as part of an enumeration of pagan-like festivals in general.

11. Iakovlev, *Tamozhennye knigi moskovskogo gosudarstva XVII veka*, 1: 242, 265.

12. S. H. Baron, ed. and trans., *The Travels of Olearius in Seventeenth-Century Russia* (Stanford, 1967), p. 142.

13. Olearius's illustration is reproduced on p. 79.

14. *Izvestiia Imperatorskago arkheologicheskago obshchestva* 6 (1868): section 2, p. 69.

15. *Rerum moscoviticarum commentarii*, p. 65b; *Descriptions of Moscow and Muscovy*, p. 19.

16. *Akty sobrannye v bibliotekakh*, 1: 62, No. 86.

17. Ibid., pp. 117, 122, 257; also "Ustavnaia gramota posadskim liudiam gor. Shui [July 7, 1606]," in A. I. Iakovlev, ed., *Namestnich'i, gubnyia i zemskiia ustavnyia gramoty moskovskogo gosudarstva* (Moscow, 1909), p. 152.

18. *Akty sobrannye v bibliotekakh*, 1: 153, 180–81.

19. "Usishcha" is apparently an abbreviated version of a longer original, which can be found in Kirsha Danilov's *Sbornik*. The shorter version was first recorded by Grigor'ev in the Pinega region at the turn of the century (1899–1901). A. D. Grigor'ev, comp., *Arkhangel'skiia byliny i istoricheskiia pesni*, 1: 382–92. Reference here will be to the more complete version of Kirsha Danilov. *Drevnie rossiiskie stikhotvoreniia sobrannye Kirsheiu Danilovym*, ed. A. P. Evgen'eva and B. N. Putilov (Moscow-Leningrad, 1958), pp. 279–82, also Appendix, pp. 632–33.

20. V. Chernyshev, "Zametki o russkikh pesniakh," *Slavia* 2 (1932):

178. Chernyshev writes that the *skomorokhi* show themselves to be accomplished comedians and entertainers in this song. Among the songs M. Speranskii regards as indisputably of *skomorokh* origin is "Usishcha." *Byliny*, vol. 1 (Moscow, 1916), p. 282.

21. The *gramota* reads, in part, as follows: "The Muryshkin brothers, with their companions, engage in brigandage day and night in many towns, killing people and burning their homes." N. Aristov, *Ob istoricheskom znachenii russkikh razboinichikh pesen'* (Voronezh, 1875), p. 34.

22. P. Avrich, *Russian Rebels, 1600–1800* (New York, 1972), pp. 65, 79.

23. *Drevnie rossiiskie stikhotvoreniia sobrannye Kirsheiu Danilovym*, pp. 632–33.

24. Ibid., pp. 281–82, ll.71–77, l.99.

25. Ibid., p. 280, ll.15–38.

26. Chernyshev, "Zametki o russkikh pesniakh," p. 178.

27. I. Beliaev, "O skomorokhakh," pp. 83–84, n. 3. The original lines are, "Ai, matushka Likova,/ Prishei k shube rukava!"

28. Ibid., p. 83.

29. An eyewitness account of the events in Moscow in 1648 can be found in L. Loewenson, "The Moscow Rising of 1648," *Slavonic and East European Review* 27 (1948): 152–57; see also the anonymous seventeenth-century chronicle *Novyi letopisets*, in *Vremennik Imperatorskago moskovskago obshchestva istorii i drevnostei rossiiskikh* 17 (1853): 193–94.

30. Avrich, *Russian Rebels*, p. 57; G. V. Lantzeff, *Siberia in the Seventeenth Century* (Berkeley, 1943), p. 85.

31. J. L. H. Keep, "The Decline of the Zemsky Sobor," *Slavonic and East European Review* 36 (1957): 114–15.

32. A. A. Morozov, "Skomorokhi na severe," p. 229. Morozov makes the additional observation that the paganism of the *skomorokhi*, so closely identified with the religion of the masses, took on a socioeconomic significance in the eyes of the authorities, who viewed it as a threat to the feudal culture with which the state was identified. A similar interpretation has recently been put forth by A. A. Belkin, *Russkie skomorokhi*, pp. 73–91.

33. Belkin, pp. 242–43.

34. Maikov, *Kniga pistsovaia po Novgorodu Velikomu kontsa XVI v.*, p. 160.

35. Ibid., pp. 263–64.

36. Ibid., p. 118.

37. P. L. Gusev, ed., "Pistsovaia kniga Velikago Novgoroda 1583–1584 gg.," *Vestnik arkheologii i istorii* 17 (1906): pt. 2, p. 143.

38. B. D. Grekov, ed., *Opis' torgovoi storony v pistsovoi knige po Novgorodu Velikomu* (St. Petersburg, 1912), pp. 68, 34.

39. Ibid., p. 22.

40. N. Findeizen, *Ocherki po istorii muzyki v Rossii*, 1: 150.

41. PSRL, 30: 189.

42. D. N. Al'shits, "Novyi dokument o liudiakh i prikazakh oprichnogo dvora Ivana Groznogo 1572 goda," *Istoricheskii arkhiv* 4 (1949): 3–71. The author maintains that the document at hand proves rather conclusively that the *oprichnina* did not disappear in 1572, as most historians contend, but survived well into the late 1570s (p. 10).

43. Ibid., p. 39.

44. Ibid., p. 13.

45. Anthony Jenkinson, *Early Voyages and Travels to Russia and Persia*, ed. E. D. Morgan and C. H. Coote, vol. 2 (London, 1886), p. 358.

46. Jerome Horsey, *The Travels of Sir Jerome Horsey*, Hakluyt Society Publications, no. 20 (London, 1856), p. 201.

47. Salomon Henning, *Lifflendische Chürlendische Chronica* (Leipzig, 1594), p. 55, as cited in Carl Stief, *Studies in the Russian Historical Song* (Copenhagen, 1953), p. 228.

48. J. L. I. Fennell, trans. and ed., *Prince A. M. Kurbsky's History of Ivan IV* (Cambridge, 1965), pp. 22–23.

49. The *Domostroi* (literally "household manual"), attributed to the priest Sylvester, who was a close advisor to the tsar in the years 1547–53, contains similarly strong language directed against the *skomorokhi*. Among the numerous editions of the *Domostroi*, that of Iakovlev contains the most explicit condemnation of the *skomorokhi* and their audiences. V. A. Iakovlev, ed. *Domostroi*, 2d ed. (Odessa, 1887), pp. 58–59.

50. Fennell, *Prince A. M. Kurbsky's History of Ivan IV*, pp. 180–81.

51. Findeizen, *Ocherki po istorii muzyki v Rossii*, p. 246. Ivan was not the first to use the *skomorokhi* in this fashion. In the late fifteenth century Archbishop Gennadii of Novgorod, in his attempt to humiliate the Judaizer heretics, on one occasion had them paraded through the streets of the city mounted backwards on old nags and dressed up like *skomorokhi*. Each heretic also bore the inscription: "This is Satan's army." P. P., "Shuty i skomorokhi v drevnosti i v noveishee vremia," *Istoricheskii vestnik* 8 (1888): 466–67.

52. Giles Fletcher, *Of the Rus Commonwealth*, ed. A. F. Schmidt (Ithaca, 1966), pp. 146–47.

53. I. E. Zabelin, *Domashnii byt' russkikh tsarits v XVI–XVII st.* (Moscow, 1869), p. 407.

54. *Perepisnaia kniga goroda Moskvy 1638 goda* (Moscow, 1881), p. 218.

55. Zabelin, *Domashnii byt' russkikh tsarits v XVI–XVII st.*, p. 432.

56. Ibid., p. 431.

57. V. A. Borisov, *Opisanie goroda Shui i ego okrestnostei*, pp. 451–52.

58. *Akty sobrannye v bibliotekakh*, vol. 3: *1613–1645*, pp. 401–5.

59. Zabelin, *Domashnii byt' russkikh tsarits v XVI–XVII st.*, pp. 443–44.

60. I. Sakharov, ed., *Skazaniia russkago naroda o semeinom zhizni svoikh predkov*, vol. 3 (St. Petersburg, 1837), Appendix, pp. 158, 162–63.

61. See N. Kharuzin's article "K voprosu o bor'be moskovskago

pravitel'stva s narodnymi iazycheskimi obriadami i sueveriiami v polovine XVII v.," *Etnograficheskoe obozrenie* 1 (1897): 143–51. N. V. Rozhdestvenskii has tried to show that the movement toward spiritual reform within the Russian Church actually began before Aleksei became tsar. "K istorii bor'by s tserkovnymi bezporiadkami, otgoloskami iazychestva i porokami v russkom bytu XVII v.," in *Chteniia v Imperatorskom obshchestve istorii i drevnostei rossiiskikh pri Moskovskom universitete* 2 (1902): pt. 4, Smes', pp. 1–31.

62. *Akty sobrannye v bibliotekakh*, vol. 4: *1645–1700*, pp. 481–82 in "Dopolneniia."

63. Ibid., p. 51–53. That same year, 1647, the tsar sent a *gramota* to the Solovetskii Monastery forbidding the elders to keep alcoholic beverages in their cells. Ibid., p. 482 in "Dopolneniia."

64. A. I. Almazov, *Tainaia ispoved' v pravoslavnoi vostochnoi tserkve*, Appendix to vol. 1, published in *Zapiski Imperatorskago novorossiiskago universiteta* 65 (1895): 217. The sixteenth-century Sofiiskii *Trebnik* contains the following question, to be asked of virgins and wives: "Did you listen to *skomorokhi* and delight in their games?" (p. 168). In the 1647 edition of the *Trebnik* all penitents were required to respond to questions related to *skomorokh* entertainments.

65. According to one cadastre, there were already thirteen *skomorokhi* in and around Nizhnii Novgorod in 1621, among them some who were quite well to do. *Pistsovaia i perepisnaia knigi XVII veka po Nizhnemu Novgorodu*, pp. 105, 108–9, 120–21, 130, 140, 143, 185, 279, 351.

66. As early as 1636, Neronov, together with some other priests from Nizhnii Novgorod, petitioned Patriarch Ioasaf I complaining about the disorderly conduct of the people during the various festival periods (*Koliada* in particular) and the nefarious influence of the bear and dog tamers, or performing *skomorokhi*. Since Michael Romanov was still on the throne, the complaint evidently fell on deaf ears. A. N. Robinson, *Zhizneopisaniia Avvakuma i Epifaniia: issledovanie i teksty* (Moscow, 1963), p. 222. See also Rozhdestvenskii, "K istorii bor'by s tserkovnymi bezporiadkami, otgoloskami iazychestva i porokami v russkom bytu XVII v."

67. "Zhitie Grigoriia Neronova, sostavlennoe posle ego smerti," in *Materialy dlia istorii raskola*, vol. 1 (Moscow, 1875), pp. 260–61.

68. *Pistsovaia i perepisnaia knigi XVII veka po Nizhnemu Novgorodu*, p. 279.

69. The incident must have occurred before the Volga had frozen over (i.e., no later than early autumn) since shortly after this Avvakum sailed for Kazan with Vasilii Petrovich Sheremetev, the newly appointed *voevoda*, or governor, of that eastern outpost. Sheremetev, Avvakum tells us, sternly rebuked him for his summary handling of the *skomorokhi*. Robinson, *Zhizneopisaniia Avvakuma i Epifaniia*, p. 144; also in translation, *The Life of the Archpriest Avvakum by Himself*, trans. Jane Harrison and Hope Mirrlees (Hamden, Conn., 1963), pp. 47–48.

70. Robinson, *Zhizneopisaniia Avvakuma i Epifaniia*, p. 144; *The Life of the Archpriest Avvakum*, pp. 47–48.

71. Olearius alludes to this coarser aspect of a *skomorokh* entertainment in his brief description of their puppet performances. Baron, *The Travels of Olearius in Seventeenth-Century Russia*, p. 142.

72. Reprinted in full in P. I. Ivanov's *Opisanie gosudarstvennago arkhiva starykh del* (Moscow, 1850), pp. 296–99. A. A. Belkin maintains that Aleksei's first *gramota* was in fact a response to a petition sent by Gavrilo Malyshev from Kursk in November of 1648. *Russkie skomorokhi*, pp. 87–88 and 173–75 for text of the Malyshev petition.

73. Only two other versions of the *gramota* have survived. One, dated 20 December 1648 and addressed to the *voevoda* of Dmitrov, Ivan Okinfeevich Shiskov, is a verbatim copy of the original. It is reprinted by Kharuzin in his article "K voprosu o bor'be moskovskago pravitel'stva s narodnymi iazycheskimi obriadami i sueveriiami v polovine XVII v.," pp. 147–49. The other is a paraphrased version dated 13 December 1649 and reproduced as part of a memorandum ("Pamiat") of the *voevoda* of Verkhotursk to the governor of the Irbitskaia *sloboda*. *Akty istoricheskie*, vol. 4: *1645–1676* (St. Petersburg, 1842), pp. 124–26.

74. Excellent examples of such verses can be found in Shein, *Velikoruss v svoikh pesniakh*, 1: 306–9; also Chubinskii, *Trudy etnografichesko-statisticheskoi ekspeditsii*, 3: 428–29, No. 161. The last mentioned vividly demonstrates the fusion of the pagan and Christian traditions, with the plow described as guided by God himself and the Virgin Mary.

75. Aleksei's order to confiscate and burn the musical instruments of the *skomorokhi* was carried out in earnest, as one eyewitness has noted. Baron, *The Travels of Olearius in Seventeenth-Century Russia*, pp. 262–63.

76. *Usen'* literally refers to the first day of spring, but here it is linked with the customs and traditions pertaining to New Year's Eve. These customs center on satirical songs and invocations of the sun as it begins its gradual return to earth. For additional bibliography see M. Vasmer, *Russisches Etymologisches Wörterbuch*, 3: 190. The *gramota* is reprinted in full by I. P. Sakharov in the Appendix to his *Skazaniia russkago naroda*, vol. 2 (St. Petersburg, 1885), pp. 228–31. No other version of this second *gramota* of Aleksei's has been preserved. On 18 January 1649 Varlaam, the Archimandrite of the Dmitrov Monastery in Kashin, sent a petition to the tsar complaining about the excesses of the *Maslenitsa* festival in his jurisdiction. In the petition Varlaam specifically mentions the *skomorokhi*, along with a host of other evils, and requests that the tsar send a *gramota* to proscribe these pagan practices. That same month, on 30 January 1649, Aleksei sent a *gramota* to Varlaam, which was presumably a copy of the 24 December 1648 document. Appropriate emendations were made in the original to reflect the particular concerns of the Archimandrite. Kharuzin, "K voprosu o bor'be moskovskago pravitel'stva s narodnymi iazicheskimi obriadami i sueveriiami v polovine XVII v.," pp. 150–51.

77. *Akty sobrannye v bibliotekakh*, 4: 138–39.

78. See n. 14 above.

79. *Iaroslavskiia pistsovyia, dozornyia, mezhevyia i perepisnyia knigi XVII v.*, in *Trudy iaroslavskoi uchenoi arkhivnoi komissii*, 4, nos. 3–4 (1913): 261, 265. On p. 263 the widow of a *skomorokh* is also recorded.

80. By 1653, for example, the *skomorokhi* were apparently more popular than ever in the Siberian province of Tobol'sk, which prompted the local archbishop, Simeon, to lodge a formal complaint in Moscow. A. N. Kopylov, *Ocherki kul'turnoi zhizni Sibiri XVII–nachala XIX v.* (Novosibirsk, 1974), p. 220.

81. L. S. Sheptaev, "Russkoe skomoroshestvo v XVII veke," *Uchenye zapiski Ural' skogo gosudarstvennogo universiteta* 6 (1949): 58. Only the 1649 version of the reissued *gramota* has been preserved. It appears in a memorandum from the *voevoda* of Verkhotursk, Raf Rodionovich, to the *prikazchik* of the Irbitskaia *sloboda*. *Akty istoricheskie*, 4: 124–26.

82. *Akty sobrannye v bibliotekakh*, 4: 95–97.

83. Ibid., p. 97.

84. A. Titov, *Troitskii Zheltovodskii monastyr u Starago Makar'ia (1435–1887)* (Moscow, 1887), p. 39.

85. V. I. Sreznevskii, *Opisanie rukopisei i knig sobrannykh dlia Imperatorskoi Akademii Nauk v olonetskom krae* (St. Petersburg, 1913), p. 464. The Russian title of this ananymous account is *Opisanii russkogo gosudarstva v 1686 g.* It was published originally in Amsterdam in 1686, with the Russian translation appearing sometime in the late seventeenth or early eighteenth century. Sreznevskii's comments on and description of the *Opisanii* appear on pp. 142–45. See also Sheptaev, "Russkoe skomoroshestvo v XVII veke," p. 48.

86. The document, no doubt of ecclesiastical provenance, dates from 1754. "Stat'ia rumiantsevskago sbornika, posviashchennaia sueveriiam," *Zapiski Imperatorskago moskovskago arkheologicheskago instituta imeni Imperatora Nikolaia II* 18 (1913): 93.

87. V. I. Dal maintains that he knew of a peasant from the province of Nizhnii Novgorod who earned a living as a practicing *skomorokh* as late as the mid-nineteenth century. He describes him as an itinerant bagpipe player who could also do a variety of bird calls. *Tolkovyi slovar' zhivago iazyka*, vol. 4, 3d ed., rev. (St. Petersburg, 1909), p. 202.

88. V. N. Tatishchev, *Istoriia rossiiskaia*, vol. 1 (Moscow-Leningrad, 1962), p. 115, n. 16.

89. For a discussion of the questions that still surround Kirsha Danilov's *Sbornik* and its authorship see B. N. Putilov's essay appended to the most recent edition of the *Sbornik*. "Sbornik Kirsha Danilova i ego mesto v russkoi fol'kloristike," in Evgen'eva and Putilov, *Drevnie rossiiskie stikhotvorenia sobrannye Kirsheiu Danilovym*, pp. 513–65. In a recent article A. A. Gorelov has tried to show that all or most of the songs in Kirsha Danilov's *Sbornik* must be attributed to a single person who was a *skomorokh*. "Kem byl avtor sbornika 'Drevnie rossiiskie stikhotvoreniia,'" *Russkii fol'klor* 7 (1962): 293–312. See also J. L. Rice, "A Russian Bawdy Song of the Eighteenth Century," *Slavic and East European Journal* 20 (1976): 353–70.

90. P. N. Sheffer, ed., *Sbornik Kirshi Danilova* (St. Petersburg, 1901), p. 195.

91. K. Golodnikov, "Ssyl'nye v tobol'skoi gubernii i vliianie ikh na nravstvennyi i ekonomicheskii byt starozhilov," *Tobol'skie gubernskie vedomosti 17* (1891): 5. See also Kopylov, *Ocherki kul' turnoi zhizni Sibiri XVII–nachala XIX v.*, pp. 220–21.

92. Sheptaev, "Russkoe skomoroshestvo v XVII veke," p. 58.

Chapter 4

1. Henning, *Lifflendische Chürlendische Chronica*, p. 55, as cited in Stief, *Studies in the Russian Historical Song*, p. 228; Baron, *Travels of Olearius in Seventeenth-Century Russia*, p. 48.

2. Gruzinskii, *Pesni sobrannyia P. M. Rybnikovym*, 1: 162–72, No. 26. An English translation of this *bylina* can be found in N. K. Chadwick, *Russian Heroic Poetry* (Cambridge, 1932), pp. 81–90.

3. Chadwick, *Russian Heroic Poetry*, p. 86, ll.191–94.

4. Ibid., p. 87, ll.225–38.

5. Miller, *Ocherki russkoi narodnoi slovesnosti*, 1: 59; Famintsyn, *Skomorokhi na Rusi*, p. 4; Findeizen, *Ocherki po istorii muzyki v Rossii*, 1: 110.

6. Miller, *Ocherki russkoi narodnoi slovesnosti*, 1: 59.

7. "Terentii muzh Danil'evich," in Evgen'eva and Putilov, *Drevnie rossiiskie stikhotvoreniia*, pp. 17–22; and "Vavilo i skomorokhi," in N. P. Andreev, ed., *Byliny: russkii geroicheskii epos* (Leningrad, 1938), pp. 436–41, No. 33.

8. In a version of the *bylina* about Vasilii Buslaev, reference is made to the hero's joining a band of *veselye liudi* (i.e., *skomorokhi*). See Evgen'eva and Putilov, *Drevnie rossiiskie stikhotvoreniia*, pp. 59–67.

9. Rybakov, *Remeslo drevnei Rusi*, p. 269, illus. 61.

10. B. D. Grekov traces the Kievan heroic tradition as far back as the Antes; unfortunately, he does not offer any evidence to substantiate this conclusion. *The Culture of Kiev Rus* (Moscow, 1947), p. 79. Somewhat dated, though still useful, is the chapter on the composition and recitation of Russian heroic poetry in Chadwick and Chadwick, *The Growth of Literature*, 2: 238–69. An excellent recent article devoted to the question of the origin of the *byliny* is Felix J. Oinas's "The Problem of the Aristocratic Origin of Russian *Byliny*," *Slavic Review* 30 (1971): 513–22.

11. *PSRL*, 2: *Ipatievskaia letopis'* (St. Petersburg, 1843), pp. 155, 180, 187.

12. *PSRL*, 7: *Letopis' po voskresenskomu spisku* (St. Petersburg, 1856), p. 151.

13. V. P. Adrianova-Peretts, ed., *Slovo o polku Igoreve* (Moscow-Leningrad, 1950), pp. 2–4, 37, 44 (in 1800 ed.), also pp. 376–77 in the Commentary.

14. M. P. Pogodin, *Izsledovaniia, zamechaniia i lektsii o russkoi*

istorii, vol. 7 (Moscow, 1856), p. 420. Pogodin's first polemic against Maksimovich appeared in the pages of *Moskvitianin* 3 (1845): 1–10; and 7–8 (1845): 47–57.

15. Pogodin, *Izsledovaniia,* pp. 426–27.

16. P. Kulish, *Zapiski o Iuzhnoi Rusi,* vol. 2 (St. Petersburg, 1857), pp. 48–57.

17. P. A. Bezsonov, ed., *Pesni sobrannyia P. V. Kireevskim,* vol. 4 (Moscow, 1862), pp. xxiii–xxvi.

18. Ibid., p. xxvii. A comprehensive study of the relationship between Russian and Ukrainian heroic poetry has recently been published by M. M. Plisetskii, *Vzaimosviazi russkogo i ukrainskogo geroicheskogo eposa* (Moscow, 1963).

19. O. F. Miller, "Velikorusskiia byliny i malorusskiia dumy," in *Trudy tret'iago arkheologicheskago s'ezda,* vol. 2 (Kiev, 1878), pp. 285–306.

20. Open letter from O. F. Miller to M. P. Dragomanov in *Drevniaia i novaia Rossiia* 9 (1875): 92.

21. V. B. Antonovich and M. P. Dragomanov, eds., *Istoricheskiia pesni malorusskago naroda,* vol. 1 (Kiev, 1874).

22. Miller, "Velikorusskiia byliny," pp. 290–94, 306.

23. *Drevniaia i novaia Rossiia* 9 (1875): 93–96.

24. N. I. Petrov, "Sledy severno-russkago bylevago eposa v iuzhno-russkoi narodnoi literature," *Trudy Kievskoi Dukhovnoi Academii* 19 (1878): 357–92. An unsigned review of Petrov's article appears in *Russkii filologicheskii vestnik* 2 (1879): 152–55.

25. Petrov, "Sledy severno-russkago bylevago eposa," p. 366. It should be noted that allusions to the plow and sowing are common not only in Ukrainian but in Great Russian Yuletide songs as well; their connection with Mikula is therefore tenuous at best. A classic study of these winter calendar songs as they have survived in Russia has recently been published by V. I. Chicherov (*Zimnii period russkogo zemledel'cheskogo kalendaria XVI–XIX vekov* [Moscow, 1957], pp. 115–65). Mikula's identification with Christ (as plowman), as well as other heroes, is the subject of André Mazon's essay, "Mikula, le prodigieux laboureur," *Revue des Études Slaves* 11 (1931): 149–70.

26. Petrov, pp. 366–68.

27. Ibid., pp. 380–82.

28. "Byli li malorussy iskonnymi obititeliami polianskoi zemli ili prishli iz-za Karpat v XIV v.," *Osnova* 10 (1862).

29. N. I. Kostomarov, "Istoricheskoe znachenie iuzhnorusskago narodnago pesennago tvorchestva," *Beseda* 12 (1872): 28–49.

30. Ibid., pp. 30–32.

31. L. N. Maikov, *O bylinakh vladimirova tsikla* (St. Petersburg, 1863), p. 31.

32. M. Khalanskii, "Velikorusskiia byliny kievskago tsikla," *Russkii filologicheskii vestnik* 3 (1884): 145. V. F. Miller and a number of his followers also assigned to the *skomorokhi* a primary role in carrying

the *byliny* to the north, though at a much later date. *Ocherki russkoi narodnoi slovesnosti*, 1: 52–64.

33. Morozov, "K voprosu ob istoricheskoi roli i znachenii skomorokhov," p. 51.

34. S. I. Dmitrieva, "Methods in the Study of Russian Epics" (unpublished paper). A copy of the paper was made available to me by Professor Felix J. Oinas of Indiana University, to whom I am most grateful.

35. Grigor'ev, *Arkhangel'skiia byliny i istoricheskiia pesni*, 1: 391–93.

36. Ibid., p. xxiii.

37. Morozov, "Skomorokhi na severe," p. 243.

38. In Rybnikov this *bylina* is entitled "Dobrynia v ot'ezde"; in Hilferding it appears under the title "Dobrynia i Alesha." It is the latter version that is referred to here. A. F. Hilferding [Gil'ferding], comp., *Onezheskiia byliny zapisannyia Aleksandrom Fedorovichem Gil'ferdingom letom 1871 goda*, vol. 3, 2d ed. (St. Petersburg, 1900), No. 215, pp. 104–13.

39. Ibid., ll.285–86. Soviet folklorists explain Prince Vladimir's less than courteous treatment in some *byliny* as a reflection of revolutionary ferment in seventeenth-century Muscovy. A. M. Astakhova, *Il'ia Muromets* (Moscow-Leningrad, 1958), p. 415.

40. M. Speranskii, ed., *Byliny*, vol. 1 (Moscow, 1916), pp. 228–38.

41. Ibid., p. 225.

42. Good, annotated Russian versions of both *byliny* can be found in D. P. Costello and I. P. Foote, eds., *Russian Folk Literature* (Oxford, 1967), pp. 121–41. English translations of both are available in Chadwick's *Russian Heroic Poetry*, pp. 134–55.

43. Gruzinskii, *Pesni sobrannyia P. N. Rybnikovym*, 2: 250–51, ll. 269–77 and 285–96.

44. Speranskii, *Byliny*, vol. 2 (Moscow, 1919), p. 281.

45. These introductory verses seem to have been recited for Hilferding almost as an afterthought or as an epilogue. He places them apart, at the end of the song. Hilferding, *Onezheskiia byliny*, vol. 1 (Moscow, 1894), pp. 455–56, ll.180–96. See also in Hilferding's second volume the introductory verses for Nos. 123 and 132.

46. The peasant narrators used the term *starina* to refer to their songs, rather than the scholarly, contrived term *bylina*.

47. Evgen'eva and Putilov, *Drevnie rossiiskie stikhotvoreniia*, pp. 194–95, ll.183–93. Some other interesting exodes can be found in Gruzinskii's *Pesni sobrannyia P. N. Rybnikovym*, 1: 246–47, ll.504–13; p. 255, ll.300–306.

48. The name *byliny-skomoroshiny* was first used by Speranskii, who includes six songs under that general heading in volume 1 of his *Byliny* (pp. 288–315): "Vavilo i skomorokhi," "Gost' Terent'ishche," "Starina o bol'shom byke," "Usishcha," "Nebelitsa," and "Foma i Erema." This list of *byliny-skomoroshiny* has been considerably expanded by V. Ia.

Propp and B. N. Putilova in their recent two-volume anthology of *byliny* (*Byliny*, vol. 2 [Moscow, 1958], pp. 391–456). L. M. Ivleva ("Skomoroshiny (Obshchie problemy izucheniia)," in *Slavianskii fol'klor*, ed. B. N. Putilov and V. K. Sokolova [Moscow, 1972], pp. 110–24) has further expanded the list (p. 119) and has taken issue with Speranskii's inclusion of "Vavilo i skomorokhi" among the *skomoroshiny* (p. 118). See also Morozov's "K voprosu ob istoricheskoi roli i znachenii skomorokhov" (pp. 58–61) for a discussion of *skomoroshiny* as a distinct genre.

49. An excellent model study of the song has been made by Walter Anderson, who also discusses its relationship to the *skomorokhi*. *Der Schwank vom alten Hildebrand*, pt. 1, in *Acta et Commentationes Universitatis Tartuensis (Dorpatensis)*, B: Humaniora, vol. 21 (Tartu, 1931), pp. 58–83. The version under discussion here is taken from Evgen'eva and Putilov, *Drevnie rossiiskie stikhotvoreniia*, pp. 17–22.

50. Evgen'eva and Putilov, *Drevnie rossiiskie stikhotvoreniia*, p. 21, ll.138–40.

51. Andreev, *Byliny*, pp. 436–41, for most recent edition. See also Grigor'ev, *Arkhangel'skiia byliny*, 1: 333–36, 376–81 and 686–87 for melody used by Krivopolenova in rendering the song.

52. A brief discussion of "Vavilo i skomorokhi" and its relationship to the Finnish "Lemminkäinen's Song" can be found in Felix J. Oinas, *Studies in Finnic-Slavic Folklore Relations*, Folklore Fellows Communications, no. 205 (Helsinki, 1969), pp. 11–12.

53. In a recent study, Professor Martti Haavio discovered a possible source of "Vavilo i skomorokhi" in an old Egyptian story that tells of a charm duel between the Ethiopian sorcerer Horus and the Egyptian priest Horus. The Russian tsar's name, Sobaka, derives, according to Haavio, from the name of the cruel Ethiopian king Shabako (Sabakós, Sabakón in Herodotus), who conquered Egypt in the seventh century B.C. and ruled there for several decades. *Suomalainen mytologia* (Porvoo-Helsinki, 1967), pp. 238–49.

54. Andreev, *Byliny*, p. 437, l.63.

55. The legend of Vavilo as a saint apparently had wide currency in northern Russia. There is, for example, in O. E. Ozarovskaia's *Piatirechie* (Leningrad, 1930), pp. 303–4, a brief description of an icon of Vavilo with *gusli* in hand. M. K. Krivopolenova (*Byliny, skomoroshiny, skazki* [Arkhangel'sk, 1950], pp. 142–44) discusses two variants of a legend with the basic theme that even a *skomorokh* can gain salvation. In the first instance he does so by renouncing his profession; in the second, by continuing to practice his art among the people.

56. Sokolov, *Russian Folklore*, p. 344.

57. "Pistsovye knigi goroda Kazani 1565–68 gg. i 1646 g.," p. 36.

58. The other military minstrels mentioned in the cadastres are simply described as *skomorokhi*.

59. V. Nechaev, ed., *Pskov i ego prigorody*, bk. 2, in *Sbornik moskovskago arkhiva ministerstva iustitsii*, vol. 5 (Moscow, 1913), p. 431.

60. *Pistsovaia i perepisnaia knigi XVII veka po Nizhnemu Novgorodu,* p. 143.

61. Cited in Stief, *Studies in the Russian Historical Song,* p. 228. Henning adds the telling comment that when the performance was not to his liking, Ivan would beat the singers with his *baculo* so that the "red notes" oozed out.

62. Baron, *The Travels of Olearius in Seventeenth-Century Russia,* p. 48.

63. Sheffer, *Sbornik Kirshi Danilova,* p. 195.

64. *Istoricheskiia pesni russkago naroda XVI–XVII vv.,* in *Sbornik otdeleniia russkago iazyka i slovesnosti Imperatorskoi Akademii Nauk* 93 (1915): 1–26. An excellent discussion of the variants of the Kazan songs is provided by Carl Stief in his *Studies in the Russian Historical Song,* pp. 227–57.

65. Stief, p. 229.

66. Ibid., pp. 246–49.

67. Miller, *Istoricheskie pesni russkago naroda XVI–XVII vv.,* No. 19, pp. 22–23, ll.13–14.

68. Ibid., No. 20, pp. 23–24, ll.1–3.

69. Ibid., No. 13, pp. 15–16, l.14.

70. The most recent study along these comparative lines is A. E. Alexander, *Bylina and Fairy Tale: The Origins of Russian Heroic Poetry* (The Hague, 1973).

71. Ibid., pp. 7–8.

72. P. V. Vladimirov, *Vvedenie v istoriiu russkoi slovesnosti* (Kiev, 1896), p. 138.

73. L. M. Brodskii, "Sledy professional'nykh skazochnikov v russkikh skazkakh," *Etnograficheskoe obozrenie* 2 (1904): 16.

74. I. I. Sreznevskii, *Svedeniia i zametki o maloizvestnykh i neizvestnykh pamiatnikakh,* pt. 2: XLI–LXXX (St. Petersburg, 1876), p. 554.

75. I. E. Zabelin, *Domashnii byt' russkikh tsarits v XVI–XVII st.* (Moscow, 1869), p. 429.

76. Ibid., p. 430.

77. Ibid., p. 431.

78. Brodskii, "Sledy professional'nykh skazochnikov v russkikh skazkakh," p. 8.

79. V. P. Adrianova-Peretts, "Narodnoe poeticheskoe tvorchestvo vremeni krest'ianskikh i gorodskikh vosstanii XVII v.," in *Russkoe narodnoe poeticheskoe tvorchestvo,* vol. 1 (Moscow-Leningrad, 1953), p. 352.

80. V. Ia. Propp, ed., *Narodnye russkie skazki A. M. Afanas'eva,* vol. 3 (Moscow, 1957), No. 428, p. 233.

81. D. N. Sadovnikov, comp., *Skazki i predaniia samarskago kraia,* in *Zapiski Imperatorskago russkago geograficheskago obshchestva po otdeleniiu etnografii* 12 (1884): No. 4, p. 41.

82. Brodskii, "Sledy professional'nykh skazochnikov v russkikh skazkakh," pp. 12–13.

83. A. Veselovskii, "Opyty po istorii razvitiia khristianskoi legendy," *Zhurnal ministerstva narodnago prosveshcheniia* 5 (1877): 90–96.

84. Shein, *Velikoruss v svoikh pesniakh*, 1: 317, No. 1070; Chubinskii, *Trudy etnografichesko-statisticheskoi ekspeditsii*, 3: 427–31, 478–79.

85. Azarin, *Kniga o chudesakh pr. Sergiia*, pp. 46–47.

86. The first comprehensive collection of Russian proverbs appeared anonymously under the title *Sobranie 4291 drevnikh rossiiskikh poslovits* (Moscow, 1770).

87. Ibid., pp. 34, 256.

88. V. I. Dal, ed., *Poslovitsy russkago naroda* (Moscow, 1862), p. 129.

89. Ibid., p. 915.

90. P. P., "Shuty i skomorokhi v drevnosti i v noveishee vremia," p. 463.

91. *Sobranie 4291 drevnikh rossiiskikh poslovits*, p. 256.

Chapter 5

1. Findeizen, *Ocherki po istorii muzyki v Rossii*, 1: 59. See also F. Kolessa, *Ukrajins'ka usna slovesnist'* (L'viv, 1938), pp. 3–80.

2. Some of the best and most fundamental research into the music of the early Kievan period has been done by F. Kolessa (*Rytmika ukrajins'-kykh narodnikh pisen'* [L'viv, 1906–7]). See also A. J. Swan's important article, "The Nature of the Russian Folk-Song," *Musical Quarterly* 29 (1943): 498–516 and N. Vernadsky, "The Russian Folk-Song," *Russian Review* 3 (1944): 94–99.

3. A. J. Swan, *Russian Music and Its Sources in Chant and Folk-Song* (London, 1973), p. 38.

4. Findeizen, *Ocherki po istorii muzyki v Rossii*, p. 60.

5. Nestor, "Zhitie prepodobnago otsa nashego igumena pecherskago, opisannoe prep. Nestorom," p. 178.

6. Findeizen, *Ocherki po istorii muzyki v Rossii*, p. 62.

7. Vernadsky, *The Origins of Russia*, pp. 154–61.

8. M. Vasmer, *Russisches Etymologisches Wörterbuch*, 1: 323.

9. A. S. Famintsyn, *Gusli: russkii narodnyi muzykal'nyi instrument* (St. Petersburg, 1890), pp. 3, 5–6.

10. Ibid., pp. 7–8.

11. Ibid., pp. 61–62, 75. A. O. Väisänen sees no generic relationship between the Baltic psaltery (including the *kantele*) and the early Russian *gusli*. "Das zupfinstrument gusli bei den Wolgavolkern," *Memoires de la Societe Finno-Ougrienne* 58 (1928): 303–30. On the relationship between the *kantele* and other Baltic musical instruments see E. Nieminen, "Finnische *Kantele* und die damit verbundenen Namen baltischer Musikinstrumente," *Studia Fennica* 10 (1963): 3–43.

12. I. Tõnurist, "Kannel Vepsamaast Setumaani," in *Soomeugri rahvaste muusika pärandist*, ed. E. Rüütel (Tallinn, 1977), pp. 149–78. See also S. Reynolds, "The Baltic Psaltery: Bibliographical Problems and Desiderata," in *The Second Conference on Baltic Studies in Scandinavia*, vol. 2 (Stockholm, 1973), pp. 7–30.

13. *Radzivilovskaia ili Kenigsbergskaia letopis'*, pt. 1: *Fotomekhani-cheskoe vosproizvedenie rukopisi* (St. Petersburg, 1902), pp. 112–13.

14. N. Kondakov, "Zametka o miniaturakh Kenigsbergskago spiska nachal'noi letopisi," in *Radzivilovskaia ili Kenigsbergskaia letopis'*, pt. 2, *Stati o tekste i miniatiurakh rukopisi* (St. Petersburg, 1902), pp. 115, 123.

15. Stasov, *Slavianskii i vostochnyi ornament*, plate 67, No. 2; plate 68, No. 25. Illustrated in Chapter 2.

16. Baron, *The Travels of Olearius in Seventeenth-Century Russia*, pp. 262–63.

17. Spiegelman, "Style Formation in Early Russian Keyboard Music," pp. 311–20.

18. Ibid., p. 313.

19. Vernadsky, *The Origins of Russia*, p. 159.

20. Iu. A. Bakhrushin, *Istoriia russkogo baleta* (Moscow, 1965), p. 7; B. V. Varneke, *History of the Russian Theatre (Seventeenth Through Nineteenth Century)*, trans. B. Brasol (New York, 1951), pp. 1–2.

21. V. Vsevolodskii-Gerngross, *Russkii teatr ot istokov do serediny XVIII v.* (Moscow, 1957), p. 12.

22. Bakhrushin, *Istoriia russkogo baleta*, p. 13; V. Krasovskaia, *Russkii baletnyi teatr ot voznyknoveniia do serediny XIX veka* (Moscow-Leningrad, 1958), pp. 14–15; Roslavleva, *Era of the Russian Ballet*, pp. 18–19.

23. It occurs in the collection of church canons attributed to Maksim, Bishop of Belgorod (1187–90), who warns his flock to shun "the dancing games" of the *skomorokhi*. S. I. Smirnov, ed., *Materialy dlia istorii drevne-russkoi pokaiannoi distsipliny*, p. 54.

24. N. Kostomarov, ed., *Pamiatniki starinnoi russkoi literatury*, vol. 1 (St. Petersburg, 1860), p. 209.

25. Stasov, *Slavianskii i vostochnyi ornament*, plate 67, No. 2; plate 68, No. 25. Both are illustrated in Chapter 2.

26. Uspenskii, *Drevnerusskoe pevcheskoe iskusstvo*, p. 52.

27. Adam Olearius, *Verhmerte newe Beschreibung Der Muscow-itischen und Persichen Reyse* (Schlesswig, 1656), p. 20. Baron does not reproduce this illustration in his translation.

28. Baron, *The Travels of Olearius in Seventeenth-Century Russia*, pp. 48–49.

29. One scholar maintains that the dancers are actually wearing masks and costumes and are acting out some sort of satirical farce. Bakhrushin, *Istoriia russkogo baleta*, p. 14.

30. Varneke, *History of the Russian Theatre*, p. 23. See also B. Malnick, "The Origins and Early History of the Theatre in Russia," *Slavonic and East European Review* 19 (1940): 212–16.

31. It was also in Aleksei's reign that the first ballet performance was staged in Russia in 1673. For details about this performance see Roslavleva, *Era of The Russian Ballet*, p. 18.

32. Varneke, *History of the Russian Theatre*, p. 22.

33. The precise meaning of the word *moskoludstvo* is still problematic. For a complete, annotated text and commentary on Luka

Zhidiata's sermon wherein this reference occurs, see A. I. Ponomarev, ed., *Pamiatniki drevne-russkoi tserkovno-uchitel'noi literatury*, vol. 1 (St. Petersburg, 1898), pp. 314–27.

34. Veselovskii, *Razyskaniia v oblasti russkago dukhovnago stikha*, p. 207.

35. *Stoglav*, chap. 41, ques. 16. See also Mahler, *Die russischen dörflichen Hochzeitsgebräuche*, p. 140.

36. Malnick, "The Origin and Early History of the Theatre in Russia," p. 205. V. D. Kuz'mina, *Russkii demokraticheskii teatr XVIII v.* (Moscow, 1958), p. 155; Belkin, *Russkie skomorokhi*, pp. 159–63. See also P. M. Berkov, ed., *Russkaia narodnaia drama XVII–XX vekov* (Moscow, 1953), and L. Warner's excellent article, "The Russian Folk Play 'Tsar Maximillian': An Examination of Some Possible Origins and Sources," *Folklore* 82 (1971): 185–206.

37. Ozarovskaia, *Piatirechie*, p. 410, n. 11.

38. Veselovskii, *Razyskaniia v oblasti russkago dukhovnago stikha*, p. 187.

39. Buslaev, *Istoricheskaia khrestomatiia tserkovnoslavianskago i drevne-russkago iazykov*, p. 381.

40. K. Waliszewskii, *Ivan the Terrible*, trans. Lady Mary Lloyd (Philadelphia, 1904), p. 70.

41. Famintsyn, *Skomorokhi na Rusi*, p. 118, n. 1. In Polish Galicia, bears were used for entertainment as early as 1421. Student Emelianov, "Puteshestviia Gill'bera de-Lannoa v vostochnyia zemli Evropy v 1413–14 i 1421 godakh," *Kievskaia universitetskiia izvestiia* 8 (1873): 35.

42. *PSRL*, 30: *Novgorodskaia vtoraia (arkhivskaia) letopis'*, p. 189.

43. Berkov, *Russkaia narodnaia drama XVII–XX vekov*, pp. 137–140.

44. A comprehensive study of the Russian puppet theater remains to be written. The earliest attempt at writing such a history was made by V. M. Perets, *Kukol'nyi teatr na Rusi* (St. Petersburg, 1895). Perets's study is quite brief, and it begins in the early seventeenth century. Among the most recent studies is N. I. Smirnova's *Sovetskii teatr kukol* (Moscow, 1963), which contains two solid chapters on the early period. A delightful fictionalized account of Petrushka's formative years has recently been published by B. Privalov, *Petrushka-dusha skomorosh'ia* (Moscow, 1963).

45. A. Alferov, "Petrushka i ego predki," in *Desiat chtenii po literatury*, 4th ed. (Moscow, 1915), p. 195. In the West the puppet theater had become a popular form of secular entertainment by the twelfth century, and there is evidence that even earlier, between the seventh and ninth centuries, puppets had been put to the service of the church. Reich, *Der Mimus*, 1: 833–34; Nicoll, *Masks, Mimes and Miracles*, p. 167.

46. In the Eastern or Byzantine Empire, the puppet theater was flourishing as early as the sixth century. Reich, *Der Mimus*, 1: 834; Nicoll, *Masks, Mimes and Miracles*, p. 167.

47. Veselovskii, *Razyskaniia v oblasti russkago dukhovnago stikha*, p. 188.

48. N. N. Martinovitch, *The Turkish Theatre* (New York, 1933), pp. 29–30; B. Baird, *The Art of the Puppet* (New York, 1965), p. 84.

49. Vysotskii and Totskaia, "Novoe o freske 'skomorokhi' v Sofii Kievskoi," pp. 50–61.

50. Baird, *The Art of the Puppet*, p. 84 and illus. p. 27.

51. K. Jettmar, *Art of the Steppes*, trans. A. E. Keep (London, 1967), pp. 95–97, 123, 125.

52. Baird, *The Art of the Puppet*, p. 35; Smirnova, *Sovetskii teatr kukol*, pp. 13–14.

53. Vernadsky, *The Origins of Russia*, p. 112.

54. For an in-depth study of these rites see W. Liungman, *Traditionswanderungen Euphrat-Rhein*, 2 vols., Folklore Fellows Communications, nos. 118–19 (Helsinki, 1937–38), esp. 2: chap. 20–21; also, M. Eliade, *Patterns in Comparative Religion*, trans. R. Sheed (New York, 1963), pp. 317–21.

55. For a comparison of *Maslenitsa* and the Western Carnival see V. F. Miller, "Russkaia maslenitsa i zapadnoevropeiskii karnaval," in *Rechi i otchet chastnoi gimnazii Perepelkinoi* (Moscow, 1884), pp. 1–49. D. Rovinskii has reproduced a series of twenty illustrations depicting the weeklong activities connected with *Maslenitsa* in eighteenth-century Russia in his *Russkiia narodnyia kartinki*, vol. 2 (St. Petersburg, 1900), pp. 351–54.

56. An interesting comparison has been drawn between the rites surrounding Iarilo and the ancient Greek Charilo by G. Calderon, "Slavonic Elements in Greek Religion," *Classical Review* 27 (1913): 79–81.

57. The *rusalki* were reputed to be the spirits of drowning victims, premature babies, and infants who died unbaptized (the last were also sometimes called *mavki*). In the spring they roamed about the fields and allegedly tickled people to death or drowned those who went near water.

58. A good description of the tug of war and scattering of the *rusalka* puppet is provided by A. N. Veselovskii, "Genvarskiia rusalii i gotskiia igry v Vizantii," p. 4. Other methods of disposing of the puppet are described by V. Vsevolodskii-Gerngross, *Istoriia russkago teatra*, vol. 1 (Moscow-Leningrad, 1929), pp. 169–70.

59. A description of *Kupalo* rituals and games can be found in Chubinskii, *Trudy etnografichesko-statisticheskoi ekspeditsii*, 3: 192–233.

60. The earliest reference to the Old Slavonic word *kukla* occurs in the fifteenth-century edition of the tenth-century Bulgarian *Khronografiia Ioanna Malaly*, where the original Greek τῶν σκηνικῶν ("of the stage," "theatrical") is rendered as *kukla*. I. I. Sreznevskii, *Materialy dlia slovaria drevne-russkago iazyka po pis'mennym pamiatnikam*, vol. 1, reprint ed. (Graz, 1955), p. 1360. The word *kukla* does not appear in any native Russian source until the early seventeenth century. Here it also carries the general connotation of "theatrical performance," in the Greek sense of the term, and appears to be borrowed from Canon 51 of the Quinisexta, or Trullan, Church Council (Constantinople, 692) where mimes and theaters are singled out for censure. N. Tikhomirov, ed., *Pamiatniki otrechennoi russkoi literatury*, vol. 2 (Moscow, 1863), p. 313.

See also V. J. Mansikka, *Die Religion der Ostslaven*, Folklore Fellows Communications, no. 43 (Helsinki, 1922), p. 254.

61. Veselovskii, *Razyskaniia v oblasti russkago dukhovnago stikha,* pp. 189–95.

62. Ibid., p. 191.

63. Baird, *The Art of the Puppet*, p. 34.

64. "O pozorishchnykh igrakh, ili komediakh i tragediakh," *Sankt-Peterburgskie vedomosti* nos. 44–46: 175–76, as cited in Smirnova, *Sovetskii teatr kukol*, p. 18.

65. Among the several meanings Sreznevskii gives for these two synonymous Old Russian words are: spectacle, performance, presentation, and show. *Materialy dlia slovaria drevne-russkago iazyka*, 2: 1090–92.

66. The earliest known reference to the word *kukla* in its modern Russian sense of "puppet" or "puppet theater" dates from 1699. S. K. Bogoiavlenskii, comp., *Moskovskii teatr pri tsariakh Aleksee i Petre: materialy*, in *Chteniia v Imperatorskom obshchestve istorii i drevnostei rossiiskikh pri Moskovskom universitete* (1914): 78.

67. Ivanov, *Opisanie gosudarstvennago arkhiva starykh del*, pp. 296, 297.

68. Relevant excerpts from Filaret's *ukaz* are cited in Famintsyn's *Skomorokhi na Rusi*, p. 182.

69. Vsevolodskii-Gerngross, *Russkii teatr ot istokov do serediny XVIII v.*, p. 60.

70. An excellent text of "Petrushka" can be found in Berkov's *Russkaia narodnaia drama XVII–XX vekov*, pp. 113–23. A badly translated, abridged English version of the play appears in P. McPharlin's anthology, *A Repertory of Marionette Plays* (New York, 1929), pp. 291–300.

71. Sreznevskii, *Materialy dlia slovaria drevne-russkago iazyka*, 2: 1090.

72. Ibid.

73. Vsevolodskii-Gerngross, *Russkii teatr ot istokov do serediny XVIII v.*, pp. 6–7.

74. Ibid., p. 6.

75. Sreznevskii, *Materialy dlia slovaria drevne-russkago iazyka*, 1: 1021.

76. Baron, *The Travels of Olearius in Seventeenth-Century Russia,* p. 142 and illus.

77. Recently some ceramic figures dating back to the mid-fifteenth century were excavated in Moscow. According to M. G. Rabinovich, they are the remains of hand puppets that he attributes to the *skomorokhi.* "K istorii skomoroshikh igr na Rusi ('Rekvizit vertepa')," in *Kul'tura srednevekovoi Rusi* (Leningrad, 1974), pp. 53–56.

78. Vsevolodskii-Gerngross, *Russkii teatr ot istokov do serediny XVIII v.*, p. 60.

79. I. Ia. Gurliand, *Ivan Gebdon—kommissarius i rezident: materialy*

po istorii administratsii moskovskago gosudarstva vtoroi poloviny XVII veka (Iaroslavl', 1903), p. 49.

80. Fortunately for the historian, this beating caused a minor diplomatic incident between Denmark and Russia. The Danish envoy in Moscow lodged a formal complaint on behalf of Kaulitz with Peter I, who ordered an investigation into the whole affair, a transcript of which has been preserved. Bogoiavlenskii, *Moskovskii teatr pri tsariakh Aleksee i Petre*, pp. 77–80.

81. Ibid., pp. 81–82.

82. Smirnova, *Sovetskii teatr kukol*, p. 19.

83. *Otchet Imperatorskoi publichnoi biblioteke za 1868 god* (St. Petersburg, 1869), pp. 205–6, as cited in Smirnova, *Sovetskii teatr kukol*, p. 19.

84. Vsevolodskii-Gerngross, *Russkii teatr ot istokov do serediny XVIII v.*, p. 60.

Index

Adrianova-Peretts, V. P., 99
Afanas'ev, A., 2, 14
Aleksei, Tsar, 10, 15, 35, 37, 48, 50, 51, 63, 64, 65, 93, 106, 108, 109, 110, 119; proscription of *skomorokhi* by, 58, 60–62; temperament of, 57, 63. *See also gramota* (first) of 1648; *gramota* (second) of 1648
Andreyev, N., 30
Antonii (abbot), 58
Antonovich, V. B., 85
Antonovyi, Ivan (Russian puppeteer), 119
Astrakhan, 55; capture of depicted in song, 96
Avvakum (archpriest): attack on *skomorokhi* by, 59–60, 140 n. 69
Azarin, Simon, 9
Azbukovnik, 6, 10

Baird, B., 113, 116
bakhari, 57, 98, 99
balalaika, 95, 107
ballet: rudiments of, 109; first staged in Russia, 149 n. 31
Balto-Finns, 105, 106
bard, 83, 84, 96, 105
basni. See skazki
bears: used in divination, 8–9
Beliaev, I., 2, 50
Belkin, A. A., xiv, 121
Berkov, P. N., 112
Best, Robert, 55

Bezsonov, P. A., 85
Bogomilism, 7
Boian, 84, 105
brigand songs: attributed to *skomorokhi*, 49–50
Brodskii, L. N., 99, 100
Budimirovich, Solovei, 92
Buslaev, Vasilii, 85, 90
Buturlin, Timofei Fedorovich, 60
byliny, 64, 81, 83, 84, 86, 87, 93, 94, 96, 97, 105, 118, 121, 145 n. 46; acting out of by *skomorokhi*, 111; editing of by *skomorokhi*, 89–92; meter in, 93; transfer from Kiev north, 84–89, 144–45 n. 32
byliny-skomoroshiny: discussed, 92–94
Byzantium, 1, 16; decline of Kievan trade with, 23

cadastres *(pistsovye knigi)*, 32; used in drawing socioeconomic profile of *skomorokhi*, 34–42
Carnival, 115, 151 n. 55
census books *(perepisnye knigi)*, 32; used in drawing socioeconomic profile of *skomorokhi*, 34–42
Chambers, E. K., xv, 32
Chet'i Minei, 28
Chobotko, 86
Christmas: pagan rituals associated with, 61, 62

155

Chronicle of Pereiaslavl-Suzdal, 8, 18, 25
church, Russian Orthodox: movement toward reform in, 57–58, 139–40 n. 61
Cosmas and Damian, Saints: patrons of *skomorokhi*, 9, 93, 94, 126–27 n. 45
court minstrels, 83, 84; *skomorokhi* as, 42, 45
Cumans: impact of on Kievan trade, 23
customs duty records *(tamozhennye knigi)*, 32; description of, 33–34; used in drawing socioeconomic profile of *skomorokhi*, 34–42

Dal, V. I.: reference to nineteenth-century practicing *skomorokh* by, 142 n. 87
dance-games: earliest link of *skomorokhi* to, 108
dancing *skomorokhi*: depicted in miniature initials, 109
Daniil (metropolitan of Moscow), 31
Daniil (prince of Galich), 84
Danilov, Kirsha, 65, 96, 97. *See also* Sbornik
David, King (the Psalmist), 29
Demidov (mill owner in Urals), 65, 96
Dionysia: similarity of to Slavic goat-grain ritual, 12
divination, 8–9, 111–12
Dmitriev, Iu. N., 27, 28, 30
Dmitrieva, S. I., 88, 121
Dobrynia Street: haven of *skomorokhi* in Novgorod, 52
"Dobrynia v ot'ezde," discussion of, 82–83
dogs: depicted in miniatures of *skomorokh*, 25; used in *skomorokh* entertainment, 64
Domostroi: strictures against *skomorokhi* in, 139 n. 49
domra, 107
Dragomanov, M. P., 85, 86
drama: cyclic ritual, 10–12, 110, 127 n. 49; secular, 111. *See also* wedding
dumy, 85, 86, 87
Dunai *(byliny* hero), 86
dvoeverie (ditheism), 60, 126 n. 36
Dvornik, F., 18

Ediger, T., 17
Epiphany: pagan rituals associated with, 60, 61

fabliaux, 92
fairy tales (Ukrainian), 85, 86
Famintsyn, A. S., xiv, 105; on origins of *skomorokhi*, 1, 2, 14
Fedor I (tsar), 55, 63
Fedor II (tsar): *gramota* condemning *skomorokhi*, of, 64
Filofei (monk): epistle against paganism of, 29–30. *See also* Pskov
Findeizen, N., xiv; map illustrating geographic distribution of *skomorokhi* by, xiv–xv, 32, 34, 131 n. 5
First Pskovian Chronicle, 27
Fletcher, Giles, 55–56
folk drama, 110

Gennadii (archbishop of Novgorod): humiliation of *skomorokhi* by, 139 n. 51
George, Saint, feast of, 86
Georgii of Zarub (monk), 24
Germany: Kievan ties with, 16–18
gęslarzy (Polish pagan priests): involved in anti-Christian rising (1034), 5, 124–25 n. 14
Glubinnye knigi ("Books of Depth or Deep Wisdom"), 7
goat (goat-grain): ancient symbol of fertility, 11
gramota (first) of 1648, 51, 52, 108, 109, 119; effectiveness of, 63–64, 142 n. 80; impact of on *skomorokhi*, 62, 63; popular practices and popular amusements enumerated in 60–61; reissuance of, 63, 142 n. 81
gramota (second) of 1648, impact of on *skomorokhi*, 62, 63; pagan rituals and practices enumerated in, 61–62
Grek, Maksim: his "Slovo protiv skomorokhov," 31; references to Satanic games of *skomorokhi* in, 32
grievances: petitions of made directly to tsar by *skomorokhi*, xvi, 56
Grigor'ev, A. D., 88, 93
gudok, 28, 48, 94, 118; popular among *skomorokhi*, 107

masks, 2, 114; use of by *skomorokhi*, 10–11, 60, 61, 110, 115, 116
Maslenitsa, 3, 15
Matveev, Artaman Sergeevich, 110
Meletovo: church of Assumption of Virgin Mary in, 27; fresco depicting *skomorokh* in, 27–30, 29, 106. *See also* Pskov
Miller, G. F., 65, 96
Miller, O. F., 85, 86
Miller, V. F., 83, 97
Miloslavskii, Prince Iliia, 51
mikhonosha (mekhonosha), 11, 12, 127 n. 56
mimes (Byzantine), 113, 114; influence of on *skomorokhi*, 16, 22; repertoire of, 21
Mitus, 84
Mongols, 30, 54, 84, 113; introduction of census in Russia by, 33. *See also* census books
Morozov, A. A., 52
Morozov, Boris, 51
moskoludstvo, 12, 110, 149–50 n. 33
Moscow, 34, 36, 48, 50, 51, 52, 53, 54, 55, 62, 63, 64, 65
Moscow Circus, 65, 111
Mozhaisk, 34, 36, 41
Mstislav (prince of Tmutorokan), 84
Muryshka, Grishka, 49
Muromets, Ilia, 64, 85, 86
Muscovite *skomorokhi*: become itinerant, 31–32; persecution of by church, 31; professionalization of, 32
musical instruments: mass burning of by Aleksei, 61, 141 n. 75; used by *skomorokhi*, 107
music: sacred and secular, 104–5

Napea, Osepp, 55
Naryshkin, Natal'ia, 110
Nasonov, A. N., 88
navki (mavki), 10
Neronov, Ivan: attacks on *skomorokhi* by, 59, 140 n. 66
Nestor, 4, 19, 20, 21, 105
Nevskii, Alexander, 84
New Year's Day: pagan rituals associated with, 61, 141 n. 76
Nicoll, A., 20
Nikitich, Dobrynia, 40, 52, 82, 83, 89, 90, 96
Nizhnii Novgorod, 34, 38, 39, 40, 41,

95; incident involving *skomorokhi* in, 59–60, 140 n. 65
nonsense rhymes, 98
Novgorod, 17, 34, 39, 51, 62, 84, 89, 92, 106, 112; as center of *Strigol'nik* heresy, 29; as refuge of *skomorokhi*, 24; colonization of northeast by, 88; initials of *skomorokhi* from, 25; political disintegration of 52–54
Novgorod *skomorokhi*, excellence of, 54

Obraztsov, Sergei, 65
Olearius, Adam, 28, 48, 96, 106, 109, 112, 116, 117, 118, 119
Olga (princess of Kiev): visit to Constantinople of, 17, 18, 129 n. 86
Oleg (grand prince of Kiev), 7
Olonets, 87
Onega, Lake, 88
oprichnina, 37; favor in decline of *skomorokhi*, 52–54
organ: Byzantine pneumatic, 20, 21, 113
organon, 19, 21
Ozarovskaia, O. E., 111

paganism: among Kievan Slavs, 6–8
Paterik, 5
Pchela, 23–24
Pecherskii, Feodosii, 19, 105
Peter I (tsar), 33, 119
Petrov, N. I., 86
"Petrushka": scences from, 118
Petukhov, V. I., 32–33, 35
Pimen (archbishop of Novgorod), 55
Pogodin, M. P., 84, 85
Ponomarev, A. I., 2, 3
Popovich, Alesha, 64, 81, 85, 89
poteshnaia palata: use of by the tsars, 56, 57
Potyk, Mikhailo, 85
Pozharskii, Prince Dmitrii, 42, 56
pozorishche (pozor), 116, 117, 118
priest: son of *skomorokh* ordained as, 37
Primary Chronicle, 3, 6, 7, 8, 13, 14, 19
proverbs: identified with *skomorokhi*, 101
Pskov, 17, 34, 38, 39, 51, 84, 95, 106; as center of *Strigol'nik* heresy, 29; as refuge of *skomorokhi*, 24;

influence of Novgorod school of illumination in, 26; link to Meletovo fresco of, 30; survivals of paganism in, 29

puppet theater, 48; identified with skomorokhi, 114–18; origins of in Russia, 112–14

Pyriatynskij, Oleksij Popovich, 85

Radunitsa, 127 n. 49

Radziwill (Königsberg) Chronicle, 106

Razboinik, Solovei, 64, 85

Razin, Stenka, 49

Riazan, 34, 39; influence of Novgorod school of illumination in, 26; initials of skomorokhi from, 25–26, 30

Romanov, Michael (tsar), xvi, 63, 81, 96, 98, 109; extensive use of skomorokhi by, 56–57

rosalia (rosaria, dies rosae), 5

Rozov, N. N., 28, 29, 30

rusalki, 6, 151 n. 57

Rusaliia, 3, 4, 6, 9; festival of, 10–11, 12, 47, 100, 104, 110, 115; origins of, 5

Russkie skomorokhi (Belkin), xiv

Russkii fol'klor (Sokolov), xvi

Rybakov, B. A., 5, 83

Sadko, 85, 90

Šafařik, P. I., 2

Saint Sophia: in Kiev, 19, 20, 29, 108, 113; in Novgorod, 29

Sbornik: of Kirsha Danilov, 65, 97, 142 n. 89

Selianinovich, Mikula, 86, 144 n. 25

serfs, skomorokhi as, 41

Serpukhov, 39

shadow puppetry (lantern pictures), 113; evidence of in Central Asia and Scythia, 113–14

Shuiskii, Prince Ivan, 42, 56

Shuiskii, Vasilii, 98

shuty (fools and dwarfs), 56

skaziteli, 88

skazki, 57; discussion of, 98–100; relationship of to byliny, 98

skomorokh: depicted on bracelet, 83, 131 n. 110; domrachei (domernik, domershchnik) (synonym), 42, 95, 96, 99; gudochnik (synonym), 42;

gusel'nik (synonym), 5, 42, 97; medvednik (synonym), 42, 53, 112; makrachei (synonym), 42; poteshnik (synonym), 42; rozhechnik (synonym), 5, 42; smychnik (synonym), 42; strunnik (synonym), 42; tsymbal'nik (synonym), 42; veselyi (synonym), 42, 53

skomorokhi: and bears (see trained bear act); as bobyli (landless peasants), 37, 41; as coryphaei, 108; as cult leaders, 2, 3; charms (zaklinaniia), use of by, 101 (see also incantations); demographic distribution of, 35–36; depicted in initials (miniature letter-figures), 24–26, 132 n. 18; dobrye molodtsy (synonym), 99; as druzhko (druzhka), 13; dudnik (synonym), 5, 42; excommunication of by church, 63; exile to Siberia, 65; as hired workers, 41; itinerant, 45–50; itinerant, lawlessness of, 48–50; legal status of, 46; malye rebiata (synonym), 98; members of, in middle class (srednye liudi), 38–39, 40; as molodshie liudi (lower taxpaying class), 37, 40, 41; molodtsy (synonym), 99; as oprichniki, 54–55; as pagan priests, xv, 2, 8–12; participation of in memorial rites, 2, 10; registered (opisnye), 45, 46, 47; as shopkeepers, 39–40; as sluzhilye liudi (lower service people), 38 (see also strel'tsy); as sorcerers, 94; transfer of from Novgorod to Moscow, 53–54; unregistered (neopisnye), 45, 46, 47; urbanization of, 37–38; veselye liudi (synonym), 3, 42, 53, 112; veselye molodtsy (synonym), 28, 92, 93, 99; as warlocks, 9, 116; in Western eyes, xvi; works on in English, xv

Skomorokhi na Rusi (Famintsyn), xiv

Skomorokhova, Matrena, 88

Skomorokhovo, village of, 34, 35

skomoroshestvo, xv, 93

skomoroshiny. See byliny-skomoroshiny

Slovo o polku Igoreve, 84, 105

Sobolevskii, A., 2

Sokolov, Iu. M., xvi, 95

"sovereign's skomorokhi," 56

Spielmänner (Spielleute), xv, xvi; influence on *skomorokhi* of, 18, 21, 22; repertoire of, 16
staircase *(skomorokhi)* frescoes, 19–21, 108
Staver, 92
Stefanovich, Diuk, 64
Stief, Carl, 97
Stoglav: references to *skomorokhi* in, xvi, 9, 13, 47, 48, 54, 55, 137 n. 9
strel'tsy, 51, 134 n. 68; *skomorokhi* as, 37, 38, 95–96, 134–35 n. 73
Strigol'niki, 29
Sudebnik (1589), 45, 46, 56, 136–37 n. 2
superstitions: common to Kievan Slavs, 3–4; common in seventeenth-century Muscovy, 61
Sviatogor, 86
Sviatoslav I (grand prince of Kiev), 7
Sviatoslav II (grand prince of Kiev), 19, 105
Sviatoslavich, Roman (prince of Tmutorokan), 84
Sviatoslav (prince of Chernigov), 3

Tatishchev, V. N.: comment on *skomorokhi* of, 64, 81
teratological ornamentation, 25; earliest school in Russia of, 26
"Terentii muzh Danil'evich": discussion of, 92–93
tiaglye liudi (taxable commoners): three classes of, 38; *skomorokhi* as, 38, 46
Tõnurist, I., 107, 121
Toropets, 34; comparatively large number of *skomorokhi* in, 36
Totskaia, I. F., 113, 122
trained bear act: association of *skomorokhi* with, 48, 54, 60, 64, 111–12; early history of, 111–12; reconstruction of early "bear comedy," 112
Trebnik (1647): questions regarding *skomorokhi* in, 58, 140 n. 64
Trinity-Saint Sergius Monastery, 9, 30, 46, 49
"Tsar' Maksimilian," 111
Tula, 34, 36, 41
Turinsk, 48, 63

uprisings, urban (1648), 50–52; in Moscow, 51; in other cities, 51
Ustiug Velikii, 39, 40, 47, 51
"Usy" ("Usishcha"), 49, 137 n. 19. *See also* brigand songs

Varlaam (metropolitan of Rostov-Iaroslavl), 58
Varneke, B. V., 109
Vasil'evich (Prince Iurii of Dmitrov), 30; 49
Vasilii II (grand prince), 52
"Vavilo i skomorokhi": discussion of, 93–94; Vavilo as saint, 146 n. 55
Vernadsky, G., 114
Veselovskii, A. N., 20, 111, 113, 116
Viatka, 34, 39
Viaz'ma, 39
Virgin Mary, 29, 86; depicted in Meletovo fresco, 27
Vitov, M. D., 88
Vladimir I (grand prince of Kiev), 6, 15, 64, 82, 84, 89, 90, 96
volkhvy, 6–7, 9, 15, 116, 126 n. 28, 128 n. 73
Vonifat'ev, Stefan, 57
voodoo doll, 116. *See also kukla*
Vostokov, A. Kh., 16
Vsevolod (prince of Pereiaslavl), 3
Vyshnevetskij, Prince Dmytrii, 85
Vysotskii, S. A., 113, 122

wedding: as dramatic performance, 12–13, 110, 118; role of *skomorokhi* in, 12–14
White Sea, 88, 93
Wojcicki, K. W., 5
women: as *skomorokhi*, 37, 134 n. 67

Zabelin, I. E., 56, 98
zachiny ("beginnings"), use of in *byliny*, 91, 92
zapevy (introductory refrains), 97–98
Zhidiata, Luka (bishop of Novgorod), 12, 110
Zigmund, Johann Christofor, 119
Zimin, A. A., 45
Zlatoust, 26
Zlatustroi, 6
Zmeev, Semen Il'ich, 61
znamenny chant, 104

DATE DUE